THE HOLY WAR

Edited by Thomas Patrick Murphy

The Holy War

OHIO STATE UNIVERSITY PRESS: COLUMBUS

Copyright © 1976 by the Ohio State University Press
Manufactured in the United States of America

Library of Congress Cataloging in Publication Data
Conference on Medieval and Renaissance Studies, 5th,
  Ohio State University, 1974.
  The holy war: [papers]

  Sponsored by the Ohio State University's Center for
Medieval and Renaissance Studies.
  Includes bibliographical references and index.
  1. Crusades—Congresses. I. Murphy, Thomas Patrick.
II. Ohio State University, Columbus. Center for
Medieval and Renaissance Studies. III. Title.
D160.C66   1974   940.1'8   76-7595
ISBN 0-8142-0245-4

Table of Contents

PREFACE

The annual Conference on Medieval and Renaissance Studies
sponsored by the Ohio State University's Center for Medieval and
Renaissance Studies is designed to make distinguished scholars in
the subject under consideration available to the faculty and students of the university and surrounding schools as well as to
interested members of the community. A scholar speaking at the
conference accepts the task of preparing a paper of sufficient
complexity to be important in its field, while remaining accessible
to nonspecialists. The papers in this volume grow out of that spirit
and thus serve, in varying degrees, as both introductions to the facts
and issues of medieval holy warfare and significant statements
about it.

The Center wished to preserve this conference in the form of a
published set of essays for two reasons. First, since the conference
was an effort to focus different academic disciplines on a single
problem with far-reaching implications within the medieval and
Renaissance world, the papers are truly interdisciplinary. But the
implications are not restricted to the past as a kind of closed
system, and the second reason for publishing the proceedings lies
in the importance of the effort made in the conference, particularly
in the panel discussion at the end of this volume, to understand

what the study of medieval holy war can tell us about war in our own times, not on the basis of superficial analogues, but only after a considered analysis of the past.

One conclusion that the conference clearly establishes is the strong connection between the intellectual climate of a culture and the likelihood of its waging a holy war. This book, therefore, is ultimately more than a work about holy war; it is a factor in our movement toward or, more hopefully, away from future holy war.

I wish to thank Stanley J. Kahrl and the Advisory Committee of the Center for giving me the opportunity to edit these proceedings. In particular, I wish to acknowledge the assistance given me by Joseph Lynch and Michael Zwettler, the excellent typing of Shari Harrison, and the extensive help of Madalene Axford Murphy.

T. P. M.

THE HOLY WAR

STANLEY J. KAHRL

Introduction

At a time of generally increased interest in the Middle Ages, the Crusades are probably not one of the particular features of the period held in high repute. Except for the dedicated band of historians led by Kenneth Setton, or the impressive work of Sir Steven Runciman, most of us are more than likely to turn our backs on the Crusades as a regrettable lapse, an unfortunate outburst of religious enthusiasm. When we do think of them at all, we are more likely to recall the bones of Peter the Hermit's crazy followers bleaching at Civetot, the sack of Constantinople, or, most probably, that awful internecine struggle, the Albigensian Crusade, portrayed with such fiery anger in the pages of Zoë Oldenbourg's *Massacre at Monsegur.*[1] An interest in the nature and origin of romantic love leads the student new to the Middle Ages inevitably to the Cathars and the Midi. There one meets not only the full horror of medieval warfare but the first excesses of the Inquisition. Alternatively one can take the comic view of Osbert Lancaster, in *The Saracen's Head,*[2] whose young knight, William de Littlehampton, found himself en route to the Holy Land in the midst of an English army officers' mess composed of public school hearties for whom the sands of Acre bear a striking resemblance to the playing fields at Eton.

Each of these aspects of the Crusades was unquestionably a part of the story, but they are not the entire story. From Urban II's sermon at Clermont to the end of the Crusades three hundred and fifty years later, the Crusaders were always impelled at least in part by a strong sense of idealism, a belief that the sacrifices they made, the hardships they endured, were for a cause more important than their own lives. One finds in the late-eleventh-century *Song of Roland* the dedication, the idealism as well as the bigotry and intolerance that seem to accompany idealism so often. In the fourteenth century Philippe de Mézières exemplified the burning sense of dedication to a cause as well as any other figure associated with the Crusades. Yet, stumping the courts of Europe to call forth once again ill-disciplined bands of knights for the expedition that ended with the disgraceful sack of Alexandria in 1365, he is clearly an anachronism. The religious fervor had shifted, had gone elsewhere. His successful response to that shift came later in his work for the cult of the Virgin.

Chaucer's Knight too is an anachronism, a man who has fought in "his lordes werre"—the ambiguity of the lower case "l" must be deliberate—wherever a Crusade was in progress, even up to and including the sack of Alexandria. The Knight himself portrays laconically the ambiguities of a Crusade in his description of Theseus's campaign against Thebes. In righting a wrong, in performing his function as a defender of the helpless, Theseus undertakes a military expedition that ultimately results in the total destruction of a city and the flight of those of its inhabitants not put to the sword. It cannot have been simply the physical and financial difficulties of mounting an expedition to the Holy Land that led finally to the end of those expeditions; there must also have been a growing recognition of the paradoxical nature of a war on behalf of the Prince of Peace.

Yet the idea of a holy war has lived on, even if attempts to realize that idea in assaults on Islam have ceased. Shakespeare's Henry Bolingbroke knew the power of the old ideal, and vowed, as had kings before him, to "make a voyage to the Holy Land, To wash this blood off from my guilty hand" (*Richard II*, 5.6.49–50) to expiate the death of Richard. Yet his vow is an empty vow, and the

Jerusalem in which he dies is a room in England. It is in act 1 of
Henry V that we see the full transformation of the idea of a holy war
from one whose participants gained spiritual sanctification through
the slaughter of unbelievers to a war for political or economic
interests for which God's support is sanctimoniously invoked.
When Henry V prophesies that generations yet unborn will curse
the Dauphin for his mocking gift of tennis balls, he sugarcoats his
political feud with the pious conclusion,

> But this lies all within the will of God,
> To whom I do appeal; and in whose name
> Tell you the Dauphin I am coming on,
> To venge me as I may and to put forth
> My rightful hand in a well-hallow'd cause.
>   (1.2.289–93)

With such sentiments we are in the world of the modern holy war.

Because the United States has just lived through a war whose
supporters often spoke as though we were engaged, not in a crusade
in Europe, as Eisenhower called World War II, but a crusade in the
East, it seemed appropriate for the Center for Medieval and Renaissance Studies at Ohio State University to bring together a group
of scholars interested in how the first holy wars of Western Christendom began. For it is our belief that many of the justifications
developed to sanction aggressive war that are in use today are
similar to the justifications developed in the Middle Ages to sanction its own holy wars. A group of speakers, whose essays appear in
this volume, were invited to address the problem of how a culture
formally dedicated to fulfilling the injunction to "love thy neighbor
as thyself" could move to a point where it sanctioned the use of
violence against the alien both outside and inside society. In order
to gain the perspective of a nonmedievalist sensitive to the issues of
war and peace, we invited a representative from the Mershon
Center for Education in National Security to take part in a concluding discussion that would consider how constant the justifications
for the use of violence against one's neighbor have been.

The papers that resulted speak for themselves. I have no intention here of summarizing them. However there are one or two
general points that I do feel need to be made. First, I admire Mr.

Cowdry's willingness to assert without qualification that after all due allowance has been made for such causative factors as the need for channeling the warlike energies of the knights into areas "at a distance from the places of their birth" (p. 14), or the effect on the priests of a rise in the social status of the knights, ultimately there is a single dominant personality that causes the course of events to bend in a new direction. All those who participated in the conference wondered what might have happened had not Urban II been so successful in carrying on the program of Gregory VII. There is no question that the Church took a decisive turn that November day at Clermont, and lost a chance to speak unequivocally as the champion of peace for European Christendom in the centuries that were to follow. At a time when historians are turning with delight to the wonders of statistical analysis so that they may better count the consequences of many daily decisions, it is good to be reminded that there are moments in time when one person, for good or ill, takes a course that changes all that follows after. The substitution of a sword for a pilgrim's staff unquestionably placed not only Urban's papacy but those of his successors as well in the position of supporting war when it was waged for religious ideals.

Certainly the holy war, as that term is now generally understood, appears to have been an invention of the West. Professor Watt's paper makes it clear that the usual image of a horde of rabid Muslims sweeping all civilization before them in a war without quarter, a horde crying "Convert or die," is, like so many faces of the enemy, a caricature. For such warriors one must go instead to the verses of *The Song of Roland* where Roland cries "Nos avom dreit mais cist gloton ont tort"[3]— "We are right but these wretches are wrong"—as he splits a pagan warrior in half. The Jihād succeeded precisely because it was *not* that sort of a war.

To say that Urban, or, for that matter, Bernard of Clairvaux, can be seen as a dominant influence in the making of the Crusades is not to say that other factors were not at work as well. There must be a catalyst, a magnetic figure, but such a figure cannot be heard where there are no ears to hear. The men at Clermont listened because they were ready to listen. The most serious conclusion to be drawn from Cowdrey's analysis of the causes of the Crusades may be his statement that "men seem in all ages to engage in the aggressive warfare of ideas less for external gains than to relieve the internal tensions and problems of their own society" (p. 28). For the medieval holy wars those tensions seem to have arisen as much as anything else from the Church's teachings on sin and penance. The songs that Professor Crocker includes are in many cases what one would expect, a soldier's regrets at parting from his loved one. But there is the other strain as well:

> He who goes with Louis, what has he to fear from hell? For surely his soul will dwell in Paradise with the angles of our Lord. (p. 84)

In a brutal world where life was cheap and short, what comfort to know with certainty that what one was doing would guarantee an eternity of bliss! What we would like to know much more about, however, is just how much the changes in the penitential teaching of the medieval Church altered attitudes toward holy war. For example, were the Crusades a casualty of the late medieval move toward internalizing penitential discipline?

Richard Southern, in his fine study of *Western Society and the Church in the Middle Ages,*[4] shows how closely related the Church's programs always were to the needs of medieval society. And in late medieval society the need was for individual roads to God. Taking the vow of a Crusader made sense in an earlier world where "the need for a binding vow was one of the common assumptions that had bound together all religious orders in the Middle Ages."[5] As the sense of the efficacy of formal vows declined, one would expect a lessened interest in taking the Cross. The Templars were destroyed, to be sure, because their wealth was coveted by Philip the Fair, but they were also by the time of their demise in the early fourteenth century an anachronism. Certainly it is becoming clear that our best road to travel into medieval psychology is the road paved with Penitential manuals. What are the links between the reforms of the Lateran Council of 1215 and the changed attitudes toward taking the crusading vow that we find in the thirteenth century? What was the effect of a lessened emphasis on external works, the increased concern for individual self-examination and private contrition we see in late medieval manuals of sin, or sermons on the Seven Deadly Sins? It would be fascinating to know whether the regularization of penitential procedures, the provision for more manageable ways to save one's soul, led to a decline in crusading enthusiasm.

Such things we may not ever know. But it is clear from the impressive array of documentation marshaled by Professor Brundage that once having decided to conduct holy wars, the medieval Church clearly felt a need to justify undertaking such endeavors. As Brundage makes plain, the concept of a just war has an ancient pedigree; and as one reads his careful delineation of what a just war involved, one realizes how strongly the concepts he sets out are still a part of our thinking. The insistence that a war to be just must be declared by a legitimate authority provided what was probably the most cogent attack on President Johnson's conduct of the Vietnamese War. The further conditions—that "there must be a reasonable and morally acceptable cause for the war: the war must be necessary, . . . and the war must be fought by acceptable means" (p. 102)—all are still recognizably current in any present discussion of the conditions under which war is justified.

What is of course of more interest to this discussion is Brundage's discussion of the subordinate category of the holy war, a phenomenon he too sees as essentially an invention of medieval European Christendom. As is so often the case, the lawyers come after the event, and codify contemporary practice. It is absorbing reading to watch the gradual development of legal justifications for participation in wars that purported to sanctify the soldiers who took part. In the first place one is struck quickly by the canonists' treatment of enemies in a holy war as beyond the pale. Weapons that were too horrible to be used against fellow Christians could be used against the infidel. The persistence of such thinking accounts in part for the current debate whether the Western Allies would have dropped an atomic bomb on Germany. Japan had certainly fulfilled all the conditions necessary to make the war in the Pacific a just war. Nevertheless, cultural differences led many to cast the

Japanese enemy in much the same mold that we find fitting the Saracens, to accord them a different status from the European enemy. Brundage is too good a historian not to point out that those horrible weapons, the crossbow and the ballista, were in fact used quite casually on fellow Christians despite the attempt to limit their use. The destruction of Dresden or the fire-bombing of Hamburg also suggest that the Allies had in fact few compunctions about what they threw at Nazi Germany. It is the attitude toward the enemy in a holy war that matters more than the actual weapons used against him, the belief that he is not to be accorded full human status, that is our unfortunate legacy from the crusading mentality.

Of course not everyone was an enthusiastic supporter of the idea of the holy war even in the Middle Ages. It is good to be reminded that Gratian did take seriously the argument that war was wrong, at least for Christians. From the canonists quoted it is clear that the defenses for a morally justifying war were hammered out in a debate where the minority view always had supporters. Could it be that the eventual defense of holy war as a variety of just war, in the Augustinian sense of that term, a defense based on supposed papal sovereignty over Jerusalem, came about because the concept of the just war was a much less exposed position to defend? It is almost as though those who were running the Crusades saw, as Stubbs later maintained, that a war for rights, for limited political gains, was more palatable than a war for ideas.

The canonists certainly did what they could to make the whole idea palatable. Whoever the antiwar critics of the Crusades were, whoever caused there to be a debate, they do not appear to have been the poets of the period. Whether the dominant literary mode of romance, focusing as it does on love and war as the theaters within which heroes win their fame, prevented any extended public criticism of the values of the Crusades or not is uncertain. One does find a surprising number of virtuous pagans in the later romances, suggesting that at least some of the poets had discovered that their enemies were as fully human as they were themselves. In *Huon of Bordeau,* for example, the world of the East is far more cultured, and far more charitable, than the court of Charlemagne.

For an outright attack on the paradox of the Church of the Prince of Peace preaching war against the infidel neighbor, one has to wait for the writings of such Christian humanists as Erasmus and More. Perhaps one has to see the horrors at firsthand to understand the abstract incongruity. Thus it is that European humanists, Italian or Dutch, see more clearly than perhaps the English the bestial, pestilential side of war in general, and, from that general perception, the incongruity of Christians visiting such horrors on any other creature of God. And yet, at the same time, there is Luther, in a direct line of descent, speaking of war as a "precious and godly" work (p. 165) when it protects the good. As Professor Greene remarks, "The conception of the soldier as godly and the sword as potentially divine sufficed to justify wars of religion for many Protestants in the terrible century that followed" (p. 165).

Though we no longer slaughter each other in the name of God, we do still treat our enemies as though we were engaged in a holy war, still think of them as less than human, beyond salvation. Our soldiers may no longer believe that their deaths in our wars will automatically absolve them of sin, but they are still capable of destroying life and property indiscriminately if it belongs to "gooks." If there is one general conclusion that the panel was drawn to, it was to underline the close connections between how we view the world, and what form our violence will take. It does not seem any more possible now than at any other time in human history to envisage a world without violence, to suppose that no one will ever again raise up another swastika over another people. But it does seem possible, if education is still to have the effect that Erasmus hoped for it, to learn that there are no infidels, only other people.

H. E. J. COWDREY

The Genesis of the Crusades: The Springs of Western Ideas of Holy War

Our subject in this volume is how men thought about war in the medieval and early modern periods, and how their thinking has contributed to contemporary outlooks upon warfare and violence. A convenient starting point for our deliberations is a comment upon changes in the Western estimate of warfare over the centuries, which William Stubbs made in the third volume of his *Constitutional History of England,* originally published in 1878. "The kings of the middle ages," he wrote, "went to war for rights, not for interests, still less for ideas."[1] For rights . . . for interests . . . for ideas. Implicit in those three phrases is a downhill progression from bad to worse in the pretexts upon which wars have been waged; and Stubbs was not without a remarkably prophetic concern that, with the French Revolution, the Europe he studied and lived in might not have embarked upon its final stage. He made his comment with King Henry V of England in mind. Henry went to war for rights. He had, or at least he professed to have, a rightful claim to the crown of France, which he was denied; his warfare was, therefore, the continuation of a judicial process by other means. If he gloried in war as the highest and noblest work of kings, his aggressive designs were, nevertheless, subject to a measure of legal justification. Such legal justification itself implied principles that, however imperfectly kings themselves may have attended to them, reinforced the doctrines of limited warfare that, at least since the early twelfth century, canonists and schoolmen had been seeking to formulate.

We move on from the fifteenth century to the seventeenth and eighteenth centuries. By then, kings such as Louis XIV and Frederick II fought for interests—like the Spanish Succession, or control of Silesia. That was a rather worse sort of warfare, Stubbs thought, than warfare for rights. No cloak of justice now hid naked selfishness. Kings advanced excuses, rather than legal justifications, for their aggressions. And yet, warfare for interests was still not too bad: it remained limited; few people were killed, and those were mostly soldiers. As regards thought about war, the centuries of warfare for interests consolidated and continued the doctrines of limited war that had gained increasing currency in the Middle Ages.

With the French Revolutionary period, however, there moved toward the center of the picture a far more destructive and fearful warfare—warfare for ideas. Stubbs was not confident that what he saw as having been the formative and stabilizing principles of European history—dynasty, nationalities, and freedom, all of them having deep roots in the Christian tradition—were in his day any longer secure.[2] In particular, the principle of nationalities, in its current form, had been "mostly unlucky in its prophet" (that is, Napoleon I); and Stubbs was also alarmed by "the first attempts at a propaganda of liberty, and the first attempts at a propaganda of nationality" in the French Revolution. He seems to have been anxious lest such unlimited warfare for ideas as had ominously marked the Revolutionary epoch and had been resurgent under Napoleon III, might become the order of the day.[3]

There were grounds for such anxiety, quite apart from those that we, with our experience of the total wars of the present century, can recognize with the benefit of hindsight. For Europe inherited from the Middle Ages another tradition about warfare, besides that of limited war. The eleventh and following centuries had witnessed the vast upsurges of the Crusades, in whose inception Stubbs had rightly seen a "war of idea." In the name of God the participants sought to extirpate those whom they saw as aliens, both inside and outside Christian society. "Scarcely a single movement now visible in the current of modern affairs," wrote Stubbs, again, "but can be traced back with some distinctness to its origin in the early middle ages."[4] The Crusades were such a point of origin; they were effectively the starting point of a view of total warfare that stands in contrast to limited hostilities for rights or interests. They left an indelible mark upon the Western consciousness, which goes far to justify Stubbs's half-articulated fear lest warfare for ideas— secularized, now, but waged with quasi-religious fervor—might again become prevalent.[5]

My concern today is with this last kind of warfare—total, ideological warfare, and the springs of its compulsion upon men. I shall try to set out what seem to me to emerge from modern scholarly inquiry as the reasons why, in the late eleventh century, men came, in the Crusade, to wage it so extensively against what seemed alien to them, and why what they then did has shaped Western ideas so profoundly. I shall then try to suggest some lessons that might today be drawn from the rise and decline of crusading ideas, and from the alternative tradition of limited warfare, which is also a medieval legacy.

When we study the First Crusade, preached at Clermont in 1095 by Pope Urban II, we are fortunate in having, in the Chronicle known as the *Gesta Francorum*, an anonymous account of it, composed by a fighting knight while it was still taking place. He was a highly sophisticated and articulate man—a skilled, professional warrior with a developed sense of feudal loyalty and social obligation. The opening words of the *Gesta* set forth the origin of the Crusade in these words:

> When that time had already come, of which the Lord Jesus warns his faithful people every day, especially in the Gospel where he says, "If any man will come after me, let him deny himself, and take up his cross, and follow me," there was a great stirring of heart throughout all the Frankish lands, so that if any man, with all his heart and all his mind, really wanted to follow God and faithfully to bear the cross after him, he could make no delay in taking the road to the Holy Sepulchre as quickly as possible.[6]

Besides the strongly religious motivation, you will notice that the knight did not focus attention upon events in the East as having been decisive for the "great stirring of heart" that led to the Crusade. We can, I think, put on one side as not of key importance a whole group of factors that historians once thought were critical—I mean factors arising in the Muslim or Byzantine East. The anonymous knight fought with and for high ideals: to suffer for the Name of Christ and to set free the road to the Holy Sepulchre.[7] But he had little real knowledge of his Muslim enemies or of what was going on in their lands: he just thought of them as heathens, who denied the faith of Christ and holy Christendom for which he had taken arms. In the mid-1090s not much was happening in the East to concentrate his mind. If there was some atrocity propaganda in the air, Western piety was not being affronted by serious Muslim attacks upon Christians. Nor, so far as we can see, did Eastern Christians themselves particularly wish to be liberated from the Muslim yoke. Such events as the burning of the Church of the Holy Sepulchre in 1009 by the mad Caliph Hakim were few and far between, and there was no major recent outrage that stirred men to the heart. Islam was by and large a tolerant religion; while subject Christians kept themselves duly humble and paid their taxes, they were not badly off. Nor was it unduly hard for Christians from the West to make their pilgrimages to Jerusalem and the other Holy Places. Pilgrims, after all, are profitable and best not deterred. The Muslims did well from their tolls, from their lodging, and from providing them with supplies. So they let them journey.

Again, in the circumstances of 1095, the Byzantine emperor, Alexius Comnenus, wanted anything but the vast and unmanageable crusading hordes that were soon to come his way. The threat of the Seldjuk Turks, so deadly when they routed the Byzantines at Manzikert in 1071, had receded by 1092, with the death of the last great sultan, Malik Shah. Thereafter, Alexius could do with—indeed he actively sought—a limited supply of mercenaries who would make his diplomacy more credible. Crusaders by the thousands, under independent command, spoiling for war, and whom he could not control, were not what the circumstances of Byzantium in 1095 called for.

Nor was frustrated trade with the East really a factor in causing the Crusade. Up to 1095, the Amalfitans—the most active in the East of the Italian merchants—traded much as they wished. During the First Crusade, the Genoese, the Pisans, and the Venetians were cautious about joining in until they saw that there was money to be made. It was not a desire for trade that stimulated the Crusade, but vice versa.

All things considered, historians would, I think, now be pretty generally agreed that the First Crusade, the "great stirring of heart" in the West, was not, at root, caused by any pull of events in the East. On the contrary, knights like the author of the *Gesta* were impelled to go by constraints and shifts within Western society itself—its social classes, its institutions, and its ideas. I shall discuss four of these constraints and shifts, taking first what I think was perhaps the least important of them in bringing about the Crusade.

First, there was the rise in the population of western Europe during the eleventh century, combined with progressively more sophisticated standards of law and order. This combination tended to produce a surplus population whose aristocracy had every incentive to seek new, external outlets for its martial ardor and its desire for land. Conditions of landownership and inheritance were especially important. They were commonly not based on anything like primogeniture, or impartible descent from father to eldest son. Especially in southern France, there was often some kind of shared possession, such as the so-called *fraternitia,* or *frérêche,* by which inheritance passed to all brothers in common, or to a more extended family circle. Some brothers could be accommodated on the family land. But younger brothers were under pressure, and they also had an interest, to seek their sustenance elsewhere—in a monastery, perhaps, or in holy orders; but, if these choices were not attractive to them, in some lay outlet compatible with their birth.

Rising standards of public order tended to restrict such outlets near home. In France, the post-Carolingian breakdown of authority, and the gravest manifestations of feudal anarchy, seem to have reached their nadir in the generation following the year 1000.

Thereafter, such expedients as the Peace and the Truce of God—by which the Church, first by itself and then with the collaboration of lay authorities, gave its peace to certain classes of society and to certain seasons of the year—curbed opportunities of brigandage and of the fortunes of the sword. Peace-breakers were stigmatized as aliens within society, to be persecuted by a kind of "war upon war" having strong religious sanctions. By 1054, at the Council of Narbonne, it was even asserted that "no Christian should kill another Christian, for whoever kills another Christian undoubtedly sheds the blood of Christ."[8]

As such limitations upon domestic warfare increased, the surplus male offspring of the military classes came under pressure to seek new outlets for their martial and predatory energies at a distance from the places of their birth.

Contemporaries were not unaware that such pressures made men ready to be stirred by the summons to the Crusade. Yet I believe that their power, though considerable, can easily be exaggerated. The internal colonization of Europe could, and did, provide for much of the rising population. So did the increasing use of merce-nary knights and the expansion of aristocratic households. Above all, we should mark how few Crusaders settled permanently in Outremer. The initial military establishment of the Kingdom of Jerusalem after 1100 seems to have been only some 300 knights and 1,200 footsoldiers. In the long run, the kingdom suffered from the endemic weakness that, although men came in plenty from the West to conquer the Holy Land, there were never enough who would stay to colonize it effectively. Pressure of population in the West was evidently not serious enough to displace sufficient men who would take up the land available in the East. Demographic or economic factors go only a small way toward explaining the popu-larity in the eleventh century of the holy war and of the Crusade.

More important—and this is my second factor—was the rise of the knights in social status, and the enhanced sophistication that attended this rise. South Italian Norman though he was, the author of the *Gesta Francorum* typified where many knights of the West had got to by about 1100. He was decidedly a *gentleman*—a man of substance and standing, who rode on horseback and fought with expensive weapons and equipment. He was proud of his knight-hood, and he had a strong professional ethic, based upon loyalty to his feudal lord, Bohemond—*bellipotens Boamundus*. Yet he was not blindly loyal. He approved of Bohemond when, in real or politic deference to the law of the land, he did not plunder town-ships in the Byzantine Balkans. But he parted company at Antioch, when Bohemond turned aside from the Crusade to establish a principality for himself. And there is no mistaking the genuinely religious conviction of our knight, as expressed, for example, in the passage that I earlier cited. Knights had not always been as highly motivated, as sophisticated, as professional, as "gentlemanly," as he. Not long since, they had often been little better than predatory toughs, without *esprit de corps* as a social group. *Knecht* in German still means servant: that indicates the level of many eleventh-century knights before, as the century went on, the elite of their class rose in the world by acquiring land and gentility, and by entering more honorable service and companionship.

This rise in the knights' standing followed changes in military technique—the development of castles, for instance, and the growth of fighting on horseback—which enhanced the standing and prestige of those who fought. But for our purpose today, it is important that the Church—the clergy—also had much to do with the upgrading and dignification of knighthood. The clergy had little choice but to assist the process. In the Carolingian heyday of strong kingship, emperors and kings had seen to the security of the Christian people and defended them from their foes. "Look favorably, O God," the Carolingian clergy had prayed, "upon the Roman empire, that the peoples [that is, its enemies] who trust in their own fierceness may be restrained by the right hand of your power." When the Roman empire—as upheld by emperors and kings—became but a shadow, the defense of the Christian people necessarily tended to devolve upon the knights. To perform their new role, they must be raised from their low estate and given something of the dignity of kings. So, from about 950, we find formulas for the liturgical blessing of the banners under which knights fought. Where the clergy once prayed for kings, they now prayed for knights, as in this *Oratio super militantes:*

> Bless, O Lord, your servants who bend their heads before you. Pour on them your stablishing grace. In the warfare in which they are to be tested, preserve them in health and good fortune. Wherever and whyever they ask for your help, be speedily present to protect and defend them.[9]

In the eleventh century, we also find formulas for the blessing of swords and weapons. There emerged a religious ceremony of knightly investiture; in France after 1070, the dubbing of knights appears widely in the sources. As kings were crowned, so knights were invested. Knighthood now was, or could be, a vocation. The Church was in direct touch with the profession of arms, without the king as an intermediary. The warfare of knights was securing a new sanction and a new prestige. It was becoming holy war.

Since the knights were becoming so important, the clergy were also concerned to effect what German historians, in a good but untranslatable word, call their *Versittlichung*—that is, the raising of their social, ethical, and religious outlook through the determination of the objectives and limits of their warfare. They supplied them with an ideology. Hence the importance of such a work as Abbot Odo of Cluny's *Life of Gerald of Aurillac,* a paradigm Christian knight who drew the sword only in defense of the poor and of righteousness. Hence, too, the Peace and the Truce of God, the "war upon war" that churchmen tried to sponsor. Churchmen sanctioned warfare, but within strict limits and with a minimum of violence. (According to his panegyrist, Gerald of Aurillac, to avoid bloodshed, fought only with the *flat* of his sword![10]) Peace should be the quality of the Christian society itself. Yet fighting was the knights' way of life, and the Church was blessing their weapons. It was difficult to accomplish the *Versittlichung* of the knights, or to enable them to fulfill their social and professional role, within Christian society. If domestic peace were to be secured, it was requisite to find outlets for knightly war outside it. So, in the eleventh century, the Church encouraged knights to take part in the Reconquest in Spain by holy wars against the Muslims there. The ethics of the *Chanson de Roland* took shape in French chivalric society. The knights had come of age. Enhanced in social status, with a novel religious sanction for their carrying of arms, and habituated to the assigning of Christian objectives for their warfare, they were being well prepared to experience a "great stirring of heart" when the call came to the Eastern Crusade.

By thus insisting upon the Church's patronage of the military classes, I have already begun to touch upon a third *sine qua non* of the Crusade within the Western world. It was a radical change in Christian thought and practice in relation to the waging of war, so that warfare for ends of which the Church approved might be proclaimed as without reservation right and meritorious. To the very eve of the First Crusade, it is astonishing how ambiguous Western Christians were in their attitude toward warfare. The clergy were blessing swords and—understandably enough in the circumstances of the time—were praying ever more earnestly for the knights' success in warfare. They were, in effect, sanctioning "holy war." And, over the centuries, one can point to various "holy wars": like the upholding of the Peace and the Truce of God, or the Spanish campaigns, which we have noticed; or like the forays against the Muslims of the Mediterranean to whose participants the ninth-century popes Leo IV and John VIII held out a martyr's crown; or tenth-century Ottonian wars against the Magyars; or Pope Leo IX's ill-starred campaign of 1053 against the Normans of South Italy, which we have not noticed; and others.

Yet right into the second half of the eleventh century, and therefore on the very eve of the First Crusade, the Christian West was also teaching that killing or wounding in warfare, however legitimate the cause, was gravely sinful and merited severe penance. From this point of view, warfare was far from having the Church's blessing and approval: it stood under its condemnation. Far from being a legitimate service in the name of Christ, the profession of arms was not really fitting for a Christian man. This ambiguity of attitude—this "double-think," as it must seem to us—on the Church's part, is nowhere better illustrated than by the Battle of Hastings in 1066. The Norman host fought under a papal

banner, in what was deemed to be a just cause, at the command of
the legitimate prince. And yet, soon after Hastings, the Norman
bishops, with a papal legate at their elbow, imposed penances upon
the warriors for their transgressions upon the field of battle: for
killing a man, a year's penance; for wounding, forty days; and so
forth. This was fully in line with the principal canon-law collection
of the early eleventh century, the *Decretum* of Burchard of
Worms.[11]

If we turn from practice to ideas, it was also in line with the
dominant official view of Western Christianity during its first
eleven centuries. For the West had never given a full and unqual-
ified blessing to the waging of war, not even of "just war," or war
waged with a greater or lesser degree of ecclesiastical backing.
True, St. Augustine of Hippo, though only in a few brief passages,
had, for the first time in Christian history, put forward a theory of
the "just war."[12] He had also come to approve of the coercion of the
Donatists as stiff-necked resisters of Catholic authority, setting all
too much emphasis upon Christ's words in a parable, *Compelle
intrare*, "Compel them to come in"; as developed by Pope Gregory I, this justification for warfare became very influential in the
Middle Ages. Moreover, the conversion of the Franks and other
Germanic peoples had long since begun to incorporate war in the
popular substructure of Christian thought, including thought about
kingship. Christianity did not extinguish Germanic warrior ideals,
so it had to accommodate what it could not destroy. For example, a
feature of the post-Carolingian period was the growing cult of the
Archangel Michael. Scholars have rightly seen in it the Christian
substitute for Woden, and it is no surprise that Michael had no
more ardent devotees than the recently converted Normans. His
sanctuary at Monte Gargano, in the Abruzzi, where he had appeared in battle late in the fifth century, became a favorite center of
Norman pilgrimage. His cult was calculated to foster a warrior
ethic within Christianity. He was captain of the hosts of heaven: if
God accepted the military service of angels, why should he not also
accept the military service of men?[13] But this was a "grass-roots"
reaction, rather than (with a few exceptions in Carolingian times)

the official view of responsible spokesmen. Far into the eleventh
century, not only canonists like Burchard of Worms but also the
ablest and most reform-minded propagandists at the papal court set
their faces against the acceptance of war. They found no place (if
they knew of it) for Saint Augustine's teaching about a "just war,"
and they had reservations about coercion. "In no circumstances,"
insisted Cardinal Peter Damiani, "is it licit to take up arms in
defence of the faith of the universal church; still less should men
rage in battle for its earthly and transitory goods."[14] Even the fiery
Cardinal Humbert deprecated the persecution of heretics by force
of arms; he argued that Christians who took the sword against them
themselves became hardened in ways of violence and rapine.[15]

Until those who spoke officially for Christianity took a different
view, anything like a Crusade—as a war promoted and blessed by
the Church, and which won only benefits for those who fought—
was unthinkable. The change of mind that occurred in the late
eleventh century was largely owing to one man, who, as Hilde-
brand, was archdeacon of Rome from 1059 to 1073, and who, as
Gregory VII, was pope from 1073 to 1085. (It was he who was
behind the giving of a papal banner in 1066 to William of Normandy.) Historians have often stressed the epoch-making character of his work. Caspar called him "the great innovator who stands
alone."[16] Tellenbach has written that "Gregory stands at the
greatest—from the spiritual point of view perhaps the only—
turning-point in the history of Catholic Christendom; . . . the
world was drawn into the church, and leading spirits of the new age
made it their aim to establish the 'right order' in [a] united Christian
world."[17] No aspect of this change of front in the so-called Gregorian Reform is more significant than the transformation of the
Church's official attitude to warfare, so that, from being inherently
sinful, it was, or at least might be, meritorious to engage in it, and
so to promote "right order" in human society by force of arms.

Let me illustrate in two ways the change that Gregory brought
about. First, he very often used in his letters the phrase *militia
Christi*—the warfare of Christ. That, to be sure, was a traditional
phrase. It harked back to Saint Paul's words about a Christian

warfare that was not against flesh and blood, and for which the Christian must be shod with the preparation of the gospel of peace. Later generations had, accordingly, thought of the *militia Christi* as the *spiritual* combat of the martyr and the monk; it stood in the sharpest antithesis to the (wrongful) warfare of earthly arms—to *militia secularis*. Gregory took the critical step of proclaiming that earthly warfare could, after all, be an authentic part of the *militia Christi*. During his struggle with Henry IV of Germany, he called, in an altogether novel way, upon the knights of all lands to dedicate their swords to the service of Christ and of Saint Peter, and to realize their Christian vocation by so doing. Second, and consistent with this, Gregory's reign saw the proclaiming of a new kind of soldier-saint. There had been soldier-saints before, like, for example, Saint Maurice, Saint Sebastian, Saint George, or Saint Martin. But if you read their legends, you will notice that, by and large, they had gained recognition as saints *despite* being soldiers. Saint Maurice, for example, was a member of the Theban legion in Gaul, who, according to the widely read legends about him, disobeyed military orders—there are different versions—either to offer heathen sacrifices, or to punish Christians. Saint Martin even sought discharge from the Roman army, declaring, "I am Christ's soldier; I am not allowed to fight."[18] Gregory began to recognize among his contemporaries soldier-saints who were saints *because* they were soldiers; like Erlembald of Milan, the fierce Patarene leader who perished in 1075 during the savage communal violence that he had provoked. In Gregory's eyes, he was a true *miles Christi*—a soldier of Christ; in 1078 he made it clear that he regarded him as virtually a saint.[19]

It was only after Gregory had so drastically revised the official attitude of the West to warfare, and after his ideas had been disseminated by such publicists as Bishop Anselm II of Lucca— only, therefore, at the very end of the eleventh century—that the preaching of a Crusade became feasible. Only then could a man like the author of the *Gesta Francorum* have heard and answered a papal summons to go eastward, traveling with words from the Gospel upon his lips, and fortified by the assurance that, far from being sinful, his warfare would avail for the remission of sins and the winning of salvation.

The factors that we have so far noticed as contributing toward the Crusade have all concerned the knights, and the secular and religious status of their warfare. Fourth, I turn to something rather different, which historians are increasingly judging to have been of cardinal importance for understanding how the First Crusade came about. It is the state of the Church's penitential discipline at the end of the eleventh century.

No reader of eleventh-century sources, especially those relating to the Crusade, can fail to be struck by men's insistent preoccupation to secure the remission of sins—*remissio peccatorum*. Now, one might well ask whether this has not always been a key matter of Christian concern. Does not the Creed say, "I acknowledge one baptism for the remission of sins (*in remissionem peccatorum*)"? Indeed. But there are historical junctures when a particular matter of Christian dogma or concern, like justification in the Lutheran Reformation or personal conversion in the teachings of John Wesley, strikes home to men with exceptional force. When the First Crusade was being prepared, it seems to have been so with the remission of sins.

One reason for this was that the penitential system of the West was in disorder and confusion. During the twelfth and thirteenth centuries, this would be put right. As a result, an instructed Christian would know pretty clearly how the remission of sins was available to him. If he fell into mortal sin, say by homicide, he would suppose that he had incurred both guilt and punishment. He must confess his sin to a priest and be absolved; that would take away his guilt and free him from eternal punishment. Left with a burden of temporal punishment both in this life and after death (that is, in purgatory), he could, by availing himself of the indulgences that the Church now offered, draw upon the boundless mercy of God and the merits of the saints to lighten this, as well. In the eleventh century, all was not so clear and simple. Penance was still being imposed under an older system that had its heyday in Carolingian times. It knew little of the clear-cut and reassuring distinctions of the later order—between guilt and punishment, eternal and temporal punishment, penance and indulgence. Originally, the Christian had done a penance that, once performed, restored him as he had been before he had sinned. There were already grounds for anxiety in this: could a man be *sure* that his penance was equal to his sin? Before long, penances were being commuted for money: still more urgently, was not more than money needed for the remission of sins? And, by the eleventh century, penitents were often restored to communion before—not, as originally, after—they completed their penance. There was now certainly much left to be done before they could be fully assured that their sins were remitted. For one reason or another, they increasingly took thought for what they might do over and above the penitential system.

For members of the upper classes, there were two courses of action in particular, either or both of which they felt pressed to consider. Best of all, a man could become a monk, and so give himself to a life that was altogether one of penance. As a less effective variant on this course, which was therefore more fraught with anxiety, he could found or endow a monastery; then, his goods and the monks' prayers these goods endowed would avail for the remission of sins at the Day of Judgement. The alternative course of action was to go on pilgrimage. The popularity of pilgrimage to places like Monte Gargano, Compostela, Rome, and Jerusalem, shows how widely the feudal classes sought by this means to gain the remission of their sins. Like the monk, the pilgrim gave up his knightly status and activities; for it was demanded of a pilgrim that he travel unarmed. He carried only his purse and his staff, so that he abandoned himself to the mercy and protection of God. But unlike the monk's, the pilgrim's change of status was only temporary. Once back from Monte Gargano or wherever it was, he reverted to his secular way of life. If many became monks, more became pilgrims. We need only recall Count Fulk Nerra of Anjou with his three journeys to Jerusalem, or Duke Robert the Devil of Normandy, to remember how the most ruthless of men were wont, in moods of penitence, to seek relief of their sins through pilgrimage. The build-up of pilgrimages, like the vast amount of monastic conversion, foundation, and endowment, shows how insistent the desire for the remission of sins became.

When the call to the Crusade was made, it fulfilled this desire more acceptably than anything that had gone before. The choices hitherto available of becoming a monk or a pilgrim required a fighting man to abandon altogether, whether for good or only for a time, his chosen way of life. He had to "drop out" of knightly activities. But now, following the change made by Gregory VII in the Church's attitude toward warfare, the Crusade offered the knight the remission of sins *in and through* the exercise of his martial skills. "If any man," ran the crusading canon of Clermont, "sets out from pure devotion . . . to liberate the church of God at Jerusalem, his journey shall be reckoned to him in place of all penance."[20] At Clermont in 1095, the Crusade emerged, quite suddenly and with the maximum of dramatic appeal, as the knight's own way of gaining remission of sins by waging the warfare that was his life, in the service of Christ and in vindication of Christ's name against the Muslims. The point was well taken by a chronicler of the First Crusade, Guibert of Nogent:

> In our own time, God has instituted a holy manner of warfare, so that knights and the common people who, after the ancient manner of paganism, were aforetime immersed in internecine slaughter, have found a new way of winning salvation. They no longer need, as they did formerly, entirely to abandon the world by entering a monastery or by some other like commitment. They can obtain God's grace in their accustomed manner and dress, and by their accustomed way of life.[21]

No wonder that knights flocked to the Crusade in their hundreds, or that its ideals could soon find expression in Saint Bernard's "praise of the new warfare"—his *De laude novae militiae;* when, as the final stage of the development, monks and knights were fused together in that hitherto unthinkable form of Christian society, the military religious order of the Templars:

> Advance in confidence, you knights, and boldly drive out the enemies of the cross of Christ; be sure that neither death nor life can separate you from the love of God, which is in Christ Jesus. . . . How famously do

such victors return from battle! How blessed are such martyrs when
they die in battle! . . . For if they are blessed who die in the Lord, how
much more are they blessed who die for the Lord?[22]

This was a far cry, indeed, from the reluctance to sanction warfare
by Cardinals Peter Damiani and Humbert less than a hundred years
before. A Christian warfare for ideas had now indelibly registered
itself in the consciousness of the Catholic West, and had done so
because of the internal changes in that consciousness, which we
have considered.

To summarize, then: I have identified four factors that, as recent
inquiry suggests, so shaped Western society that it was not only
ready to rally to the Crusade, but also was subject to those pressures within itself that (rather than external causes) were principally
responsible for bringing the Crusade into being. They were: pressure of population and growth of internal order; the increasing
social and religious sophistication of the knightly class; a radical
change in the official Christian ethic of war; and the strains and
stresses set up within society by the Church's penitential system.
Severally and together, they reached their full potency at the end of
the eleventh century, and only then. Thus, the last decade of the
century could witness the critical step in beginning the Crusades.
But what, exactly, was this critical step? What was it that enabled
these pressures to break forth and so produced the Crusade?

The Swabian chronicler Bernold had no doubt. "The lord pope,"
he wrote, "was the prime author of that expedition";[23] the critical
step was his preaching. Bernold was probably right. Pope Urban II
was the very man to bring to a head the developments we have
examined. As Odo de Lagery, he sprang from a noble family in
Champagne, and thus understood, from within, the aspirations,
ethics, and institutions of French military society. As prior of the
great Burgundian monastery of Cluny, he could appreciate men's
quest for the remission of sins and their readiness to undertake
penitential exercises in order to secure it. As cardinal-bishop of
Ostia under Gregory VII, he knew that pope's work at first hand,
and he declared himself the inheritor of its essential aims.[24] I
cannot myself doubt that, since Urban was such a man, the Crusade

became what he intended it to become, and that his preaching was critical in shaping it.

The eleventh century had, of course, seen some actual or planned campaigns that in some ways anticipated the First Crusade; but these serve only to emphasize the novelty of Urban's initiative. Apart from the Norman Conquest of England, French knights had crossed the Pyrenees to take part in the Christian Reconquest. To one campaign, Pope Alexander II had attached a promise of spiritual benefits not unlike those associated with the First Crusade. Such holy wars against the infidel undoubtedly prepared the way for the Crusade. Yet, when compared with it, they were on a smaller scale; there was nothing equivalent to the Crusader's vow; and they wholly lacked the characteristics of pilgrimage that (as I shall suggest in a minute) were of the essence of the Crusade as Urban preached it.

Gregory VII, too, had in 1074 tried to organize a kind of Crusade to the East, which looks still more like the First Crusade. He proposed himself to lead a military expedition, primarily to help Byzantium against the Turks. He hoped thereby to reconcile the Roman and the Byzantine churches, and also the Armenians who had been dissident from Rome since the fifth century. He hoped, as well, that his host might worship at the Holy Sepulchre. As protector of the Roman Church while he was away, he proposed to leave Henry IV of Germany, who for the moment seemed to be obedient because of his preoccupation with the Saxon rising. Gregory planned to travel in the company of pious ladies—the Empress Mother Agnes and Countess Beatrice of Tuscany. Not surprisingly, the knights of western Europe made no response to so bizarre a summons. Its unrealistic conception illustrates the weakness of all Gregory's plans to enlist knights in the *militia Christi,* as a warfare with the sword waged directly for papal ends. Strong as were the tendencies that favored a Crusade, they could not be straightly harnessed, as Gregory hoped, to the hierarchical ends of the papacy. Far from preparing the way for the Crusade of 1095, Gregory went far to alienate the military classes by adopting too direct and hierarchical an approach.

Urban II was more understanding and diplomatic. Whereas Gregory imposed his own view of obedience to the vicar of Saint Peter, Urban played upon the constraint that men felt to perform works that would bring remission of sins. Whereas Gregory asserted his own political and military leadership, Urban saw that his expedition must be commanded by the natural leaders of French chivalry—men like Raymond of Saint-Gilles, count of Toulouse. Gregory worked across the grain of lay society; Urban worked with it.

Our problem in determining just how he provoked the "great stirring of the heart" is difficult, because we have no authentic record of what he said and little evidence of what he may have said. Historians are not agreed as to the probabilities. But our evidence strongly suggests that, from the start, the Crusaders thought that they were taking part in a *peregrinatio,* or pilgrimage, and, less certainly, that they were going to Jerusalem to worship, and to free the churches of the East from Jerusalem to Constantinople. The author of the *Gesta Francorum,* for instance, regarded his companions as *peregrini.* (For up to the thirteenth century, neither Latin nor the vernacular languages had words for "crusade" or "crusader.") But Urban's Crusade was quite unlike earlier *peregrinationes.* In the past, the many who had become pilgrims could expect spiritual benefits only if they went *unarmed.* The First Crusade was an *armed* pilgrimage. Its members looked for remission of sins because they went not only to pray but also to fight. It seems likely that Urban's critical step was to announce his expedition as, in effect, a pilgrimage whose members could claim spiritual benefits although they went armed—or, rather, *because* they went armed. He thereby linked together two things that hitherto had been incompatible—pilgrimage and holy war. A pilgrimage to Jerusalem, with appropriate spiritual benefits, provided a framework into which a holy war against the Muslims was now fitted.

Whatever the precise content of Urban's preaching, it struck the right note. Its spark lit the fire that the deeper trends within western Europe during the previous decades had been preparing. For those experiencing the pressure of population and the constraints of public order, it offered an overseas expedition with new lands to conquer or new booty to win. To knights with an enhanced social standing and a new religious sanction, it presented a worthy opportunity for a fight. Since Gregory VII had dispelled qualms about the licitness of warfare even in a Christian cause, it provided a call to arms that promised spiritual benefits. Those who felt the need for the remission of sins could now find it in and through the activities of their own order of society; they need not abandon them for the cloister or an unarmed pilgrimage. Seldom in human history has one man's initiative satisfied so many and such various aspirations. When Urban spoke at Clermont, it was indeed true, in Gibbon's words, that "a nerve was touched of exquisite feeling; and the sensation vibrated to the heart of Europe."[25]

As we look back across nine hundred years to the age of Gregory VII and Urban II, we cannot fail to recognize it as one of the most powerfully formative periods in our common culture, outlook, and institutions. It saw the reversal of a thousand years of Christian tradition, when the Gregorian papacy accepted warfare without reservation as a meritorious activity, and the profession of arms as a Christian vocation so long as it was directed toward the extirpation of what is alien to Christianity both inside and outside Christian society. It is because of this reversal that the Crusade could mold Western ideas so profoundly, and modern views about war could take shape. The Crusade itself, as a kind of war aimed at propagating one set of ideas and habits of life, the Christian, as against another set, such as the Muslim, has exercised an especial influence in this century. Did not Eisenhower describe his part in the Second World War in terms of a "Crusade in Europe"?

Yet the real lessons to be drawn from the Crusade are deeper and more complex. I revert to Stubbs's dictum with which I began: "The kings of the middle ages went to war for rights, not for interests, still less for ideas." As the words "still less for ideas" remind us, long before the Middle Ages were over, such total warfare as the Crusades, fought for ideas, tended to give place to limited warfare for rights or interests, which has itself yielded only in quite recent times to renewed warfare for ideas. It seems fair to suggest that, however deeply warfare for ideas may have penetrated the Western consciousness and shaped Western attitudes, it tends, when it becomes a danger, to be so as the result of such sets of domestic circumstances as provoked the Crusades. The Crusades began at a time of uncertainty and unsettlement in the institutions and ideas of a society undergoing rapid change, which prompted a search for alien elements within and outside it to serve as targets of ideological and physical aggression. (We may recall how the People's Crusade of 1096, which I have left outside the scope of this paper, directed itself not only against the Muslims in the East but also, in the first major outbreak of the anti-Semitism that found its high-water mark in Nazi Germany, against the Jews of the Rhineland.) Men seem in all ages to engage in the aggressive warfare of ideas less for external gains than to relieve the internal tensions and problems of their own society.

Such reflections are calculated to make us sceptical of the credentials of warfare for ideas. With our experience of twentieth-century ideological war, few of us, perhaps, would dissent from the verdict that stands at the end of Runciman's *History of the Crusades:*

> The triumphs of the Crusade were the triumphs of faith. But faith without wisdom is a dangerous thing. By the inexorable laws of history the whole world pays for the crimes and follies of each of its citizens. In the long sequence of interaction and fusion between Orient and Occident out of which our civilization has grown, the Crusades were a tragic and destructive episode. The historian as he gazes back across the centuries at their gallant story must find his admiration overcast by sorrow at the witness that it bears to the limitations of human nature. There was so much courage and so little honour, so much devotion and so little understanding. High ideals were besmirched by cruelty and greed, enterprise and endurance by a blind and narrow self-righteousness; and the Holy War itself was nothing more than a long act of intolerance in the name of God, which is the sin against the Holy Spirit.[26]

That is a severe judgement, but I think it is a just one. A conclusion that we may well draw from the study of the Crusades is that societies, like individuals, should strive for the self-knowledge that lays bare and relieves the internal pressures that generate wars of ideas and "holy wars," and so render them powerless to issue in aggression, whether psychological or physical.

Are we, then, committed to an antiwar ideology? We should probably hesitate. Counterideologies often tend toward the very evils that they profess to oppose. And, given the limitations of human nature, it is hard to envisage an order of things in which force, exercised under due authority, is not called for as the sanction of justice, both within and among states. Perhaps we would do well to look again at the view of war that emerged during the centuries when (as Stubbs reminds us) wars were, on the whole, not total but were limited to the pursuit of rights and interests. This view itself looked back behind the Crusades to the teaching of Saint Augustine about the "just war," which spokesmen in the eleventh century ignored. It was discussed by the canonists and schoolmen of the twelfth and thirteenth centuries, but more fully worked out in early modern times, notably by Spanish Dominicans like Vitoria and De Soto, and Jesuits like Suarez and Molina. "It is the acme of barbarity," wrote Vitoria, "to look for and take pleasure in reasons for killing and destroying men whom God has created and for whom Christ died."[27] As against wars of ideas that arise from the internal strains of individuals and societies, this view sanctions only limited wars that can be shown to arise from the facts of a given situation. Wars may be fought only for causes and reasons that are clearly defined and just, and at the command of a legitimate ruler. There must be no other feasible means of gaining the objectives that are envisaged, and the ruler must be under an overwhelming obligation to secure them. The damage that may be foreseen must not be disproportionate to the attainable objectives, and a ruler may apply only the minimum force that is necessary to gain them.

I do not suggest that this historical tradition about war can simply be adopted by our generation without further thought or modification. But it indicates a historical approach to the problem of war, which deserves to be considered as an alternative both to the holy war tradition and to radically antiwar ideologies. I venture the

opinion that the conscious adopting of such an approach, and the
general recognition of its validity, are among the conditions of
survival for liberal and democratic societies, and for mankind.

Bibliographical Note. Modern discussion of the origin of the Crusades centers upon Carl
Erdmann, *Die Entstehung des Kreuzzugsgedankens,* Forschungen zur Kirchen- und
Geistesgeschichte 6 (Stuttgart: W. Kohlhammer, 1935). This work has found no translator,
and no apology is needed for drawing heavily upon its argument in this paper. The second
chapter of H. E. Mayer, *The Crusades,* trans. J. Gillingham (Oxford: Oxford University
Press, 1972) is also fundamental. See, too, E. O. Blake, "The Formation of the 'Crusade
Idea,'" *Journal of Ecclesiastical History* 21 (1970): 11–31. For the status of eleventh-
century knights see P. van Luyn, "Les *milites* dans la France du XIe siècle," *Le Moyen Âge*
77 (1971): 5–51, 194–238. Gregory VII's attitude toward war is examined by I. S.
Robinson, "Gregory VII and the Soldiers of Christ," *History* 58 (1973): 169–92. Urban II's
preaching at Clermont is discussed by Dana C. Munro, "The Speech of Pope Urban II at
Clermont, 1095," *American Historical Review* 11 (1906): 231–42, and H. E. J. Cowdrey,
"Pope Urban II's Preaching of the First Crusade," *History* 55 (1970): 177–88. For the
Peace and Truce of God in relation to the Crusade, see Cowdrey, "The Peace and the Truce
of God in the Eleventh Century," *Past and Present,* no. 46 (February 1970), pp. 42–67.
Saint Augustine's attitude toward coercion is discussed by Peter Brown, *Religion and
Society in the Age of St. Augustine* (London: Faber & Faber, 1972), especially pp.
260–78, 301–31; and medieval developments are reviewed in Helmut Beumann, ed.,
Heidenmission und Kreuzzugsgedanke in der deutschen Ostpolitik des Mittelalters,
Wege der Forschung 7 (Darmstadt: Wissenschaftliche Buchgesellschaft, 1963), especially
the papers by Beumann and Hans-Dietrich Kahl. There are useful references to the canonists
and schoolmen in Gaines Post, *Studies in Medieval Legal Thought: Public Law and the
State, 1100–1322* (Princeton: Princeton University Press, 1964). Joshua Prawer, *The
World of the Crusaders* (London and Jerusalem: Weidenfeld and Nicholson, 1972), pp.
147–52, includes comments on the vitality of crusading ideas into the fifteenth century. For
the Spanish Dominicans and Jesuits, see Bernice Hamilton, *Political Thought in
Sixteenth-Century Spain* (Oxford: Clarendon Press, 1963), especially pp. 135–57, 169–
70; and for the whole development, G. Combès, *La Doctrine politique de Saint Augustin*
(Paris: Les Petits-fils de Plon et Nourrit, 1927), pp. 417–26.
I am grateful to the Cambridge University Press for allowing me to quote the concluding
paragraph of Sir Steven Runciman's *History of the Crusades.* I also thank Dr. Henry
Mayr-Harting, who read and commented upon a draft of this paper; I owe a number of
valuable points to him, and he has improved it in many ways.

1. William Stubbs, *The Constitutional History of England,* Clarendon Press Series,
5th ed., 3 vols. (Oxford, 1891–1903), 3:75.
2. See Stubbs's "Inaugural" of 1867, as Regius Professor of Modern History at Oxford,
in his *Seventeen Lectures on the Study of Medieval and Modern History* (Oxford:
Clarendon Press, 1887), p. 17.
3. Stubbs developed his views in two lectures delivered in 1880, "On the Characteristic
Differences between Medieval and Modern History," printed in his *Seventeen Lectures,*
pp. 238–76; see especially pp. 272–73.
4. Stubbs, *The Constitutional History of England,* 3:75.

5. Stubbs, however, regarded the Crusades with too great approval for him fully to establish the connection. For his judgment of them, see especially *Seventeen Lectures*, pp. 180–81, 253–54.

6. *Gesta Francorum et aliorum Hierosolymitanorum: The Deeds of the Franks and other Pilgrims to Jerusalem*, ed. and trans. Rosalind Hill, Medieval Classics (London and New York: T. Nelson, 1962), p. 1.

7. Ibid., p. 62.

8. Canon 1, Joannes Dominicus Mansi, *Sacrorum conciliorum nova et amplissima collectio*, vol. 19 (Venice: Anthony Zatta, 1774), column 827.

9. On liturgical prayers see Erdmann, *Die Entstehung*, pp. 24–26, 40, 72–78, 326–35. For those cited, see pp. 25 n. 71 and 327–28.

10. The Latin text of the *Life of Gerald of Aurillac* is in J. -P. Migne, ed., *Patrologiae cursus completus . . . series Latina*, 221 vols. (Paris: J. -P. Migne, 1844–64), 133: 639–704 (hereafter cited as *PL*); there is an English translation in *St. Odo of Cluny*, ed. and trans. Gerard Sitwell (London and New York: Sheed and Ward, 1958), pp. 90–180. For Gerald's manner of fighting see *PL*, 133:646–47; for English translation see *St. Odo*, ed. Sitwell, p. 100.

11. See H. E. J. Cowdrey, "Bishop Ermenfrid of Sion and the Norman Penitential Ordinance following the Battle of Hastings," *Journal of Ecclesiastical History* 20 (1969): 225–42.

12. See especially his *Quaestiones in Heptateuchum* 6.10, ed. I. Fraipont and Donatien de Bruyne, Corpus Christianorum, Series Latina 33 (Turnhout: Brépols, 1958), pp. 318–19 and *De civitate Dei* 1.21, ed. B. Dombart and A. Kolb, Corpus Christianorum, Series Latina 47 (Turnhout: Brépols, 1955), p. 23.

13. For the new emphasis that was placed upon the militant aspects of Saint Michael in Carolingian and Ottonian times, see J. J. G. Alexander, *Norman Illumination at Mont St. Michel, 996–1100* (Oxford: Oxford University Press, 1972), pp. 85–100.

14. *Ep.* 4.9 (*PL*, 144:316). Peter's idea of the proper, i.e., spiritual, warfare of a Christian is well illustrated by his *Vita sancti Romualdi*, cap. 7 (*PL*, 144:962). For a severe judgment upon a smith who took to making weapons of war, see *Opusculum* 43, cap. 3 (*PL*, 145:681–82).

15. *Adversus simoniacos* 2.18, ed. F. Thaner, *Monumenta Germaniae Historica* (hereafter *MGH*): *Libelli de lite*, 3 vols. (Hanover: Hahn, 1891–97), 1:159–60.

16. E. Caspar, "Gregor VII. in seinen Briefen," *Historische Zeitschrift* 130 (1924): 30.

17. Gerd Tellenbach, *Church, State and Christian Society at the Time of the Investiture Contest*, trans. R. F. Bennett, Studies in Mediaeval History, no. 3 (Oxford: Basil Blackwell, 1940), p. 164.

18. For Saint Maurice, see especially the *Passio Acaunensium martyrum*, ed. Bruno Krusch, *MGH: Scriptores rerum Merovingicarum*, 7 vols. (1885–1920), 3:32–39; for Saint Martin, see Sulpicius Severus, *Vita Sancti Martini*, cap. 4, ed. C. Halm, Corpus Scriptorum Ecclesiasticorum Latinorum, vol. 1 (Vienna: G. Geroldi, 1866), p. 114.

19. Berthold, *Annales, a.* 1077, ed. George H. Pertz, *MGH Scriptores*, 32 vols. (Hanover: Hahn, 1826–1934), 5:305–6. Gregory's change of view was to some extent anticipated in the Ottonian Empire, when, for example, Saint Maurice, a soldier-saint *from a long-distant past*, began to be venerated as an active patron of tenth-century warfare and politics. See especially Albert Brackmann, "Die politische Bedeutung der Mauritius-Verehrung im frühen Mittelalter," *Gesammelte Aufsätze*, 2nd ed. (Darmstadt: Wissenschaftliche Buchgesellschaft, 1967), pp. 211–41, and Helmut Beumann, "Das Kaisertum Ottos des Grossen: ein Rückblick nach tausend Jahren," *Wissenschaft vom Mittelal-*

ter (Cologne and Vienna: Böhlau, 1972), pp. 411–58, especially pp. 435–43. Other saints of Christian antiquity came to be similarly regarded, but no *contemporary* warrior was venerated as a saint.

20. *The Councils of Urban II,* ed. Robert Somerville, Annuarium historiae conciliorum, Supplementum, vol. 1 (Amsterdam: Hakkert, 1972–), vol. 1, *Decreta Claromontensia,* p. 74.

21. *Historia quae dicitur Gesta Dei per Francos,* cap. 1, in *Recueil des historiens des Croisades: Historiens occidentaux,* 5 vols. (Paris: Imprimerie nationale, 1844–95), 4:124.

22. *De laude novae militiae,* cap. 1. (*PL,* 182:922).

23. *Chronicon, a.* 1096 (*MGH: Scriptores,* 5:464).

24. *Ep.* 1 (*PL,* 151:283–84).

25. Edward Gibbon, *A History of the Decline and Fall of the Roman Empire,* ed. J. B. Bury, 7 vols. (London: Methuen, 1909–14), 6:268.

26. Sir Steven Runciman, *A History of the Crusades,* 3 vols. (Cambridge: Cambridge University Press, 1951–54), 3:480.

27. Cited by Hamilton, *Political Thought,* p. 157.

LINDA V. SEIDEL

Holy Warriors: The Romanesque Rider and the Fight Against Islam

Equestrian figures, which flourished in the sculptural decoration of Romanesque churches, have come to be regarded, by historians and art historians alike, as a quintessential manifestation of the Renaissance of the twelfth century. Both Christopher Brooke and Erwin Panofsky considered the large-scale figures to be faithful copies of the celebrated ancient statue of Marcus Aurelius, which stood, until the sixteenth century, outside the Lateran Palace in Rome (fig. 1).[1] Since the Middle Ages believed that this monumental bronze represented Constantine, scholarly tradition has assumed that the Romanesque carvings likewise portrayed the first Christian emperor. Emile Mâle even hypothesized that commemorative trinkets of the equestrian statue, brought back by French pilgrims in Rome, provided the impetus, during the early twelfth century, for the representation of mounted figures on church façades. The relief at Parthenay-le-vieux, one of many such riders in western France, is the best preserved and most celebrated among these carvings (fig. 2).[2] Mâle's theory accords well with the widespread view of Romanesque as an art that drew its intellectual instruction primarily from the Church in Rome and its artistic inspiration, particularly in southern Europe, from local civic monuments that had survived from the period of Roman colonization.

But why elevate Constantine to such a position of prominence on the outside of ecclesiastical buildings? There is no evidence of a cult of Constantine in either France or Spain at the time and no tradition of the Roman convert as benefactor of the churches on which he appears.[3] Moreover, if the rider image was inspired by a statue in Rome, why didn't the type proliferate in territories adjacent to Italy? A few riders do appear on sculptures in southern France, but these are small and belong to narrative episodes on capitals (fig. 3).[4] And certain features of these works, such as the figure trampled underfoot and the accompanying woman, characteristics as well of the Aquitainian cavaliers, do not appear on the Roman work.[5] Neither the western French riders nor the Provençal equestrians bear significant formal relation to the monumental Antique bronze.

Two types of riders had, in fact, been bequeathed by Antiquity to the Middle Ages. The sedate image of the victorious leader, familiar from public monuments such as the one in Rome, persisted in early Christian Imperial sculptures and on official coins; it also inspired representations of Christ's entry into Jerusalem.[6] A second, animated depiction of an aggressive cavalier, found originally on pagan funerary slabs and subsequently on Imperial Roman coins, became associated with the military saints, George, Demetrios, Theodore, who were seen, in Byzantium, as the defenders of Christianity.[7] Kingsley Porter suggested that this diverse group of Eastern warrior saints, rather than the individual Imperial rider, influenced the invention of the lively Western cavaliers.[8]

Alternatives to the Constantinian explanation of the twelfth-century equestrians do, in fact, emphasize the active quality of many of the Romanesque riders. The Spanish have held that the horseman is Saint James as he legendarily appeared in a dream to Charlemagne urging the Frank to fight the Moors and liberate the Saint's basilica in Galicia (fig. 4).[9] A Poitevin sigilographer, observing the similarity between the representations of armed riders on the seals of the lords of Parthenay and the riders that grace the tympana of two churches in that town, suggested that these particular equestrian carvings had something to do with local nobility;

perhaps they commemorated a victory by an eleventh-century member of their line over a local heresy.[10] The French archeologist Paul Deschamps observed that the "Constantinian" subject on a capital of French workmanship from Syria might allude to the twelfth-century fight against Islam.[11] Abstract explanations have also been offered. The riders have been related to mounted personifications of *Superbia,* sometimes shown wearing the trappings of a soldier. The identification of that awful Vice with cavaliers has been interpreted as a warning to members of the powerful fighting class not to abuse their power and commit the sin of Pride.[12] At the same time, the triumphant riders have been viewed as the embodiment of Virtue[13] and, along with a frequent companion, the lion-fighter, they have been interpreted as the dual powers in medieval society, Kingship and Priesthood (fig. 5).[14]

Each of the non-Constantine suggestions attempts to relate the riders to developments and themes of the period in which they were carved; each is, in part, persuasive. The difficulty with the explanations lies not so much with their arguments as with their evidence: the riders, in every instance, are viewed incompletely and are treated, more or less, as independent entities. It is as though the association of the twelfth-century rider with the Roman statue transferred to the medieval carving an illusion of self-containment, a quality that, while appropriate to the art of Antiquity, is not applicable to the mural sculpture of the Romanesque period. The twelfth-century figures occur without exception as part of vast sculptural programs and architectural installations; they are merely fragments of façades. When the riders are viewed within the contexts of the mural programs of which they form a part, several fascinating themes consistently assert themselves. These themes reveal an irresistible attraction not to the Antique but to Islam and point unambiguously toward a comprehensive interpretation of a significant group of Romanesque monuments.

West façades in western France are characterized by multiple arched openings carefully aligned in two tiers and divided by a band of corbels (figs. 6, 7). The doorway is the central element in a series of richly framed nichelike units, which invariably number three on the lower story and which have been compared to Roman triumphal arches.[15] The equestrian typically occupies the deep niche to the left or the north of the façade and is seen often in the second register but, at times, as at Parthenay, is introduced into the lower one as well.

The rider, in large or small scale, is one of the standard iconographic types in the decoration of these screenlike structures. Other prevalent themes that recur in the ornamentation of the voussoirs of the main door and around the niches of the second story are the Parable of the Wise and Foolish Virgins, the Psychomachia, and a combined Zodiac and Labors of the Months, which includes a *horseman* as the workman for May. The first two themes sustain the idea of victory, suggested as well by the triumphal form of the façade.[16] The themes are often combined. The rider is united with the Psychomachia at Aulnay, where a fragment of the horse survives,[17] at Civray, at St-Hilaire-de-Melle and at Notre-Dame-de-la-Couldre at Parthenay. On the latter church, identical pairs of Prudentius's warring Virtues and Vices adorn the second row of voussoirs around the central doorway; angels and elders in turn surround them. Fragmentary reliefs of a rider and a lion-fighter can still be seen in the arched niches to either side (fig. 8). On the façade at St-Jouin-de-Marnes, also in western France, a lunging horseman about to spear a serpent is shown at the top of a lofty engaged double column to the left of of the central window (fig. 9). The figure penetrates the zone of the gable where a frieze of the faithful is shown proceeding toward a standing Virgin. Immediately above is Christ, seated in front of a huge cross, His arms lowered and extended to either side.[18] At Civray, the theme of salvation or triumph is conveyed in more jubilant form by the presence of rejoicing angels within the medallions that frame the arched niche surrounding the rider (fig. 7).[19]

One of the Vices, in particular, is singled out for representation on several façades in the Saintonge-Poitou. *Luxuria,* so dramatically rendered on the porch at Moissac farther south,[20] assumes a variety of less strident, and at times even obscure, aliases on the Aquitainian monuments, as well as on some of the Spanish ones in which the rider appears. On the façade at St-Jouin, chained apes, a well-known image of obscenity,[21] adorn the capital that supports the modish companion of the rider to the right of the central window (fig. 9). At Sangüesa, in the spandrel adjacent to a tympanum with the Last Judgment, a now headless nude woman is shown crouching in front of the horseman.[22] *Unchastity* herself, a woman agonized by serpents at her breasts, is depicted on the archivolt directly beneath a partially restored horseman (and among the warring Virtues and Vices) at Melle and another such figure ornaments the engaged capital to the left and above the rider at Parthenay-le-vieux (fig. 10). Groups to either side of Saint James in the tympanum in the south transept at Compostela have been interpreted as the women who were liberated from Muslim harems after the saint's miraculous intervention at Clavijo (fig. 4).[23]

The curious busts of nude women in baskets on the voussoirs surrounding the Parthenay figure can be added to this group (fig. 2). In fact, these unusual figures provide the key to the meaning of the *Luxuria* motif. The presentations resemble the scene of the Virgin Mary being bathed as it appears in the capital frieze on the Royal Portal at Chartres, ca. 1150 (fig. 11).[24] But such an interpretation can hardly be applied to thirty-seven women. The hefty little figures recall the novel representation of a nude woman in a basket that is carried on horseback behind a cavalier in an animated depiction of a siege (figs. 12a & b). The complex scene decorates a Persian plate of early thirteenth-century manufacture in the Freer Gallery, Washington. Although depictions of nudity are uncommon in Islamic art, a few sources locate representations of unclad figures in harem's quarters and in bath houses. Following this, Ettinghausen suggested that the figure on the ceramic probably represents a dancer or entertainer of low social or moral standing brought along for the amusement of the soldiers.[25] Such portable objects of Muslim manufacture, the plates rather than the women, were readily available in the Mediterranean ports that traded heavily with North Africa; they were even copied in French workshops. An enameled copper washbasin of thirteenth-century Limoges manufacture, in the Detroit Institute of Arts, is decorated with a mounted falconer in the central medallion and with dancing girls in the surrounding lobes. A comparable Islamic dish dated to the mid-twelfth century is presently in Innsbruck.[26] Oleg Grabar has shown that this type of object popularized previously restricted princely themes in response to the tastes of twelfth-century Muslim patrons, aristocratic as well as bourgeois.[27] It is certain that such ceramic work from the Eastern Mediterranean was imported into the West, for traces of Syrian lustre ware have been found embedded into the façade of a house built by a wealthy feudal lord of St-Antonin, a town not far from Toulouse, toward the middle of the twelfth century (fig. 13).[28]

The women in baskets represent a substitution of an Islamic motif for a conventional Christian one in a theme closely associated with Romanesque riders. Additional evidence of western Europe's contact with and appreciation of Muslim art is found in other equestrian carvings of the period. The rider on a capital from Avignon, now in the Fitzwilliam Museum, Cambridge, England, presents such a curiously feminine mien that he was recently suspected of being a woman (fig. 14).[29] The figure actually recalls the type of Islamic prince, clean-shaven but often long-haired and mustachioed, who appears in hunting scenes on precious ivory boxes produced largely in Spain and Sicily from the tenth century on. The resemblance of the stone carving to Mozarabic work is enhanced by the similarity of the pearly ribbons that meander above and behind the head of the figure on the sculpture to the jeweled bands that enclose riders in lobed medallions on a tenth-century casket in London (fig. 15).[30] Contemporary literary descriptions emphasized the Moorish attire of Provençal lords, their shaven faces, parted hair and Arab steeds, all well observed aspects of this remarkable representation.[31]

Fascination with Islamic forms may also have encouraged the inclusion of a musician alongside the rider on the Avignon capital and on the frieze at Notre-Dame-de-la-Couldre, Parthenay (fig. 16). Such an alliance of figures was common on the cosmopolitan Saracenic ceramics to which western Europe had easy access and which Christian aristocrats clearly enjoyed possessing and displaying.[32] In addition and in contrast to this courtly expression, Old Testament associations are evoked by the presence of a *crowned* harpist, David, alongside the rider on capitals at Lérida and Narbonne (figs. 17, 18a, b). David also slew a lion, and with great humility. The lion-fighter on the Lérida capital, juxtaposed with the crowned harpist, appears to evoke the legend of the youthful Hebrew king rather than the story of Samson, the biblical hero who has often been identified as the lion-fighter at Parthenay and at La Rochette (fig. 5).[33]

Three important characteristics emerge from our consideration of the Romanesque rider thus far. It has been seen that the equestrian figure in western France is generally part of a large mural arrangement in which his frequent companions are Old Testament heroes, musicians, lion-fighters, and women. Second, the idea of Triumph is implicit in the arcuated frame of these monumental ensembles and in the themes of the Psychomachia and Wise Virgins usually found around the central doors. Finally, the handling of certain motifs closely resembles Muslim workmanship and suggests sophisticated appreciation of and knowledgeable borrowing from the art of Islam.

These several elements associated with the rider reliefs are the essential ingredients of contemporary texts in which the eighth- and ninth-century struggles of Charlemagne's army against the Muslims are celebrated.[34] *The Chronicle of Pseudo-Turpin,* also known to us as Book IV of the pilgrimage compilation *Jacobus,* the songs of the *William Cycle,* and of course the brilliant *Song of Roland,* all of which can be dated like the sculptures within the first half of the twelfth century, celebrate encounters between Carolingian and Saracen armies.[35] The battles described therein take place in western France (around Agen and Saintes), in northern Spain (in Sahagún and Saragossa), and in Provence (at Orange and Narbonne), precisely the regions in which the rider figures proliferated. The texts reveal a passionate concern for the triumph of Virtue, with an immutable allocation of right to Christians and wrong to heathens, a belief in instant martyrdom and a moralizing tendency to rationalize or justify defeat, all of which parallel the themes of the sculpture. There is also a marked tendency in both the *Song of Roland* and the sculpture to employ repetition, "of artfully varied occurrences" in Erich Auerbach's words, in order to make events more intense.[36]

The author of the *Chronicle of Pseudo-Turpin* "moralizes at the drop of a hat."[37] In this text, the fight against the Moors is likened to the more general fight against evil. In chapter 9, the reader is reminded to prepare his weapons, that is to say his Virtues, before undertaking the battle against Vice, just as Charles's warriors made ready their weapons before battle. "Who-so puts virtue before vice, his spear shall sprout and his victor's soul shall be crowned in heaven."[38]

The entire *Song of Roland* can be read as a contrast of Virtue and Vice. The *Song* begins with the wily deceitfulness of the Saracens who try to buy off Charlemagne and who initially succeed by dint of their lavish gifts to persuade the Frank of their intention to convert to Christianity. The traitor Ganelon encourages Charlemagne to accept the peace proposal and the emperor's naive agreement to withdraw from Spanish territory is the occasion for the blood bath at Roncesvalles.[39]

Interestingly enough, the *Pseudo-Turpin,* which covers some of the same ground as the *Song,* labors to explain why it happened that good Christians were slaughtered by pagans in the Pyrennean pass. The massacre is blamed on the fact that on the night before the retreat, some of the Christians had slept with Saracen women, one thousand of whom were sent to Charlemagne as part of the treacherous tribute by the Moorish king.[40] Indeed, the longer editions of the *Pseudo-Turpin* go on to warn warriors not to take wives or women on campaigns for it is neither decent nor expedient.[41] Weakness of the flesh then justifies the death of Roland and the twelve peers. Yet the *Chronicle* hastens to explain that by dying in the fight against the Infidel, the sinful soldiers overcame prior transgressions. They are immediately crowned among holy martyrs in the Kingdom of Heaven.[42] It might be noted here parenthetically that a less exalted reward was described for those who survived their sinful acts and lived to repeat them. The punishment for *Unchastity* was vividly described in Book V of the *Jacobus,* the *Pilgrim's Guide,* in a passage that calls the reader's attention to the figure of a partially clad woman in one of the tympana on the Puerta de las Platerías at Santiago:

> And don't forget to notice the woman who is found alongside the Temptation of The Lord: she holds between her hands the fetid head of her lover which was cut off by her own husband and which she must kiss two times a day, on his order. Oh what a terrible and just punishment for the adulterous woman, it must be told to all.[43]

The *Pseudo-Turpin* has recently been described as possessing the essential qualities of a really good children's book; it is witty, full of action, packed with fascinating detail.[44] Whatever its purpose, it certainly became immensely popular. The fact that Aymery Picaud (or Picand) from Parthenay, a prominent town on the pilgrimage roads, is identifiable as one of the editors or contributors to the compilation, may explain in part why the imagery of a church in that town shows such rapport with the jocular spirit as well as the substance of the text (figs. 2, 6, 10).[45]

One could cite numerous passages from the literature to clarify ambiguities in the interpretation of the sculptures. For example, the descriptions of Roland's fight with the giant Ferragut may have inspired emphatic contemporary representations of the young David shown pitted against a huge and horrible Goliath.[46] A passage in the *Song of Roland,* in which Charlemagne dreams that he is struggling with a fierce lion, may help to explain the recurrent appearance of lion-fighters on capitals and church façades. The dream occurs the night before the Christian emperor's meeting with the Muslim Emir Baligant in a battle that clearly pits good against evil.[47] But Lejeune and Stiennon have already studied such relationships,[48] and moreover I do not seek to suggest that the sculptures merely serve as illustrations of popular texts. They are, rather, analogues of the manuscripts. As the texts relate to an oral tradition of folklore,[49] so the images depend upon venerable pictorial customs. And just as the authors sought their raw material in the events of Carolingian political history, so, I believe, the sculptors found some of their forms in the artistic monuments associated with Charlemagne and his court.

In particular, two objects of Carolingian metalwork, known only through old drawings, closely resemble in design and iconography Romanesque façades in western France. The arrangement of the tiers of jeweled arches on the so-called *Escrain de Charlemagne* recalls the two-dimensional organization of a façade such as the one at Tauriac (figs. 19, 20).[50] The distinctive ingredient of such a Romanesque portal, the association of a rider with an arched entry, is known from the *Arc of Eginhard,* a late ninth-century miniature metalwork arch that served as the support for a cross (fig. 21).[51] The triumphal imagery on this monument groups Christ, the Apostles, and the Evangelist symbols in the attic story while below, pairs of nimbed, armored figures holding standards adorn the short sides and, on front and back, four similarly garbed individuals, holding lances and shields, flank the opening. Guarding the inner passage are two armed riders trampling serpents. Weitzmann has modified the traditional identification of the riders, often called the rulers of the East and West, Constantine and either Charlemagne or Louis the Pious, and suggested that perhaps the more comprehensive idea of the ongoing veneration of the cross by Christian emperors past and present is represented.[52] The upper part of the façade at St-Jouin, with its culmination in the Triumphant Cross accompanied by the rider immediately below, recalls the disposition of the imagery on the diminutive Carolingian arch (fig. 9).

The influence of metalwork on the rebirth of monumental sculpture during the eleventh century was amply stressed half a century ago by Paul Deschamps.[53] Since then, resemblances between liturgical furniture and specific Aquitainian façades, such as those of Notre-Dame-la-Grande in Poitiers and the Cathedral at Angoulême, have been mentioned but not pursued.[54] Although the argument for these associations has previously been based primarily on form, the discussion here provides content and context. A possible mode of transmission can be suggested as well. Eginhard's reliquary shrine has been related to small architectural models that are known to have been employed in the construction of

Carolingian churches.[55] Some of these may well have survived and persisted in later usage.

The *Torhalle* at Lorsch, a monumental Carolingian interpretation of a triumphal arch, has previously been related to western French façades primarily because of the absence of any of the presumed Gallo-Roman models for the Romanesque churches (fig. 22).[56] But the murality of the French façades and the regularity and multiplicity of openings along their surfaces genuinely recall the treatment of the Carolingian interpretation rather than that of the *Torhalle*'s own Antique prototype, the Arch of Constantine (fig. 23).[57] During Charlemagne's programmatic revival of fourth-century Antiquity, the imposing plastic forms of selected Roman monuments had been recast and reinterpreted into delicate and decorative elements. These medievalized forms became, for a while, in the twelfth century, more accessible, both aesthetically and intellectually, than surviving remnants of provincial Roman culture.[58]

Why should a revival of Carolingian themes be centered in western France along the pilgrimage road? Quite simply because this was the seat of the oldest commital dynasty in France, one that traced its line back to Charlemagne.[59] The region's nobility was actively engaged in the twelfth-century fight against the Moors in Spain and was, at the same time, mindful of its dynastic attachments to heroes of the eighth-century struggle, in particular, the first Count William of Toulouse, Duke of Aquitaine, who ended his days as a monk in an abbey he founded at Gellone, not far from Montpellier.[60] This historic William emerged in the twelfth century as the hero of a cycle of *Chansons* that recount struggles against the Moors at Nimes and Orange.[61] These poems provide the parallels, perhaps even the sources, for the small-scale riders that decorate a number of capitals from Provence (figs. 3, 17, 18).[62] William's church was one of the high spots of the pilgrimage roads and was renamed St. Guilhem-le-désert in his honor. In a *Life* composed (ca. 1125) by the monks of his abbey, the historic William was amalgamated with the current count William of Aquitaine,[63] who in 1120, like his distinguished eighth-century predecessor, had fought in Spain, assisting Alfonso in the Spanish king's victory over the Moors at Cutanda. This William was also a bon vivant who loved music and women. In fact his participation in the Spanish campaign may have been, in part, an act of contrition following a defiant liaison for which he had been excommunicated.[64]

Protection of the count was the task of a group of castellans whose châteaux proliferated throughout Aquitaine from the tenth century on. During the eleventh and twelfth centuries, these castellans gained increased independence from the count and they, rather than the monks, were actively involved in church foundations and constructions in this area.[65] The Seigneurial House of Parthenay, whose lords were active both in the First Crusade and on the Pilgrimage, had become one of the most influential in the Poitou by the beginning of the twelfth century. By then the lords had usurped much of the power originally granted to the court.[66] A contemporary copy of the sculpture at Parthenay-le-vieux, which was the lords' burial church,[67] exists at Brinsop in Herefordshire on the Welsh border in England; it affords additional insight into the probable significance of the French monument (fig. 24). George Zarnecki explained that Oliver de Merlimond, founder of churches in Hereford, made a pilgrimage to Compostela via France during the 1130s. The falcons and cape that encumber the dragon killer on the English sculpture are not a traditional part of Saint George's iconography and appear to be directly quoted from the French carving. Zarnecki suggested that artists in Oliver's retinue returned home with sketches of monuments observed en route.[68] The English nobleman and warrior who had just completed a pilgrimage unquestionably admired and probably identified with the insignia on the Parthenay church; otherwise, why should he have had them copied?

Thus, the rider image had, in the eyes of contemporaries, become identified with the struggle against Islam. In combating this last and greatest of heresies,[69] Christians, as we have seen, had become attracted to some of its rival's characteristic modes of expression. Perhaps by imitating Islam's forms and by popularizing them, the West thought it could mitigate the powerful challenge of its enemy.[70] The proliferation of the *Luxuria* theme on Aquitainian portals may be part of this mystique. For in this geographical milieu, an image of *Unchastity* would serve as both a condemnation of heathen manners and a caveat to the Christian feudal class, as Meyer Schapiro long ago observed, to avoid excesses through which it could be drawn away from the guidance of the Church.[71] In falling prey to the Vice, Christians were reminded that they risked identification with Islam.[72]

The Romanesque fascination with the rider fused the concepts of triumphant ruler, aggressive warrior, and cosmopolitan courtier. Images of the mounted figure thus evoked associations with the state, the Church and the trusty knight who served them both.[73] Who then can we finally say the Romanesque rider represents? He represents no single individual but stands instead for a class of heroes, big and small, past and present, each of whom battled, metaphorically, alongside Charlemagne in the fight for Christianity and for country.[74] Like their colleagues in the epic poems, the riders epitomize the valor of the feudal aristocrat. Both are at once emblems of past glory and guarantors of continued triumph. In literature as well as in art, the past is perpetuated not by renaissance, but by reformulation in the Romanesque present.[75]

This twelfth-century revitalization of a once discrete Imperial motif had remarkable progeny. It is not inappropriate in the context of this meeting to look ahead to the figure's repercussions during the Renaissance. Those equestrians that flourished in Mediterranean Europe in centuries to follow, even though they were free-standing, made of metal, and posed like the Imperial bronze, continued in fact to celebrate and commemorate the prowess of local heroes (fig. 25). The Venetian Colleoni was, like our Romanesque rider, a Christian adventurer in service of God and country.

The research for this paper was carried out during several seasons and profited from discussions with numerous colleagues and friends. I am especially grateful to Ernst Kitzinger for his generous and careful criticism of key aspects of this work. A study of pilgrimage sculpture, supported by the Canaday Fund of Harvard University during the summer of 1967, first directed my attention from the issue of style to the problem of meaning. Versions of this study were presented to the Medieval Seminar at Columbia University in January 1973 and at the meeting of The College Art Association in January 1974.

1. Christopher Brooke, *The Twelfth Century Renaissance* (London: Thames and Hudson, 1969), pp. 15–17; Erwin Panofsky, *Renaissance and Renascences in Western Art* (New York: Harper and Row, 1969), p. 57. See J. S. Ackerman, "Marcus Aurelius on the Capitoline Hill," *Renaissance News* 10 (1957): 71–72, for a discussion of the history of the Roman statue's identification and E. Babut for comments on its possible ninth-century location, "Les statues équestres du Forum," *Mélanges d' archéologie et d'histoire, École française de Rome* 20 (1900): 209–22.

2. Émile Mâle is generally credited with having popularized the theory of the Constantinian identification of the Romanesque rider, although he was not the first to make the association, *L'Art religieux du XIIᵉ siècle en France* (Paris: A. Colin, 1922), p. 247. The earlier literature, including an enumeration of the Romanesque examples, is well summarized in Henri Leclercq's entry, "Cavaliers au portail des églises," in *Dictionnaire d'archéologie chrétienne et de liturgie*, ed. Fernand Cabrol, 15 vols. (Paris: Letouzey, 1907–53), vol. 2, prt. 2, cols. 2690–2700. An updated account of scholarship on the subject, touching on several of the problems considered here, is given by René Crozet, "Nouvelles remarques sur les cavaliers sculptés ou peints dans les églises romanes," *Cahiers de civilisation médiévale* 1 (1958): 27–36, with a final reconsideration in "Le thème du cavalier victorieux dans l'art roman de France et d'Espagne," *Principe de Viana* 32 (1971): 125–43. Few, if any, of the figures can be dated precisely, but the vast majority of them have been attributed to the first half of the twelfth century. For a general discussion of the sculpture of this region, including the problem of dating, see René Crozet, *L'Art roman en Poitou* (Paris: H. Laurens, 1948) and *L'Art roman en Saintonge* (Paris: A. and J. Picard, 1971). Restoration of the Parthenay sculpture replaced losses, particularly among the voussoirs, but appears not to have tampered with the surviving original elements.

3. Jean Adhémar's arguments supporting this position in *Influences antiques dans l'art du moyen âge français* (London: The Warburg Institute, 1939), pp. 208–9, and Leclercq's in "Cavaliers," cols. 2699–2700, have been rejected by Crozet, "Nouvelles remarques," pp. 31–32. To be sure, Constantine was evoked by the partisans of Gregory VII in their defense of the supremacy of the Church over the laity. But no specific relationship between this late eleventh-century dispute and the imagery considered here can be shown. See the recent comments by I. S. Robinson, "Gregory VII and the Soldiers of Christ," *History* 58 (1973): 169–92.

Hubert Le Roux has recently stressed that the name Constantine appears far more frequently in eleventh- and twelfth-century documents from western France, the precise region in which the rider sculptures proliferated, than in the charts of any other area of France. He suggests that the riders may, in many cases, be "donor" portraits of the churches' benefactors seen, perhaps, as allegories of Constantine. At Melle, he notes, two successive donors actually bore that name. "Figures Equestres et Personnages du nom de Constantin au XIᵉ et XIIᵉ siècles," *Bulletin de la Société des Antiquaires de l'Ouest et des Musées de Poitiers,* 4th ser. 12 (1974): 379–94. A previously neglected reference to Constantinus prefectus romanus, a Christian warrior in the service of Charlemagne, occurs in the *Pseudo-Turpin,* chap. 13. On the text and the question of its relationship to the problems of the riders, see below and note 35.

4. A Constantinian interpretation of the carvings in the cloisters of Saint-Trophîme at Arles and Saint-Sauveur at Aix has nevertheless been put forth. See Abbé P. M. Tonnelier,

"Reflexions sur les cavaliers des portails romans," *Bulletin de la Société historique et scientifique des Deux-Sèvres* 9 (1952): 229.

5. Harald von Roques de Maumont suggested that the crouching figure that medieval texts described beneath the hoof of Marcus Aurelius's horse was a medieval invention; the animal's foot is fully modeled and indicates no sign of attachment (fig. 1). Moreover, the figure is not in a warring pose. See *Antike Reiterstandbilder* (Berlin: de Gruyter, 1958), pp. 55–58. Charles Daras, likewise noting the lack of resemblance between the French riders and the Roman bronze, stressed the importance of indigenous Gallo-Roman prototypes for the Roman equestrians. "Réflexions sur les statues équestres représentant Constantin en Aquitaine," *Bulletin de la Société des Antiquaires de l'Ouest et des Musées de Poitiers,* 4th ser. 10 (1969): 152, 157.

6. See the discussions in André Grabar, *L'Empéreur dans l'art byzantin* (Paris: "Les Belles Lettres," 1936), pp. 45 ff. and pls. 28–29; E. Kantorowicz, "The 'King's Advent' and the Enigmatic Panels in the Doors of Sta. Sabina," *Art Bulletin* 26 (1944): 215–16; E. Kitzinger, "The Mosaics of the Cappella Palatina in Palermo," *Art Bulletin* 31 (1949): 279–80.

7. Von Roques, *Reiterstandbilder,* pp. 52–53, 55, and A. Grabar, *L'Empéreur,* pp. 47–48, with illustrations.

8. A. Kingsley Porter, *Romanesque Sculpture of the Pilgrimage Roads,* 10 vols. (Boston: Marshall Jones, 1923), 1:187–92.

9. The theme is discussed by A. de Apraïz, "La representación del caballero en las iglesias de los caminos de Santiago," *Archivo español de arte* 14 (1941): 384–96.

10. F. Eygun, "Un thème iconographique commun aux églises romanes de Parthenay at aux sceaux de ses seigneurs," *Bulletin archéologique* (1927): 387–90, and *Sigillographie de Poitou* (Mâcon: Protat frères, 1938), pl. XVIII, no. 533 and p. 236. But the rider had appeared on the seals of other nobles in western France earlier in the century. See the seals of Duke William IX and Aimery I of Châtellerault, ibid., pls. I, no. 1 and VIII, no. 207. By the end of the century, the period to which the Parthenay seals can be attributed, riders were used as personal insignia by the House of Lusignan and the Vicomte of Thouars, ibid., pls. LVII, no. 415 and LVIII, no. 532.

11. "Un chapiteau roman provenant de Terre-Sainte," *Bulletin des Musées de France* (1929): 244, and "La sculpture française en Palestine et en Syrie," *Monuments Piot* 31 (1930): 94–95. See also the catalogue by M. Aubert and M. Beaulieu, *Description raisonnée des sculptures du moyen age, de la Renaissance et des temps modernes* (Paris: Musée National du Louvre, 1950–   ), vol. 1, *Moyen Age*, pp. 81–83, no. 105. Crozet also associated a relief in Tudela, showing a mounted soldier with a turbaned Moor at his feet, with the fight against Islam, "Recherches sur la sculpture romane en Navarre et en Aragon," *Cahiers de la civilisation médiévale* 3 (1960): 127.

12. L. K. Little, "Pride Goes before Avarice: Social Change and the Vices in Latin Christendom," *American Historical Review* 76 (1971): 34–35.

13. C. Daras discussed the theme of warring and riding figures as illustrations of the Virtues and Vices. "Les cavaliers de la Rochette," *Mémoires de la Société archéologique et historique de la Charente* (1957): 1–5. See also his "Réflexions sur les statues équestres," pp. 151–57.

14. Y. Labande-Mailfert interpreted the rider and lion-fighter as *regnum* and *sacerdotium* in "L'iconographie des laïcs dans la société aux XIe et XIIe siècles," in *I Laici nella "Societas Christiana" dei secoli XI e XII,* Miscellanea del centro di Studi Medioevali 5 (Milan: Vira e pensiero, 1968), pp. 515–18.

15. René Crozet, "Survivances antiques dans l'architecture romane du Poitou, de l'Angoumois et de la Saintonge," *Mémoires de la Société nationale des Antiquaires de France*," 9th ser. 3 (1954): 198–99.

16. See the studies on the Psychomachia theme in art by P. Deschamps, "Le Combat des Vertus et des Vices sur les portails romans de la Saintonge et du Poitou," *Congrès archéologique*, vol. 79, no. 2 (1912), pp. 309–24, and Adolf Katzenellenbogan, *Allegories of the Virtues and Vices in Medieval Art*, trans. Alan J. P. Crick (New York: W. W. Norton, 1964), especially p. 9. Enumerations of the iconographic themes represented on churches in western France are included in Crozet, *L'Art roman en Poitou*, passim, and in E. L. Mendel, *Romanesque Sculpture in Saintonge*, Yale History Publications, History of Art 2 (New Haven: Yale University Press, 1940), pp. 86–88. See Porter, *Romanesque Sculpture*, 7, pl. 997 for an illustration of the doorway at Fenioux with a rider on the outermost voussoir.

17. G. Dez, "Encore le 'Constantin' de Notre-Dame-la-Grande et celui d'Aulnay de Saintonge," *Bulletin de la Société des Antiquaires de l'Ouest et des Musées de Poitiers*, 4th ser. 12 (1973): 265—74.

18. See the discussion of the whole façade in E. Maillard, "La Façade de l'église romane de St-Jouin-de-Marnes en Poitou," *Gazette des Beaux-Arts*, 5th ser. 9 (1924): 137–50. See also the plates in Porter, *Romanesque Sculpture*, especially pl. 947.

19. For the plate, ibid., pl. 1123.

20. Ibid., 4, pl. 371.

21. Horst W. Janson, *Apes and Ape Lore in the Middle Ages and Renaissance* (London: The Warburg Institute, 1952), pp. 29 ff, especially pp. 50–51. Illustrated in Porter, *Romanesque Sculpture*, 7, pl. 948.

22. Ibid., 6, pl. 749.

23. Crozet, "Le thème du cavalier," p. 135, n. 18.

24. Adelheid Heimann touched on the iconography in "The Capital Frieze and Pilasters of the Portail Royal, Chartres," *Journal of the Warburg and Courtauld Institutes* 31 (1968): 76.

25. The plate is illustrated in and dated by Arthur Pope, ed., *A Survey of Persian Art*, 9 vols. (London and New York: Oxford University Press, 1938–39), 3:1465. See the brief discussion on nudity with reference to this dish by G. D. Guest and R. Ettinghausen, "The Iconography of a Kāshān Luster Plate," *Ars Orientalis* 4 (1961): 43–45, and n. 70. Renata Holod has recently studied the dish in an as yet unpublished paper. Meyer Schapiro pointed out that the unchaste women appeared in Arab literary accounts of the afterlife, although such representations were unknown to him in art. "From Mozarabic to Romanesque in Silos," *Art Bulletin* 21 (1939): 328.

26. H. Buchthal, "A Note on Islamic Enameled Metalwork and its Influence in the Latin West," *Ars Islamica*, vols. 11/12 (1946), pp. 195–98.

27. André and Oleg Grabar, "L'essor des arts inspirés par les Cours princières à la fin du premier millénaire; princes musulmans et princes chrétiens," in *L'occidente e l'islam nell'alto medioevo*, Settimane di Studio del Centro Italiano di studi sull'alto medioevo 12 (Spoletto, 1964), pp. 845–92; Oleg Grabar, "Les arts mineurs de l'Orient musulman à partir du milieu du XIIᵉ siècle," *Cahiers de civilisation médiévale* 11 (1968): 181–90, and "Imperial and Urban Art in Islam: The Subject Matter of Fatimid Art," in *Colloque International sur l'Histoire du Caire* (Cairo: Ministry of Culture of The Arab Republic of Egypt, 1969), pp. 173–89.

28. M. Schapiro, "The South Transept Portal of Saint-Sernin at Toulouse," *Parnassus* 1, no. 2 (1929): 22. Muslim houses of the twelfth and thirteenth centuries were decorated

with comparable themes carved in stone. See the tympanum of a rider illustrated in M. S. Dimand, *A Handbook of Mohammedan Art*, 3d ed., rev. and enl. (New York: Metropolitan Museum of Art, 1958), pp. 97–98, fig. 57. For additional photos of the façade decoration, see Porter, *Romanesque Sculpture*, 4, pls. 358–59.

29. A. Borg, "A Further Note on a Marble Capital in the Fitzwilliam Museum Cambridge," *Burlington Magazine* 110 (1968): 312–16. The piece had previously been published by M. R. Taylor, "A Marble capital from the Toulouse region," *Burlington Magazine* 106 (1964): 539.

30. See the illustrations in John Beckwith, *Caskets from Cordoba* (London: H. M. Stationery Off., 1960) and Perry B. Cott, *Siculo-Arabic Ivories* (Princeton: Department of Art and Archaeology, Princeton University, 1939). E. Cruikshank Dodd has recently discussed artistic exchanges between Christian Europe and the Muslim world: "On the Origins of Medieval *Dinanderie:* The Equestrian Statue in Islam," *Art Bulletin* 51 (1969): 220–21, 225–29. The basic study on Islamic influence in the West remains A. Fikry, *L'Art roman du Puy et les influences Islamiques* (Paris: E. Leroux, 1934); on this point especially p. 162. See also E. Mendel's comments on the possible influence of Muslim ivory boxes in western France, *Romanesque Sculpture in Saintonge*, p. 4. James Kritzeck's valuable review article, "Moslem-Christian Understanding in Medieval Times," *Comparative Studies in Society and History* 4 (1962): 388–401, touches on the Christian fascination with and interest in Islam, especially pp. 392–93, 395.

31. See Raoul Glaber's description of richly attired southern lords in his *Historiae sui temporis; Recueil des historiens des Gaules et de la France,* 10:42, cited in Robert Briffaut, *The Troubadours* (Bloomington: Indiana University Press, 1965), p. 84. Similar comments appear in A. Kelly, "Eleanor of Aquitaine and her Courts of Love," *Speculum* 12 (1937): 15. The well-traveled Benjamin of Tudela provided a description of the exilarch of Baghdad (ca. 1168) that concentrated both on the elegance of his attire and on the riding ceremonies in which he participated. In J. R. Marcus, *The Jew in the Medieval World: A Source Book* (New York: Atheneum, 1969), pp. 186–87.

32. Certain themes, common in the sculpture of the region, have been related to Muslim concerns; see for example Ernst Kantorowicz's discussion of the archer as Ishmael in "The Archer in the Ruthwell Cross," *Art Bulletin* 42 (1960): 57–59, and Meyer Schapiro, "The Angel with the Ram in Abraham's Sacrifice: A Parallel in Western and Islamic Art," *Ars Islamica* (1943): 134–47.

33. For Parthenay, see Crozet, *L'Art roman en Poitou,* pp. 13, 185–86; on la Rochette, see Daras, "Les Cavaliers de la Rochette." The capital at Lérida was briefly discussed by Labande-Mailfert, *I Laici,* p. 518, and by Crozet, "Cavaliers sculptés," p. 35, n. 31. On the Davidic identity of the lion-fighter, see also B. de Montesquiou-Fézensac, "L'Arc d'Éginhard," *Cahiers archéologiques* 8 (1956): 171, n. 3.

34. The literature on the subject is vast and no attempt has been made to be comprehensive in the bibliographic references. In addition to two fundamental nineteenth-century studies, Gaston Paris, *Histoire poétique de Charlemagne* (Paris: Librarie A. Franck, 1865), especially pp. 67ff., and Gerhard Rauschen, *Die Legende Karls des Grossen im 11. und 12. Jahrhundert,* Publikationen der Gesellschaft für Rheinische Geschichtskunde 7 (Leipzig, 1890), the following recent works offer valuable presentations of the material including a review of the literature: Barton Sholod, "Charlemagne: Symbolic Link between the Eighth and Eleventh Century Crusades," in *Studies in Honor of M. J. Benardete*, ed. Izaak Langnast and Barton Sholod (New York: Las Americas, 1965), pp. 33–46; and Barton Sholod, *Charlemagne in Spain: The Cultural Legacy of Roncesvalles* (Geneva: Droz, 1966); R. Folz, *Le Souvenir et la Légende de Charlemagne dans l'Empire germanique médiévale,* Publications de l'Université de Dijon, n.s. 7 (Paris: "Les Belles Lettres," 1950), especially bk. 3, pp. 134ff.

35. See the study by H. M. Smyser, ed. *The Pseudo-Turpin,* Mediaeval Academy of America Publication, no. 30 (Cambridge, Mass., 1937), and the review by H. M. Powicke in *Speculum* 13 (1938): 364–66. Valuable articles by A. Hamel, "Überliegerung und Bedeutung des Liber Sancti Jacobi und des Pseudo-Turpin," *Sitzungsberichte der Bayerischen Akademie der Wissenschaften,* Philosophische Klass 2 (Munich, 1950), pp. 1–75, and M. L. Berkey Jr., "The *Liber Sancti Jacobi:* The French adaptation by Pierre de Beauvais," *Romania* 86 (1965): 75–80, have been surpassed by Christopher Hohler's recent "A Note on *Jacobus,*" *Journal of the Warburg and Courtauld Institutes* 35 (1972): 31–80.

On the *chansons,* see W. T. H. Jackson, *Medieval Literature* (New York: Collier Books, 1966), pp. 70–72, 160–74, and on their historical situation, specifically, R. Louis, "L'épopée française est carolingienne," in Ramon de Abadal, et al., *Coloquios de Roncesvalles,* Publicaciones de la Facultad de Filosofía y Letras, Zaragoza (Saragosa, 1956), pp. 327–460, and J. Frappier, "Réflexions sur les rapports des chansons de geste et de l'histoire," *Zeitschrift für romanische Philologie* 73 (1957): 4–8. G. Frank's "Historical Elements in the Chansons de Geste," *Speculum* 14 (1939): 209–14, considers the theoretical problem of the chansons' "origins." The relationship between the *Chansons de Geste* and the pilgrimage to Compostela has been emphasized by George Zarnecki in a recent work, *The Monastic Achievement* (New York: McGraw-Hill Book Company, 1972), pp. 55–59.

36. Erich Auerbach, *Mimesis* (Princeton: Princeton University Press, 1953), p. 104: see also Mario Pei, *French Precursors of the Chanson de Rolande* (New York: Columbia University Press, 1948), p. 36.

37. Smyser, *Pseudo-Turpin,* p. 5.

38. Ibid., pp. 24, 63–64.

39. See Auerbach's discussion in *Mimesis,* pp. 98–122. Jackson suggested that the Christian soldiers are personifications of Christian Virtues in the *Song* whereas the Pagans personify the Vices. *Medieval Literature,* p. 76.

40. Smyser, *Pseudo-Turpin,* chap. 25, pp. 40, 81–82.

41. Ibid., p. 14.

42. Ibid., p. 83. Roland and the French barons enjoy similar instant salvation in *The Song of Roland,* trans. D. L. Sayers (Baltimore: Penguin Books, 1957), lines 1127–35 and 2374–97. See recently, J. S. Preus, "Theological Legitimation for Innovation in the Middle Ages," *Viator* 3 (1972): 14–16.

43. Jeanne Vielliard, ed., *Le Guide du Pèlerin de Saint-Jacques de Compostelle,* 3rd ed. (Mâcon: Protat, 1963), pp. 102–3. For the illustration, see Porter, *Romanesque Sculpture,* 6, pl. 679.

44. Hohler, "*Jacobus,*" p. 71.

45. Ibid., pp. 40, 56.

46. On this subject, see Rita Lejeune and Jacques Stiennon, "Le héros Roland, 'Neveu de Charlemagne,' dans l'iconographie médiévale," in *Karl der Grosse: Lebenswerk und Nachleben,* ed. Wolfgang Braunfels, 5 vols. (Düsseldorf: L. Schwan, 1966–68). vol. 4, *Das Nachleben,* ed. Wolfgang Braunfels and P. E. Schram (1967), p. 216, where the David parallel is mentioned, and J. M. Lacarra, "El combate de Roldán y Ferragut y su representación gráfica en el siglo XII," *Anuario del Cuerpo facultativo de archiveros, bibliotecarios y arqueólogos* 2 (1934): 321–38. For the text, see Smyser, *Pseudo-Turpin,* chaps. 20–21, pp. 31–33, 74–78.

47. Sayers, *Roland,* lines 2549–53. The authenticity of this section of the poem has been studied and supported most recently by W. G. van Emden, "Another Look at

Charlemagne's Dreams in the Chanson de Roland," *French Studies* 28 (1974):257–71, and J. J. Duggan, *The Song of Roland: Formulaic Style and Poetic Craft* (Berkeley: University of California Press, 1973), especially pp. 63–104.

48. Rita Lejeune and Jacques Stiennon, *La Légende de Roland dans l'art du moyen âge* (Brussels: Arcade, 1966).

49. Albert B. Lord, *The Singer of Tales* (New York: Atheneum, 1971), pp. 202 ff. and Duggan, *The Song of Roland*, on oral tradition in *The Song of Roland*.

50. See V. Elbern, "Liturgisches Gerät in edlen Materialen zur Zeit Karls des Grossen," *Karl der Grosse*, vol. 3, *Karolingische Kunst*, ed. Wolfgang Braunfels and Herman Schnitzler (1966), p. 140 and figs. 13, 22. The treasure, which served during the Gothic period as a container for relics of Saints George, Theodore and Apollinaris, was melted down during the French Revolution; the basic study is by Jean Hubert, "L' 'Escrain' dit de Charlemagne au Trésor de St-Denis," *Cahiers archéologiques* 4 (1949): 71–77. See also the recent study by Peter Lasko, *Ars Sacra*, 800–1200 (Harmondsworth, 1972), pp. 24 ff.

51. B. de Montesquiou-Fézensac, "L'Arc de Triumphe d'Einhardus," *Cahiers archéologiques* 4 (1949): 79–103, and "L'Arc d'Eginhard," *Cahiers archéologiques* 8 (1956): 147–74. See also Lasko, *Ars Sacra*, p. 21, and *Das Einhardkreuz*, Abhandlungen der Akademic des Wissenschaften in Göttingen: Philologisch-Historische Klasse, 3d folge, 87 (1974).

52. K. Weitzmann, "Der Aufbau und die unteren Felder der Einhard-Reliquiars," *Das Einhardkreuz*, pp. 33–49, esp. p. 41.

53. "Étude sur la renaissance de la sculpture en France à l'époque romane," *Bulletin monumental* 84 (1925): 5–98.

54. P. Héliot, "Sur la façade des églises romanes d'Aquitaine à propos d'une étude récente," *Bulletin de la Société des Antiquaires de l'Ouest et des Musées de Poitiers*, 4th ser. 2 (1952): 247, 264, and "Observations sur les façades décorées d'arcades aveugles dans les églises romanes," *BSAO*, 4th ser. 4 (1958), 441 ff. Also C. Daras, "Les façades des églises romanes, ornées d'arcatures en Charente; leur origine, leur filiation," *Bulletin monumental* 119 (1961): 122–23.

Virtues, a frequent theme on the Western façades under consideration, are also found on reliquary shrines of the Rhine-Meuse area after the middle of the century. See Katzenellenbogen, *Allegories*, pp. 46–48.

55. See Jean Hubert, Jean Porcher, and W. F. Volbach, *The Carolingian Renaissance*, trans. James Ennons, Stuart Gilbert, and Robert Allen (New York: G. Braziller, 1970), p. 345, no. 29. A text mentioning the use of a wax model for the renovation of St-Germain in Auxerre is given in R. Louis, *Les Églises d'Auxerre des origines au XIe siècle* (Paris: Clavreuil, 1952), p. 38.

56. See note 15 above, and Crozet, *L'Art roman en Saintonge*, pp. 105–6.

57. R. Krautheimer, "The Carolingian Revival of Early Christian Architecture, *Art Bulletin* 24 (1942): 35–36; E. Günther Grimme, "Novus Constantinus," *Aachener Kunstblätter* 22 (1961): 7–20.

58. For evidence of such remains, and an alternate analysis, see Crozet, "Survivances antiques," passim. Panofsky summarized briefly evidence of the Ottonian revival of Carolingian art, *Renaissance and Renascences*, pp. 53–54, n. 1. The association of a rider with an arch or a gate, known from Roman coins, appears, similarly, to have entered the Romanesque vocabulary via the Carolingian example. For the coins, see Von Roques de Maumont, *Antike Reiterstandbilder*, figs. 22, 23; T. L. Donaldson, *Ancient Architecture on Greek and Roman Coins and Medals* (1859; rpt. Chicago: Argonaut, 1966), no. 55, pp. 218–21, and E. Baldwin Smith, *Architectural Symbolism of Imperial Rome and The Middle Ages* (Princeton: Princeton University Press, 1956), pp. 39–40, fig. 28.

The importance of late Roman Imperial monuments for the development of medieval iconography, in particular the Arc of Eginhard, is discussed by Yves Christe, "La colonne d'Arcadius, Sainte-Pudentienne, l'arc d'Eginhard et le portail de Ripoll," *Cahiers archéologiques* 21 (1971): 34 ff. and Weitzmann, "Der Aufbau . . . des Einhard-Reliquiars," pp. 33 ff.

59. S. Painter, "Castellans of the Plain of the Poitou in the Eleventh and Twelfth Centuries," *Speculum* 31 (1956): 243–57.

60. On William, ninth duke of Aquitaine and seventh count of Poitiers, see R. Bezzola, *Les Origines et la formation de la littérature courtoise en occident, 500–1200*, 3 vols. (Paris: Champion, 1944–63), vol. 2, pt. 2, 243 ff.; P. Boissonnade, "Les relations des ducs d'Aquitaine, comtes de Poitiers, avec les États Chrétiens d'Aragon et de Navarre," *Bulletin de la Société des Antiquaires de l'Ouest*, 3d ser. 10 (1934): 265–316; and A. Richard, *Histoire des Comtes de Poitou, 778–1126*, 2 vols. (Paris: A. Picard and fils, 1903), vol. 1.

61. Madeleine Tyssens, *La Geste de Guillaume d'Orange dans les manuscrits cycliques*, Bibliothèque de la Faculté de Philosophie et Lettres de l'Université de Liège 178 (Paris: "Les Belles Lettres," 1967). See also the work of Martin de Riquer, *Les Chansons de Geste français*, trans. Irénée Cluzel, 2d ed. (Paris: Librarie Nizet, 1957), pp. 122 ff., and J. Frappier, *Les Chansons de Geste du Cycle de Guillaume d'Orange*, 2 vols. (Paris: Société d'édition d'enseignement supérieur, 1955–65). A. de Mandach has closely associated the *Geste de Guillaume* with the *Liber Santi Jacobi* dating the former as early as 1129. "La genèse du Guide du pèlerin de saint Jacques, Orderic Vital et la date de la Geste de Guillaume," *Mélanges offerts à Rita Lejeune*, 2 vols. (Gembloux: J. Duculot, 1969), 2:811–27. The introduction by Joan Ferrante to her new translation, *Guillaume d'Orange, Four Twelfth-Century Epics* (New York: Columbia University Press, 1974), corroborates many of the points made here.

62. Taylor, in publishing the Avignon capital (fig. 14), suggested that the figures illustrated a legend ("A marble capital," p. 539). The elements may come from different parts of the William cycle: the bird from the *Enfances du Guillaume*, the musician-companion from the *Chanson de Guillaume*, and the ball held by the rider from *La Prise d'Orange*. See C. A. Knudson, "Le Thème de la Princesse sarrasine dans la Prise d'Orange," *Romance Philology* 22 (1969): 459 ff.

The crowned rider on the Narbonne capital (fig. 18b) is possibly Charlemagne, the legendary liberator of the city. See R. Folz, "Aspects du culte liturgique de Saint Charlemagne en France," *Karl der Grosse*, 4:92. In fact, Narbonne had been taken from the Moors in 759 by Pepin only to be lost and recaptured under William in the decade between 793 and 806. J. Lacam, "Vestiges de l'occupation arabe en Narbonnaise," *Cahiers archéologiques* 8 (1956): 93–115 and *Les Sarrazins dans le haut moyen-âge française* (Paris: G. P. Maisonneuve, 1965), pp. 18–30. For the tale of the eighth-century siege of the town by the emperor's forces with William's father at the head, see L. Demaison, *Aymeri de Narbonne, Chanson de Geste*, ed. Louis Demaison, 2 vols. (Paris: F. Didot, 1887). The recent study by A. Zuckerman, *A Jewish Princedom in Feudal France, 768–900* (New York: 1972), makes selective and highly provocative use of the material in the William songs. For a review of this work see the *American Historical Review* 78 (1973): 1440–41.

In addition to the capitals with riders at Arles (fig. 3) and at Aix, cavaliers were depicted elsewhere in the vicinity. A capital with a rider figure was mentioned in the church of Alet, near the south side door by A. Burgos and J. Nougaret, "Préliminaires à l'étude de la décoration figurée des églises romanes de Bas-Languedoc," *Mélanges offerts à René Crozet*, ed. P. Gallais and Y-J Riou, 2 vols. (Poitiers: Société d'études médiévales, 1966), 1:492. According to Louis Noguier, a rustically carved figure of a mounted rider decorates a historiated capital in the cloister at the abbey of Fontcaude, founded in 1154 at Caxoulsles-Béziers, in the diocese of Saint-Pons. "Les Vicomtes de Béziers," *Bulletin de la Société archéologique, scientifique et littéraire de Béziers* 13 (1885): 495–96, n. 9.

63. *Les Deux Redactions en vers du Moniage Guillaume*, ed. Wilhelm Cloetta, 2 vols. (Paris: Firmin-Didot, 1906–11), 2:37 and n. 3. On the metamorphosis of the historic figure into the legend, see R. Van Waard, "La postérité de saint Guilhem et la formation de sa légende," *Neophilologus* 31 (1947): 153–61, and H. Grégoire, "Les monuments inspirateurs: Comment Guillaume de Toulouse devint Guillaume d'Orange," *Provence historique* 1 (1950): 32–44.

64. F. Villard, "Guillaume IX d'Aquitaine et le Concile de Reims 1119," *Cahiers de civilisation médiévale* 16 (1973): 295–302. Local cults around other, little known, military saints flourished in the eleventh and twelfth centuries in the Garonne Valley along the pilgrimage road. Etienne Delaruelle, "Les saints militaires de la région de Toulouse," *Cahiers de Fanjeaux* 4 (1969): 173–83.

65. Painter, "Castellans," passim, and G. T. Beech, *A Rural Society in Medieval France: The Gâtine of the Poitou in the Eleventh and Twelfth Centuries*, The Johns Hopkins University Studies in Historical and Political Science, ser. 82, no. 1 (Baltimore: Johns Hopkins Press, 1964). Ch. Higounnet discussed the development of this system, "Le Groupe aristocratique en Aquitaine et en Gascogne," *Les Structures Sociales de l'Aquitaine, du Languedoc et de l'Espagne au premier âge féodal*, Colloques internationaux du Centre Nationale de la Recherche Scientifique (Paris, 1969), pp. 221–37. The remarks of P. Van Luyn on "Les Milites dans la France du XIᵉ siècle," *Le Moyen Age* 77 (1971): 5–51 and 193–238, emphasize that this group formed an elite professional class of land-holders who fought on horseback. See also R. Crozet, "Aspects sociaux de l'art du moyen-âge en Poitou," *Bulletin de la Société des Antiquaires de l'Ouest et des Musée de Poitiers* 4th ser. 3 (1955): 8–10. Joan Evans noted that only two of the churchers in western France on which a rider relief appeared were Cluniac, *Cluniac Art of the Romanesque Period* (Cambridge: The University Press, 1950), p. 33, no. 5.

66. Beech, *Rural Society,* especially pp. 42, 56 ff., 101 ff.

67. Ibid., p. 127. Ebbo, Lord of Parthenay between 1087 and 1110, was generous to the priory at Parthenay-le-vieux, mentioned in 1092. The lords were also responsible for building Notre-Dame-de-la-Couldre and St-Croix in the precinct of their château. Ibid., p. 59, and Crozet, *Poitou,* pp. 13, 76.

68. *Later English Romanesque Sculpture,* Chapters in Art 22 (London: A. Tiranti, 1953), pp. 9–13.

69. Peter the Venerable quoted by R. W. Southern, *Western Views of Islam in the Middle Ages* (Cambridge, Mass.: Harvard University Press, 1962), p. 38.

70. Cf. the thesis of Américo Castro, that the attraction of Saint James's shrine developed as a "Counter-Kaaba," a defensive or protective imitation of Moorish religious belief. I am grateful to Oleg Grabar for having called my attention to this work, *The Structure of Spanish History,* trans. Edmund L. King (Princeton: Princeton University Press, 1954), especially pp. 130 ff., 147, 152, 219. See also H. Adolf, "Christendom and Islam in The Middle Ages," *Speculum* 32 (1957): 103–15, and for a modified interpretation, J-J. Saunders, "The Crusade as a Holy War," in *Aspects of the Crusades* (Christchurch, New Zealand: 1962), pp. 56–58.

71. M. Schapiro, "Silos," pp. 326–27. See the photo of the voussoir sculptures on the portal of Ste-Croix in Bordeaux in Porter, *Romanesque Sculpture,* 7, pl. 921.

72. On the presumed immorality of the Moors, see D. C. Munro, "The Western Attitude Toward Islam during the Crusades," *Speculum* 6 (1931): especially p. 332; C. M. Jones, "The Conventional Saracen of the Songs of Geste," *Speculum* 17 (1942): 201–5; G.

Herman, "Nationality Groups in the Old French Epic" *Annuale mediaevale* 10 (1969): 81–82.

73. Compare A. Gérard's view of the *Song of Roland* as a Christian, National, and Monarchic epic in which the barons battle for faith, for country, and for empire. "L'Axe Roland-Ganelon: valeurs en conflit dans la Chanson de Roland," *Le Moyen Age* 75 (1969): 462. D. D. R. Owen emphasized the purely feudal aspects in "The Secular Inspiration of the Chanson de Roland," *Speculum* 37 (1962): 390–400.

74. Likewise Weitzmann, in his discussion concerning the standing soldiers around the base of Eginhard's reliquary arch, recommends that the figures be interpreted as a group of milites Christiani who pledge devotion to the cross and who fight in the name of Christ. "Der Aufbau . . . des Einhard-Reliquiars," p. 46.

75. Stimulating remarks on historic perspective in the contemporary *chansons* are found in S. G. Nichols, Jr., "The Interaction of Life and Literature in the *Peregrinationes ad Loca Sancta* and *The Chansons de Geste*," *Speculum* 44 (1969): 51, 71. Duggan remarks that in oral tradition "the reproduction of a song consists not in a phrase by phrase rendering of the previous version, but in a re-creation," *Roland,* p. 102.

Fig. 1. Marcus Aurelius, Piazza del Campidoglio (photo: Anderson).

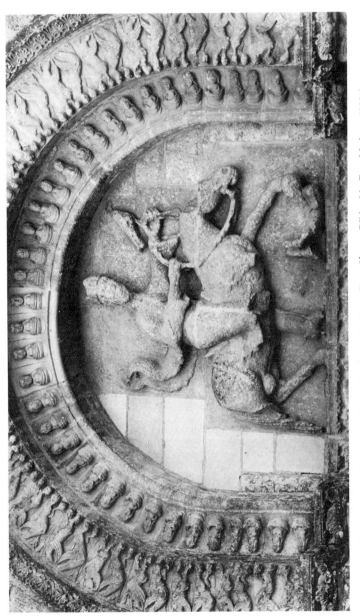

Fig. 2. Equestrian figure, left bay of west façade (Parthenay-le-vieux, Deux-Sèvres, Bildarchiv Foto Marburg 40901).

Fig. 3. Mounted figure accompanied by woman, capital in cloister of St-Trophîme, Arles (Bouches-du-Rhône; Bildarchiv Foto Marburg 31557).

Fig. 4. Saint James on horseback, tympanum in interior of south transept, Santiago de Compostela (Bildarchiv Foto Marburg 55443).

Fig. 5. Man astride lion, right bay of west façade, Parthenay-le-vieux, detail of fig. 6 (Bildarchiv Foto Marburg 161406).

Fig. 6. Parthenay-le-vieux, west façade (Bildarchiv Foto Marburg 161401).

Fig. 7. St-Nicholas, Civray (Vienne), west façade (Bildarchiv Foto Marburg 180137).

Fig. 8. Notre-Dame-de-la-Couldre, west façade (Bildarchiv Foto Marburg 40872).

Fig. 9. St-Jouin-de-Marnes, west façade (James Austin).

Fig. 10. *Luxuria,* capital at left of façade, Parthenay-le-vieux, detail of fig. 6 (Bildarchiv Foto Marburg 40898).

Fig. 11. The Virgin being bathed, detail of capital frieze on Royal Portal, Notre-Dame, Chartres (James Austin).

Fig. 12a. Scene of a Siege, Persian plate (Courtesy of the Smithsonian Institution, Freer Gallery of Art, Washington, D.C. 43.3).

Fig. 12b. Riders in a Cavalcade, detail of fig. 12a.

Fig. 13. Gallery of the façade of the Hotel-de-ville, St-Antonin-Noble-Val (Tarn-et-Garonne; Harvard Fine Arts Library, A. K. Porter Collection).

Fig. 14. Rider, marble capital from southern France (Fitzwilliam Museum, Cambridge; photo: Stearn and Sons).

Fig. 15. Rider with bird, Hispano-Arabic ivory box (Crown Copyright. Victoria and Albert Museum).

Fig. 16. Musician, detail of capital illustrated in fig. 14 (photo: Stearn and Sons).

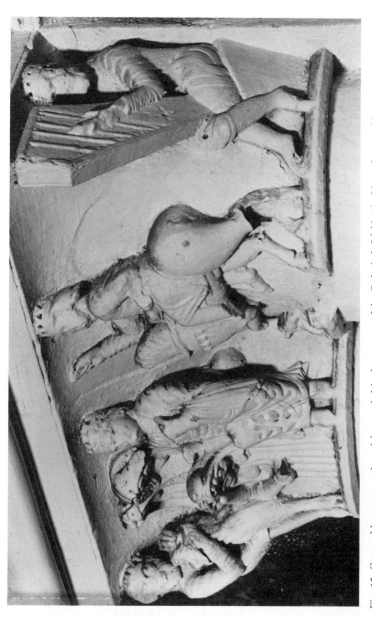

Fig. 17. Crowned horseman and musician, capital in the transept of the Cathedral, Lérida (Archives photographiques).

Fig. 18a. Musician, capital in the Palais des Archevêques, Narbonne.　　Fig. 18b. Crowned rider, detail of fig. 18a.

Fig. 19. Escrain de Charlemagne, Paris, Bibliothèque Nationale, Cabinet des Estampes, Recueil Le, 38c (Bibliothèque Nationale).

Fig. 20. St-Etienne, Tauriac (Gironde), west façade (James Austin).

Fig. 21. Arc d'Eginhard, Paris, Bibliothèque Nationale, MS Fr. 10440, fol. 45 (Bibliothèque Nationale).

Fig. 22. Gatehouse, Lorsch (Bildarchiv Foto Marburg 187534).

Fig. 23. Arch of Constantine, Rome (Bildarchiv Foto Marburg 53966).

Fig. 24. St. George, tympanum of St. George's church, Brinsop (Herefordshire; photo: National Monuments record).

Fig. 25. Bartolommeo Colleoni, equestrian monument by Verrocchio, Venice (photo: Alinari).

RICHARD L. CROCKER

Early Crusade Songs

Crusade songs came to us almost entirely from the repertories of the troubadors and trouvères.[1] That in itself seems to be a fact of great importance, for coexisting in the musical spectrum of the twelfth and thirteenth centuries were other important repertories. Alongside the secular, vernacular chant of troubadors and trouvères there was, on the one hand, the Latin sacred chant still cultivated in the monasteries, and, on the other hand, an entirely distinct repertory, that of the new polyphonic or "part-music," which flourished not at court nor in the monastery but in the great urban cathedrals of the north, especially at Notre Dame de Paris. The remarkable aspect is that—as far as I can determine—this polyphonic repertory has practically no instance of Crusade songs, certainly none as explicitly connected with the Crusades as those we will see here.[2]

Let me explore this situation briefly. In the last half of the twelfth century, polyphony, heretofore practiced on an experimental basis, developed into a systematic musical style with artistic achievement and international recognition.[3] This development took place under stylistic conditions that can be called "Gothic," that is to say, in an environment shared with Gothic architecture and using musical techniques specifically analogous to those of the new architectural style manifested at Saint Denis, Notre Dame de Paris, and elsewhere. Indeed the center of the new polyphonic art was at Notre Dame and remained in Paris for the next hundred years. This kind of music was characteristically composed and executed by clerics—but not monks—attached to urban cathedrals as permanent musical staff. Sometimes these musicians were associated also with the university, specifically the one on the Left Bank. The kind of music they cultivated required new skills and special training; it could not be sung by a traditional trouvère, and only slowly did it penetrate the courtly environment. After 1250 we find polyphonic works—*motets*—with secular vernacular texts and themes of courtly love, but with increasingly bourgeois tone. Up until that point, however, the new polyphony had apparently no contact with the courts, and it would seem that the virtual absence from the polyphonic repertory of references to the Crusades reflected a lack of interest on the part of northern urban, bourgeois, intellectual, and clerical circles. It suggests that the Crusades were simply not a concern of these segments of society, being rather associated with the landed baron and his entourage. The polyphonic repertory abounds with references to contemporary events—and with moral, political, and social satire and criticism, so it is not the case that polyphony was isolated from the world of events. Rather, I would guess it was the courtly trouvères who were becoming isolated: in purely musical terms the future belonged to polyphony, and the monophonic trouvère repertory was about to go out of existence. The same might be true, perhaps, of the social groups these repertories represented.

In general terms, the troubador repertory contains songs whose texts are Provençal. The repertory emerged around 1100 and continued past 1200, but was seriously inhibited by the Albigensian Crusade, which laid waste many of the southern courts where the art of the troubadors flourished. The art was under noble patronage, beginning with William IX of Aquitaine, and indeed some noblemen are credited with songs—which probably means the texts rather than the melodies. But it does not seem possible to equate troubador with noble singer, and there seem to have been professional singers included under this term as well. Only around 270 troubador melodies are preserved, although the number of texts is much greater.

Trouvère songs have French (that is, northern French) texts. This repertory began about the same time, around 1100, but flourished uninterrupted through the thirteenth century. Noblemen were sometimes involved, but the professional element is perhaps more clearly apparent in the north than in the south; also apparent in the north toward 1300 is an eventual spread from the courtly environment to a bourgeois one, and in the course of this shift the trouvère repertory lost much of its aristocratic tone.

Both repertories are preserved in anthology manuscripts dating from the thirteenth century—manuscripts composed after the fact and several steps removed from whatever form the songs originally took. Upon this fact depend the various uncertainties concerning this kind of song. The uncertainties mostly relate to the music: the texts are fairly secure, except for the order of stanzas for a given song preserved in several sources, where the order may vary substantially. In the case of the melodies, however, there is enough variation in manuscript sources to make us wonder whether melody and text were ever composed as an inseparable unit, or whether instead a given text could be sung to whatever melody the performer fancied. There are a number of cases where one text is provided with three or four completely independent melodies. This circumstance casts certain aspects of the music in doubt.

During the past century scholars produced categorical answers to many of these questions, though more recently there has been a tendency to admit that during two centuries of development things might have been done differently at different times. The best example concerns the rhythm of the songs. The manuscripts, in most cases, give no indication of the relative length of notes in a song. Shortly after 1900 several scholars tried to read these songs in so-called modal rhythm, a system involving long and short notes known to have been used in other repertories—specifically polyphonic music—developing around 1200 in northern France. The modal interpretation was energetically pursued: in one of the more spectacular episodes of musical research, two investigators, Jean Beck and Pierre Aubry, contested each other's priority in making the interpretation; when the question could not be resolved, they dueled. Aubry was killed; Beck came to this country and settled in Philadelphia. More recent interpretations, alas, tend to be nonmodal, and range from the declamatory mode of performance proposed by Hendryck Van der Werf to free, chantlike rhythms.

The matter of instrumental accompaniment has been—and still is—vigorously debated. You can hear modern recorded performances with elaborate instrumental preludes and accompaniment based upon a hypothesis of near-Eastern, specifically Arab, influence.[4] It is true, of course, that Western musicians made contact at this time with Arabs, both in the Iberian peninsula and on Crusade; whether this contact resulted in the transplant of instrumental practice is hard to say. It is admitted that the melodies themselves were not affected. In general, there is no hard evidence for any specific kind of instrumental practice at this time. I myself am a supporter of the indigenous Latin chant theory, which holds that the music of troubadors and trouvères can be satisfactorily explained as a consequence of the thriving, extensive repertories of sacred Latin chant composed by Franks during the ninth, tenth, and eleventh centuries. And in spite of Arabian influence proposed for the rhyme schemes of Provençal verse, still the technique of rhyme and especially scansion have much in common with the eleventh century Latin *versus*.[5]

In considering transfer from one culture to another, an image, visual motif, or artifact being transferred as a self-contained detail is one thing; a musical idiom or technique is something quite different, for the meaning of a musical motif depends almost entirely on convention and context, and these require substantial periods of time for effective transplant. In any case, substantial Arabian influence on musical practice seems firmly documented only after the thirteenth century.

While the overall effect of Van der Werf's study may be felt to be negative, pruning back as it does a century's categorical and over-enthusiastic conclusions, still Van der Werf provides a very believable picture: the texts are at the center of troubador and trouvère art; the text is what the named artist composes. This text is then sung by the professional musician as part of his personal repertory. He draws upon a stock of melodic formulas, which are as standardized in outline as the lengths of the lines of the poetry. Perhaps a text would acquire several different ones. In either case the melody was a vehicle for the text. These melodic formulas can be derived from, or at least understood in terms of, the vigorous repertory of sacred chant currently composed during the eleventh century.

Indeed, the earliest Crusade song I know about happens to be in Latin and comes from a monastery. The song, *Jerusalem mirabilis,* appears in the famous Aquitanian MS Paris B.N. Latin 1139 (early twelfth century), which also contains a dazzling collection of the new rhyming, scanning Latin *versus,* the first Provençal songs, the liturgical play *Sponsus,* and some early polyphony.[6] All

Jerusalem mira - bi-lis, urbs be - a - ti - or a - li - is,

quam permanens obta - bilis gaudenti bus te angelis.

of this simply demonstrates the conflux of new ideas in art and music at the Abbey of Saint Martial in Limoges, where the manuscript originated. The song itself, said to have been written for the First Crusade in 1095, is a simple exhortation, set to a strophic melody characteristic of the eleventh-century hymn repertory. Typical emphasis is placed upon the Holy Land as the place where Jesus lived: then strophe 7 says,

> Illic debemus pergere
> nostros honores vendere
> templum dei adquiere
> Sarracenos destruere.

[There must we go, selling our goods to buy the temple of God, and to
destroy the Saracens.]

The most famous troubador Crusade song is surely that of
Marcabru, the troubador with the most notorious character—self-
conscious, self-assured, disdainful. The song, *Pax in nomine
Domini,* has a Latin incipit; the rest of the text goes on to describe
the *Lavador*—cleansing place—that God has prepared overseas,
and also memorializes Marcabru's Duke William. The structure of
the stanza is more complex than that of a hymn, and so is the
melody.[7]

The rest of my examples are taken from the trouvère repertory, and from the basic study by Bedier and Aubry, *Les Chansons de Croisade,* which includes a collection of some thirty of the best, most representative Crusade songs; I am using the texts and melodies as established in that study. As with all aspects of the trouvère repertory, no systematic morphological treatment makes sense: basic lines of development are not known, basic laws or categories cannot be established. Individual songs can, however, sometimes be dated on internal evidence or on the basis of attribution (although both grounds are often shaky), and a presentation following the chronological order set out by Bedier seems preferable to a systematic one.

Songs from the earliest Crusades are rare; most date from the end of the twelfth century and after. *Chevalier, mult estes guariz* has been dated 1146, at the time of the Second Crusade (Bedier and Aubry, pp. 3–16). The text is an exhortation to follow King Louis VII on his Crusade to avenge the sack of Edessa (Rohais in the song) in 1144; this was the event that also evoked the participation of Saint Bernard. The lines of the text are relatively short—eight syllables instead of the more usual ten or eleven—while the stanza is relatively long—twelve lines, including a refrain. The refrain sets forth what seems to be the motto of Crusade songs:

> He who goes with Louis, what has he to fear from hell? For surely his soul will dwell in Paradise with the angels of our Lord.

The simple idioms of the melody group the twelve lines into sixes, and beyond that into pairs. The simpler phrases show the kind of melodic idiom easily associated with the declamatory rhythm.

Another of the earlier songs, *He Amours! con dure departie* attributed to Conon de Béthune, typifies the love song, specifically the farewell song, that became popular with the Crusades (Bedier and Aubry, pp. 27–37). The song is dated after 1189; Conon died in 1204. The poet explores the conflict between commitment to the Crusade and love of his lady: his conclusion is embodied in the refrain,

> Se li cors va servir Nostre Seingnour,
> Li cuers remaint du tout en sa baillie.

[If my body goes to serve our Lord, my heart remains faithful to her.]

The text alternates lines of ten and eleven syllables, in an eight-line
stanza—one of the most favored arrangements. Masculine and
feminine rhymes are paired, and the first two pairs are sung to the
same music in a musical structure frequently encountered: this
structure establishes a clear block of material at the opening of the

stanza—the opening couplet. The first pair ends "open," that is, on a musical tone that requires continuation, while the second pair ends "closed." The third and fourth pairs, in this particular piece, are similarly arranged.

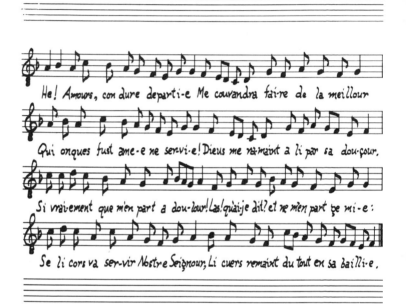

The formal principles embodied here are characteristic of the trouvère repertory as a whole: articulation of the stanza, in text and music, is always foremost in the trouvère's mind. There is, on one hand, a wide variety of stanza constructions, on the other, a concentration on the particular form seen here.

This song comes to us with three melodies; in this second melody you can hear an analog of the stanza construction of the first, expressed in a completely different melodic inflection. From hearing *one* melody for a given song, we are impressed, I think, with the care and purpose with which text and melody are matched;

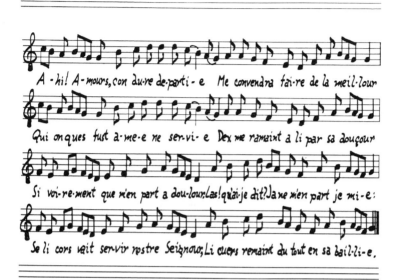

A - hi! A-mours, con du-re de-parti - e   Me convendra fai-re de la meil-lour

Qui onques fust a-me-e ne ser-vi- e   Dex me ramaint a li par sa douçour

Si voi-re-ment que m'en part a dou-lour Las! qu'ai-je dit? Ja ne m'en part je mi-e:

Se li cors vait ser-vir nostre Seignour, Li cuers remaint du tout en sa bail-li-e.

but from hearing *two* melodies we can begin to understand how the matching is due not so much to individualized creation but rather to standardized, interchangeable parts. This modular quality of construction is characteristic of several things at once: first, of the end of a phase of development, in which the original impulse of Latin song spread out and spent itself in the secular repertories; second, characteristic of the Gothic style of the late twelfth and thirteenth centuries, which maximized modular construction in many ways; and characteristic, finally, of the art of the trouvère, singing texts with the help of a standardized, memorized repertory of melodic settings.

Many of the Crusade songs are songs either of love or exhortation, such as the examples we have seen. Those on love are easily understandable as the perennially popular subject of song given added poignancy by the special event; those on exhortation are equally understandable as propaganda. A significant number of

other songs, however, include comment or even criticism—
sometimes bitter—on circumstances attendant upon the manage-
ment of the Crusades.

Bien me deüsse targier, also attributed to Conon and dated
1188, starts as a love song, then in a more obscure passage seems to
refer critically to a tax levied on the Crusades by Phillip Augustus,
but subsequently used in the struggle with Henry II (Bedier and
Aubry, pp. 41–50).

> I should put off to some other time the making and singing of songs,
> since I must leave my beloved; and I can make this boast—which is
> true—that I am doing more for God than any other lover; this gives me
> great joy for my soul, but for my body nothing but sorrow. . . . No, no
> matter how much I desire, I would not stay here with these tyrants who
> have taken up the cross so that they may tax clerks, citizens, and
> soldiers. Greed has made more Crusaders than has faith. But this cross
> that they bear will not be their salvation. In the case of this kind of
> Crusader, God will indeed be patient if he does not soon avenge himself

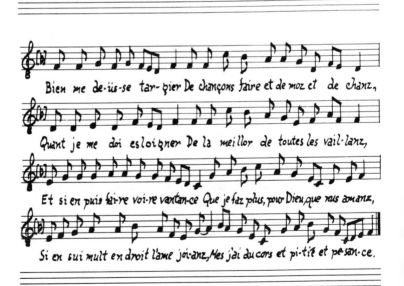

Bien me de-üs-se tar-gier De chançons faire et de moz et de chanz,

Quant je me doi esloigner De la meillor de toutes les vail-lanz,

Et si en puis faire voi-re vantan-ce Que je faz plus, pour Dieu, que nus amanz,

Si en sui mult en droit l'ame joi-anz, Mes j'ai du cors et pi-tié et pesan-ce.

of them. You who tax the Crusaders, do not spend in this way the proceeds of this tax; for by that you become enemies of God. Alas, what will His enemies do, when the righteous tremble with fear before Him who never lies? The sinners will fare badly if His pity does not prevail on His power.

The melody is less problematic: there is a straight-forward opening couplet with open and closed endings, then four more phrases of different melodic substance.

Sometimes it is hard to distinguish songs of exhortation from moral criticism, especially if the song is addressed—as *Parti de mal* seems to be—to the barons (Bedier and Aubry, pp. 67–73).

Having renounced evil and turned to good, I wish to make my song heard by the people, for God has called us to help Him, and no *preudome* should fail Him; He has deigned to die for us on the cross, for which He should be paid back, for by His death are we all redeemed. Neither counts, nor dukes, nor kings with their crowns can easily divest themselves at their death; for when they have amassed

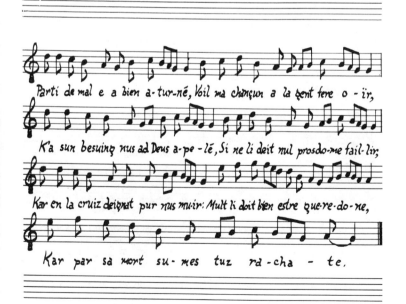

Parti de mal e a bien a-tur-né, Voil ma chançun a la gent fere o-ir,

K'a sun besuing nus ad Deus a-pe-lé, Si ne li deit mul prosdome fail-lir;

Kar en la cruiz deignat pur nus murir: Mult k doit bien estre que-re-do-ne,

Kar par sa mort su-mes tuz ra-cha - te.

such great wealth, it is only with the greatest pain that they must
abandon it. It is better for them to depart in good faith, for when they are
buried in the earth, what good is city or château?

This particular text is complex in thought and diction; it has a point
to make. So it may be surprising, but is entirely characteristic, that
the melody is relatively simple.

In contrast is *Li nouviaus tanz,* a love song attributed to the
"Chatelain de Couci," that is, Gui II of Couci, drowned on Crusade
shortly after 1200 (Bedier and Aubry, pp. 87–96). *Li nouviaus
tanz* seems uncomplicated in thought, exhibiting all the rich sonor-
ous language developed by several generations of trouvères.

> Li nouviaus tanz et mais et violete
> Et lousseignolz me semont de chanter,
> Et mes fins cuers me fait d'une amourete
> Si douz present que ne l'os refuser.
> Or me laist Diex en tele honeur monter
> Que cele ou j'ai mon cuer et mon penser
> Tieigne une foiz entre mes braz nuete
> > Ainz que voise outre mer.

[Spring, and May, and violets, and nightengale, summon me to sing, and my fair beloved makes me a present of love so sweet that I cannot refuse. May God grant me grace to rise so high that I might hold her naked in my arms before I go overseas.]

The melody, then, is relatively elaborate, with ambitious arching phrases and complex stanza structure.

A group of songs is connected to Thibaut IV, count of Champagne. Thibaut prepared for his Crusade between 1235 and 1239, then departed for Acre. We have perhaps four songs from him, two of exhortation, two of farewell to his lady.[8] *Seigneur, sachiez* is provided in one source with a sophisticated wide-ranging melody representative of the best—although not the most popular—of what the trouvères produced. Another farewell song by a poet in Thibaut's following, Chardon de Reims, has a melody somewhat less ambitious, but more songlike and more accessible—and thereby more typical of the great mass of trouvère songs. Chardon's thought is much like the previous farewell songs: "Just because my body goes to serve our Lord, that does not mean I forget my fair love."

As a last example of the love song, I would like to present a song put in the mouth of the girl left behind, but attributed by at least one manuscript to a male trouvère (Bedier and Aubry, pp. 109–17). She sings,

> I will sing to comfort my heart, for in spite of my great misery I do not wish to die, and yet I see no one return from that savage land, where he has gone who quiets my heart when I hear news of him.

> O, when they cry "Overseas," dear God, help the pilgrim for whom I tremble; for the Sarracens are bad.

The melody, though very simple and repetitive, has great charm.

Chanterai por mon cora-ge Que je vueill reconforter,

Car avec mon grant dama-ge Ne vueill morir n'afoler,

Quant de la ter-re sauva-ge Ne voi nului retorner,

Ou cil est qui m'asso-a - ge Le cuer, quant j'en oi parler.

Dex, quant cri-e-ront Outre-e, Sire, aidiez au pelerin

Por qui sui espo-en-te - e, Car felon sunt Sarrazin.

Finally, Bedier and Aubry include several fascinating songs of circumstance dating from the first half of the thirteenth century. (Some of these have no melodies in the sources.) The texts depart from the themes of love and exhortation, responding to specific needs of the moment; they often take the form of complaints. They always continue to represent the high moral purpose of the Crusades, as understood by the ideal knight.

A song attributed to Huon de Saint-Quentin, *Jerusalem se plaint,* was shown to correspond closely to that poet's *Complainte de Jerusalem contre Rome* (Bedier and Aubry, pp. 145–51). The subject is the withdrawal of a crusading force under the counts de Bar, de la Marche, de Nevers, and the dukes of Bavaria and Austria against Cairo, 1219–21. After a long siege, the Crusaders were eventually harassed by the plague and had to withdraw, leaving behind prisoners. The song complains bitterly about the fate of these prisoners, as well as about mismanagement in high places, and especially about the arrangements countenanced by prelates in Rome to permit certain Crusaders—especially barons—to be "de-crusaded" *(decroisié)* or relieved of their vows and allowed to return home. The issue of the POWs remained a difficult and a painful one.

In November of 1239 there was an ill-advised and disastrous raid by forces newly arrived in Syria; the raiders were ambushed, many were killed and many prisoners taken, among them Philippe de Nanteuil, who was taken to Babylon. He is credited with the song *En chantant veil mon duel faire,* which was apparently brought back to the West (Bedier and Aubry, pp. 217–25). The song laments the loss of the counts of Monfort and Bar, complains that the Hospitaliers and Templars might have saved the situation, and begs for rescue or ransom. Another song, anonymous, *Ne chant pas que que nus die,* complains further about the idleness of the barons subsequent to the same event (Bedier and Aubry, pp. 229–34). The poet fears that if the pilgrimage accomplishes nothing, the return will be shameful. He recalls the glory of the departure of the flower of France's nobility. It is not the fault of the knights, the lower echelons, who have sacrificed all to go on Crusade, and who have no one to redeem them when captured.

In December of 1244, King Louis, desperately ill, and confronted with the news of another disaster in the Holy Land, made
his own resolve to go on Crusade. This dramatic event was celebrated in the song *Tous li mons doit mener joie,* (Bedier and
Aubry, pp. 237–45). Another song, *Un serventois plait de de-
duit,* raised a call to arms to follow Louis; in elaborate rhymes but
simplistic thought, the poet foretold how easily the king would
conquer "Romanie," baptize the sultan of Turkey, free the world
(Bedier and Aubry, pp. 249–55). "May he reconcile Pope and
Emperor, cross the sea with a great fleet; the pagans will not be able
to resist him, he will conquer Turkey and Persia, and will be
crowned in Babylon." After the battle of Mansourah (8 February
1250) and retreat from Egypt, where Louis had been captured and
ransomed, the expedition withdrew to Acre, again leaving behind
prisoners. During June the king debated whether to return to
France, hearing counsel from his barons. A song, written apparently during the deliberations, was circulated in an effort to influence the king's decision. The song, *Nus ne porrois de mauvais
raison,* begins

> No one can make or sing a good song on a bad theme; nor do I wish to
> try. Yet I see the land of *outremer* so hanging in the balance that I want
> to beg the King not to believe the cowards when he should avenge his
> honor and God's.

He goes on to say that the king will lose all if he forsakes the
Crusade at this point, that it will be betrayal not only of the dead
and the prisoners but also of Jesus for whose sake they were
martyred. The song had its desired effect; at any rate, the king
decided to stay.

If such was indeed the locale and purpose of the song, then we
are here witnessing the Crusade song in its natural surroundings; it
addressed the "flower of chivalry," assembled in camp, and set
forth the high ideals of that way of life. Even if this particular song
was not used in this fashion, I think it is clear that the Crusade songs
as a group were identified with this social group.

But I think it is also clear that the social group for whom the
troubadors and trouvères spoke—the group of which they were an
integral and characteristic part—was not all of society; its ideals

and ambitions should not be taken as representative of the society as a whole. That is to say, I do not think that, from the songs of exhortation, or from all the rest of the material that articulated the Crusaders' intent, we can conclude that the society as a whole approved of or was involved in the Crusades.

With that conclusion I address myself to the question of how "a culture formally dedicated to fulfilling the injunction to love thy neighbor as thyself could move to a point where it sanctioned the use of violence against the alien both outside and inside society." That is to say, I do not think one can conclude from the fact of the Crusades that "the culture" as a whole sanctioned this particular use of violence. But it also seems to me that the major premise is in doubt. I seriously question the commitment of the society as a whole to the Christian ethic as a real guide to action. This is certainly too much for a music historian to assert; but my observations of medieval culture from the ninth century on lead me to believe that neither peasants nor bourgeoisie nor barons— especially not the barons—ever gave up a basic Frankish orientation that can well be summarized in the words of Jeeves (speaking of a later political philosophy): "Collar everything you can and sit on it." The greed and violence apparent in the Crusades seem to me perfectly compatible with what I know of medieval society; indeed, eminently characteristic of it.

Nor would I think it unusually inconsistent for such a society to entertain, on the one hand, the ideals that Christian saints and martyrs tried to teach it, and, on the other hand, the ideals of the Crusades. For these ideals (the trouvère songs tell us) were not of violence. One of the important mechanisms of the Crusades must have been the insulation of the violent reality from the ideals expressed in the songs. Here the language of the songs, I think, is very informative. The Crusader did not really go forth to war, he went on a pilgrimage, as a pilgrim. He did not join an army—at least, not a secular one; rather he made a personal decision, more in the nature of a conversion, to join the sacred army of God's saints. The foes he was to fight were internal foes, those perennial temptations and obstacles to the pure life. The battle, perhaps its most exciting part, might take place in France, at the time the Crusader makes his agonized decision, as in the case of King Louis. The external foes, the Saracens, are merely extensions of the inner ones; they are not a real people, not a real enemy—at least for the observer in France. This, it seems to me accounts for the naive conceptions, the never-never quality of language referring to the Crusaders' destination: he goes *outremer;* the Saracens are bad; the king will easily baptize the sultan. The Holy Land is the place where Jesus lived and died; the Crusader is to go where He went, live and perhaps die so as to be with Him in Paradise.

From the songs I get the impression that this inner spiritual experience was at the core of the popular understanding of the Crusades. Most important, this understanding seems perfectly at home in the courtly environment of the twelfth and thirteenth centuries—and only there. Other conceptions were present too, of course: the material motivations, the booty, the fiefs to be carved out of Syria, were perhaps quietly discussed among the barons, and these motivations eventually surfaced in the trouvères' complaints; but even then they were felt to be sins against the faith as much as crimes against the state. Essential to an understanding of the Crusade songs, I think, is the distinction between what is the case and what can be said in an art form. Only certain things were given artistic form; we need both to accept those things, that inner spiritual experience for what it is, and at the same time recognize all the other things that were true, too.

1. The best recent account is Hendryk Van der Werf, *The Chansons of the Troubadours and Trouvères: A Study of the Melodies and their Relation to the Poems* (Utrecht: Oosthoek, 1972). A useful anthology (with reservations, however, about the rhythm of the transcriptions) is Friedrich Gennrich, *Troubadours, Trouvères, Minne- und Meistergesang,* Das Musikwerk, eine Beispielsammlung zur Musikgeschicte 2 (Cologne: Arno, 1951). The special study by Joseph Bedier and Pierre Aubry, *Les Chansons de Croisade* (Paris: H. Champion, 1909), hereafter cited in the text as Bedier and Aubry, forms the basis for the present account. For examples 3–11 I have used the melodic versions established by Aubry, but have transcribed them from his "square-notation" into modern notation. All English translations are my own.

2. A recent recording, *Music of the Crusades,* Early Music Consort of London, David Monrow conductor (Argo 2RG 673, 1971), does indeed include several polyphonic works;

but of these some make only a tenuous and debatable reference to the Crusades, and the rest (as the record commentary ingenuously admits) have no connection with the Crusades.

3. For special studies, see William G. Waite, *The Rhythm of Twelfth Century Polyphony,* Yale Studies in the History of Music 2 (New Haven: Yale University Press, 1954), and Ernest Saunders, "The Medieval Motet," in *Gattungen der Musik in Einzeldarstellungen,* ed. Wulf Arlt et al. (Bern and Munich: Francke, 1973), pp. 497–573.

4. Hear the disc cited in note 2, and especially *Chansons der Troubadours* Studio der frühen Musik, Thomas Binkley, conductor (Telefunken SAWT 9567, 1971).

5. See the brief account in my *History of Musical Style* (New York: McGraw-Hill, 1966), pp. 47–54.

6. Paris B.N. MS Latin 1139, fol. 50–50v. Even though the notation is diastematic, transcription is problematic and uncertain in several important respects; the version given here is only provisional.

7. Gennrich, *Troubadours,* p. 12, but in a different rhythmic interpretation.

8. *Seignor, saichiez* (Bedier and Aubry, pp. 169–74), *Au tans plains de felonie* (177–87), *Dame, einsi* (189–95), *Li donz penser* (199–206).

JAMES A. BRUNDAGE

Holy War and the Medieval Lawyers

Violence has always been a problem for human societies. Western European societies, which have traditionally identified themselves as Christian, tend to find this problem especially vexing. The Christian ethic, after all, gives particular prominence in its value system to love of one's neighbor, and violent behavior is the very antithesis of the virtue of love. Yet both private mayhem and organized public hostilities have continued to erupt in Western European societies. This fact presents a notable difficulty for Christian thinkers and writers, who have commonly felt a need to try to reconcile the violent, warring actions of men, including Christian men, with the theological values they profess.

War represents the ultimate degree of organized violence between communities. War has, accordingly, always been a thorny subject for Christian writers and the Church's attitude has been markedly ambivalent on this subject. Despite their pacific ideals, Christian moralists and theologians were compelled to recognize that war was a fact of life. During the Middle Ages, Western intellectuals began to analyze in some detail the various aspects of war. Their treatments of the subject became increasingly sophisticated during the years between about 1000 and 1300. Out of the discussions of war in this period there emerged a fundamental transformation of the way in which the problem was treated. This change involved a transition from a consideration of war as primarily a moral and theological problem to a conception of war as fundamentally a problem of law. Likewise, as the Church's enforcement powers increased, theological moralizing tended to be replaced by a more rigorous categorization of hostile action.

One result of this transition from theological-moralistic thinking about war to a legal treatment of these activities was a change in the kinds of problems that were addressed. There was considerable overlap, of course. Both theologians and lawyers were concerned about such matters as whether a given war was just or unjust, licit or illicit. But they tended to be interested in these questions for different reasons and to judge them by different criteria. Both groups needed to deal with the problem of who has the power to declare war, but again they did so for rather different reasons and might arrive at differing conclusions. Other problems were far more central to the concerns of lawyers than of theologians—questions of property rights, for example, questions about liability for damage resulting from war, the legitimacy of conquest, its implications for possessory and jurisdictional rights.

Finally, there emerged the concept of holy war, of war that was not merely justifiable but justifying and spiritually beneficial to those who participated in it. This category was certainly theological in its basis; but this category, too, was transformed during the high Middle Ages into a fundamentally legal concern, with a resulting change in emphasis.

In order to make sense out of the ways in which medieval writers dealt with holy war, it is necessary to look first at the problem of war and its place in the juridical structure, as medieval lawyers saw it. We must begin by saying something, however brief and superficial, about the theological background and its scriptural basis. Medieval thinkers were, of course, aware that the Old Testament dealt rather ambiguously with war. Some passages in the Scriptures treated war as an evil, as a punishment inflicted upon the people of Israel for their sins.[1] But other Scriptural texts spoke of war in much more positive terms. They described God as the author of victory in war, victory which Yahweh granted to His people when He was pleased with them.[2] God accompanied the Israelites' army, watched over it, and, when not otherwise engaged, might even serve as its commanding officer, in conjunction with His priests.[3]

The treatment of war and violence in the New Testament was even more ambivalent and medieval writers were aware of this inconsistency. If Saint Paul spoke, in standard Old Testament fashion, of the Lord as the author of victory,[4] he also spoke of Him as a God of peace.[5] Even more emphatic in the new dispensation than in the old, was an aversion to violence: "Those who take the sword will perish by the sword" are words attributed to Jesus.[6] Still more pointedly, Jesus was represented in Saint Matthew's Gospel as repudiating the approval given in the Old Testament to strong-armed resistance to aggressors. The Mosaic Law had accepted resistance and retaliation as appropriate responses to attack;[7] the Gospel rejected this conduct and proposed instead the ethic of nonresistance.[8] The Christian, it might seem, was obliged not to repay evil with evil, violence with violence; rather he was expected to overcome evil with good, to counter force with love.[9] Thus it might appear that Christianity from the outset was opposed to works of violence, that no Christian could with propriety dedicate himself to military affairs. Against this background it might seem that the concept of a holy war, sanctioned and supported by the Christian Church, must be an absurdity.[10]

Yet things are not so simple as they might at first glance appear. Historically it is clear from the evidence of Tertullian (ca. 160–ca. 250) and other early authors, that numerous Christians did in fact serve in the ranks of the Roman army and that pacifism was by no means a universally accepted stance in early Christian communities.[11] The words of Christian writers echoed the actions of Christian believers. The Fathers of the Western Church, at least by the fifth century, had begun to face up to the ambivalence of the Scriptures on the matter of violence and were trying to rationalize the apparent contradictions that they found. In this process, as in many others, the voice of Saint Augustine (354–430) was especially prominent.

Augustine conceived of God as the author of wars, or at least of some wars.[12] Augustine was, moreover, persuaded that righteous men were sometimes forced to wage war as a result of the wrongdoing of the wicked.[13] All wars, in Augustine's view, were fought in order to secure peace.[14] Hence the peaceful objectives of a war were not adequate criteria to determine whether or not a particular war was morally acceptable. Rather, in order to make a judgment as to the morality of a particular war one must, according to Augustine, consider the circumstances of the war's origin together with the motives and the moral authority of the combatants.

Augustine, then, distinguished between just wars and unjust wars. This distinction was not, to be sure, very novel. It can be found, for example, in Cicero.[15] But in Roman thought the term "just war" tended to have as much ceremonial as moral content. A *bellum iustum et pium* was a war that had been properly declared, with full observance of the appropriate public ceremonies and religious rites.[16] Still, the Roman concept of just war was not utterly devoid of moral content: *aequitas* required that a just war have a just cause. This normally meant a violation of Rome's legal interests in foreign territories, infringement on Roman territory itself by foreign powers, or disrespect for the immunities of Rome's allies or her representatives on alien soil.[17] Augustine's notion, however, went beyond such considerations as these. Although he adopted Cicero's terminology and the basic notion that *aequitas* distinguished just wars from unjust ones, Augustine analyzed the justice of war in terms of four basic criteria. There must be a declaration of war by a legitimate authority; there must be a reasonable and morally acceptable cause for the war; the war must be necessary, that is, there must be no other way of achieving the legitimate objective; and the war must be fought by acceptable means.[18]

From the fifth century onward Augustine's views shaped the basic attitude of most Christian thinkers toward organized public conflict.[19] The Augustinian analysis, often in a somewhat simplified form, provided the matrix for the treatment of war by medieval canon lawyers. But one thing Augustine did not give us precisely was a doctrine of holy war. It is one thing to deal with just war, with war that is morally tolerable and not reprehensible in itself; it is quite another and distinct matter to take the further step of conceiving of war as sanctifying, and as an activity that actually confers spiritual merit on the warrior.

The history of the Christian doctrine of holy war is complex; numerous strands, often of strongly clashing colors, are woven into its fabric. It is not necessary to untangle all of those strands here; but it will be useful at least to mention some of them in passing.[20]

There is, for one thing, a suggestive parallel between Christian holy war and the Muslim *jihād*.[21] No one to date has been able to demonstrate a direct influence of the one upon the other. There is, in fact, a good argument to be made that what they really have in common with each other is a common root in more ancient ideas.[22]

Certainly, too, early medieval Christian wars against pagans, both in the Carolingian period and later, were a factor in the development of holy war ideology in the West. The expansionist wars of Carolingian and Ottonian monarchs, activities in which bishops and other prelates often figured prominently, were accompanied by the conversion of conquered populations to Christianity. The role of churchmen in these wars and the conversions that resulted from them led to an association of war with salvation; and military success was naturally ascribed to God's pleasure in seeing the number of the faithful increased.[23] Warfare, indeed, became a Christian duty for bishops in Ottonian Germany, and there was a strong inclination to take the further step of pronouncing participation in warfare as spiritually meritorious—provided, of course, that the war was just.[24]

In part, too, one can trace the roots of the holy war idea to a Christian transformation of more ancient German heroic traditions. As a newly converted Christian society gradually remodeled its older values into new forms, the pagan husks of the older heroic tradition were soon enough discarded and new, Christian outer wrappings substituted for the old ones.[25]

One striking example of this transformation may be found in the liturgical evidence.[26] In the tenth century, when the Church began to bless knights and their weapons, in order to consecrate them to the defense of true religion and ecclesiastical possessions, Christian society was clearly shifting its attitude toward giving a more positive value to warfare and to the warrior in the scheme of salvation. All this was not quite the same as saying that war was holy and sanctifying; still it was not a startling leap from the notion that weapons (at least when destined for proper use) should be blessed and that their users (at least in principle) were consecrated persons to the further notion that the activities in which the consecrated warriors employed their blessed weapons were themselves pleasing in the sight of God.[27] By the eleventh century Christian warriors who worried about the salvation of their souls could avail themselves of another reassurance: under certain conditions they might march into battle under a sacred banner, blessed by the Church. The banner symbolized the justness of their cause and evidenced ecclesiastical approval of the warriors' martial activities often at the exalted level of Saint Peter's successor in Rome.[28] It was only a short further step from fighting under the banner of Saint Peter to fighting with a Crusader's cross sewn on one's cloak.[29]

The papacy itself was not directly involved in the active organization and direction of armies until the ninth century, when it faced the problem of defending its territories from attacks by Muslim invaders in central Italy.[30] The really radical change in papal policy toward warfare, however, occurred during the reign of that most warlike of pontiffs, Pope Gregory VII (1073–85).[31] It has been argued, with considerable justice, that Gregory VII revolutionized the Christian view of warfare and that he was the principal inventor of the holy war idea in medieval Christendom.[32] Gregory demonstrated his passion for sanctifying the grubby business of organized fighting on several different levels. In the realm of political theology and political rhetoric, there is much to be learned from his use of the metaphor of the sword.[33] In the more immediate and practical realm of action, one can also learn much from a study of his concept of the Christian army and the Christian knight.[34]

What is more to the point here, Gregory seems to have entertained the notion that those who died in battle on behalf of righteousness were automatically and deservedly freed from their sins.[35] Other popes before Gregory VII had spoken in roughly similar terms—notably Pope Leo IV in 853,[36] Pope John VIII in 878,[37] Pope Leo IX in 1053,[38] and Pope Alexander II in 1063.[39] Gregory VII's pontificate gave a new twist to the older idea that soldiers dying in battle for a just cause might thereby be saved. Whereas his predecessors had spoken primarily of defensive situations, of encounters in which Christian soldiers were defending persons and property against hostile incursions by non-Christians, Gregory carried the notion of justification by war into situations where active expansion of the Christian world and aggressive activities on behalf of papal interests were at issue.[40] Moreover, the notion of warfare as a holy activity was markedly more prominent in Gregory's thought and actions than it was in the works and words of earlier popes.

Gregory VII has been described, with justice, as one of the forefathers of the Crusade, which embodied the holy war in its most characteristic medieval form. Certainly by the time that Urban II (1088–99) inaugurated the First Crusade at Clermont in 1095, the holy war was well on its way to becoming a fixture of papal policy and religious discourse in the West. Urban II's primary contribution was to bring together a number of accepted and relatively popular ideas in a new form, one that had the good fortune to achieve a spectacular and impressive success. This new institutional entity was the Crusade.[41]

By the pontificate of Urban II Western churchmen had in principle embraced the concept of holy war and viewed warfare as a positive value in the Christian life. "Such is the history of society," wrote Cardinal Newman, "it begins in the poet and ends in the policeman."[42] And one might paraphrase his observation by saying that the history of the medieval Church begins in the Gospel and ends in the Military Orders.[43]

But what of the lawyers, especially the canon lawyers, in all of this? Certainly it would be true to say that they played a role in it; but prior to the time of Gratian (fl. ca. 1140) theirs was a subordinate role. Before Gratian, canon law was not a science, certainly, nor even a very consciously defined discipline.[44] It was not clearly distinguished or distinguishable from moral theology. The growth of canon law as a distinct instrumentality in the life of the Western Church was largely a twelfth-century development.

Still, there were canonists before Gratian, and some of them had dealt with the problem of warfare and its relationship to Christian life. Anselm of Lucca (+1086), for one, devoted the thirteenth book of his *Collectio canonum* to the theme of violence and the use of coercive force by the Church.[45] And the great Ivo of Chartres (+1116), writing just at the time when Urban II was launching the First Crusade, dedicated one book in each of his major canonistic collections to the problem of Christian violence and warfare.[46]

Although these earlier canonists played a part in the process, it is hard to escape the conclusion that Gratian did much more than any of his predecessors to transform the law of war into an ecclesiastical institution.[47] In Causa 23 of his *Decretum,* Gratian examined in detail the whole problem of violence and Christian life. In this context, he dealt with war as a particular species of violence.[48] Throughout his treatment he employed the familiar metaphor of the sword to express the general concept of coercive force. Two swords were in play: the spiritual sword and the material sword. These metaphorical swords, however, did not stand for "Church" and "State." Rather, they stood for two different kinds of coercive force—spiritual coercion (i.e., interdict, excommunication, and other spiritual penalties that might be employed against the offender) and material coercion (i.e., physical force and violence). The Church, according to Gratian, had the right to use both swords when necessary to secure obedience to legitimate commands.[49] It is clear that when Gratian spoke of the Church's right to use material coercion, he meant that the Church had the right to employ physical force, including the right to kill or to mutilate the offender, in the exercise of its functions.[50] The use of physical force by the Church, however, was subject to one significant limitation: violence was not to be employed directly and immediately by clerics; rather it was employed indirectly and mediately, through the agency of laymen.[51]

Within this general theoretical context, then, let us examine Gratian's treatment of war. In Causa 23, in his usual fashion, Gratian outlined a basic situation, from which he then isolated a series of specific questions for discussion. The situation described in this Causa is one in which some heretical bishops have been using threats and force to compel the faithful roundabout to embrace their heresies. The pope, in turn, has commanded the other bishops of the vicinity to defend the faithful from the wayward shepherds and their helpers and to compel the heretics to return to the Catholic fold. The obedient bishops thereupon assembled soldiers to do battle with the heretical forces. In the fighting some of the heretics were slain, others jailed and imprisoned; and thus they were forced to return to the unity of the Catholic faith.[52]

Given this situation, Gratian then posed eight questions, which he discussed in the light of the canonical sources: Is it sinful to make war? What is a just war? Should one use arms to ward off injuries done to others? Ought one to take revenge? Is it sinful for judges and other officials to kill guilty persons? Ought evil persons be forced to be good? Should heretics be despoiled of their goods? Do those who take the goods of heretics in fact take the possessions of other people? Can bishops or clerics take up arms on their own authority or on that of the pope or the emperor?

From Gratian's discussion of these questions and from the welter of authorities whom he cited, I should like to abstract four themes for comment here: first, the treatment of the evils of war and its sinfulness; next, the problem of the salvation of soldiers; third, the justifications for war; and finally, Gratian's approach to war as a legal category.

As to the first of these, Gratian's treatment of the sinfulness of war, it may be thought that in some sense Gratian was setting up a straw man, destined from the beginning for demolition. I am not wholly persuaded that this was so. At the least, Gratian's arguments for the proposition that war is morally wrong and not to be tolerated in a Christian society represented very fairly a continuing viewpoint among Christians. He cited the scriptural authorities for a nonviolent position, and he developed with some vigor the argument that the practice of war and violence is foreign both to the spirit and the explicit teaching of the Gospels.[53] Further, he cited a passage from Origen (although he attributed it wrongly to "Gregory") to show that various Old Testament passages that seem to condone war and physical violence ought to be interpreted in a Christian context as referring to spiritual struggles.[54] In short, although Gratian finally rejected the position that war is inherently sinful and wholly incompatible with Christian values,[55] he did report that position and gave it a reasonable presentation in the *Decretum*. Gratian, to put it another way, was fully conscious of the arguments that Christians should reject war, and he rejected that position consciously.

Next, Gratian held that it was no sin for a Christian to serve as a soldier. For this position he found support among the Fathers of the Church, principally from Saint Augustine.[56] There was a significant reservation in Gratian's thought on this matter, however: for Gratian distinguished between those who fight and kill on their own authority, which he thought wrong, and those who do so on the command of public authority, which he thought allowable.[57] This distinction was both basic and important. By introducing the notion of public authority into the discussion, Gratian really transformed his treatment of war into legal, rather than moral, categories. Public authority, to be sure, was not the only factor involved in distinguishing the righteous war from the unrighteous. A just war must be fought for a good reason, to serve just and proper ends,[58] in addition to having the sanction of legitimate public authority. Given these necessary conditions, there emerged in Gratian's treatment a Christian obligation to fight under certain circumstances. Wars are fought by Christians in order to protect the good and repress the evil, according to Gratian's doctrine; thus those who fail to oppose evildoers are in fact their helpers.[59] The man who did not help to put down the unjust and to protect the righteous was in effect consenting to evil and rejecting the good. So there were some circumstances, according to Gratian, where the Christian had a positive duty to engage in war.[60]

For Gratian, that war was just which was fought by sanction of rightful authority. But he also taught that wars to redress wrongs were just and he implied that this was true whether they were proclaimed by public authority or not.[61] He cited some precedents, too, in order to make his meaning clear: as for example a war fought in order to maintain a right-of-way,[62] a war fought to protect the faithful against heretics,[63] a war fought to protect one's homeland against barbarians,[64] and a war fought to ward off robbers and pirates.[65]

This in turn led Gratian to a discussion of property rights in war. He concluded his discussion of this topic by determining that property captured and appropriated in a just war was rightfully taken and that title to it legitimately passed to the victor.[66]

It is reasonably clear, I think, that Gratian took the moral-theological category of the just war, as it had previously been treated by theologians, and transformed it into a judicial institution. He defined the circumstances under which war was just and lawful. Then he added the further basic premise that only a just war resulted in legitimate legal consequences. Rights to tangible property and intangible rights might both be won in a just war, but not in an unjust war.

Both the criteria and the consequences of this legal category of the just war were explored and developed more fully by Gratian's successors. A few of the decretists who commented on the *Decretum* chose not to deal with Gratian's treatment of war, or did so very scantily,[67] but most of them gave the subject full-scale treatment, as befitted a matter of continuing practical importance.[68] In the decades following Gratian there gradually took shape as well a body of new law, mainly derived from papal decisions in specific cases, but stemming partly also from the decrees of the great twelfth- and thirteenth-century councils. The treatment of war in this new law, and in the writings of the decretalists who commented on it, extended and refined, but did not supersede, the fundamental principles set down in Gratian's *Decretum*.

This canonistic literature is enormous; the portions of it dealing with warfare alone are very sizeable, and I do not propose to make anything like a complete survey of all of it here.[69] It will be worthwhile, however, to take a brief look at some of this literature in order to understand how the holy war fit into the lawyers' analysis of warfare as a whole. There are four topics I should like to touch on, before coming to grips with the lawyers' views on holy war. These topics are: (1) the authority to initiate war; (2) the power to wage war; (3) limitations on armed conflict; and (4) property rights and liability for damages suffered as a result of hostilities.

As to the first of these topics, the basic rule laid down in the *Decretum* was followed by subsequent generations of legal writers: namely that a legitimate public authority must declare a war, since to kill a person without public authority was homicide.[70] Thus it was not a substantial question for the canonists whether a public authority was required. What did trouble them and what they did disagree about was the question of whether or not the pope and the bishops were public authorities entitled to declare war. Paucapalea (fl. 1140–48), the earliest of Gratian's pupils to write a *Summa* on the *Decretum,* thought that no cleric, not even the pope, had the right to initiate a war. He did concede that the clergy could properly exhort princes and secular rulers to take up arms in order to defend the oppressed or to resist the machinations of God's enemies.[71] Rolandus Bandinelli (who later reigned as Pope Alexander III, 1159–81) likewise held that clerics, since they were prohibited from fighting in wars, also lacked the power to declare war.[72] A later generation of decretists, however, was not so certain of this point as the early commentators had been. Huguccio, writing about 1188 or 1190, was at least willing to admit that there was some point to an argument that justified the declaration of war by ecclesiastical judges.[73] The *glossa ordinaria* to the *Decretum* (first compiled by Johannes Teutonicus between 1215 and 1217; later edited by Bartholomaeus Brixiensis ca. 1245) adopted the position that ecclesiastical princes had the power to declare war.[74]

One of the more interesting and original commentators on this matter was Pope Innocent IV, who wrote his *Apparatus* on the *Liber Extra* amid the crises and distractions of his pontificate (1243–54). In his opinion, clerics as a general rule were forbidden to declare war and would be subject to ecclesiastical penalties if they did so.[75] But there were important exceptions to this generalization. Clerics could properly initiate a defensive war, for one thing; and they could likewise declare war in order to recover their possessions from an illegal taker.[76] Further, Innocent believed that bishops who held territorial jurisdiction could undertake wars to protect that jurisdiction, although they could not personally participate in the prosecution of such a war.[77] Hostiensis (+1271), another great thirteenth-century canonist, agreed in large part with the positions taken on this question by Innocent IV,[78] but added one further observation that is particularly significant for our purposes here. Ecclesiastical authorities, said Hostiensis, could properly declare war against the enemies of the Christian faith and against those who attacked the Church or rebelled against it.[79]

It is worth noting, too, that Gulielmus Durantis (1237–96), writing shortly after Hostiensis, taught that when the cause of a war arose out of a matter falling under ecclesiastical jurisdiction, any ecclesiastical judge had a right to declare war. Otherwise, he thought, such jurisdiction would be delusory.[80]

The power to wage war is closely linked with the power to declare war, and the canonistic writers reflected this connection. From quite early times, ecclesiastical regulations provided that the shedding of blood, even in a just war, constituted an impediment to the reception of holy orders and forbade clerics to use weapons, even in self-defense.[81] Gratian's *Decretum* incorporated these viewpoints. Priests should be concerned with the law, not with war, according to one of the canons,[82] and when force was required for the protection of the Church and its interests, then recourse should be had to the secular power for defense.[83] Bishops and other clerics might, under some circumstances, accompany an army, but their role was to assist it with prayers and spiritual aids, not to fight in its ranks.[84]

Later legal writers sometimes qualified this stance. Rolandus Bandinelli, for example, admitted that there was a case to be made for clergymen bearing arms, but concluded that it was always illicit for priests to do military service. Clerics in minor orders, however, could, in his opinion, wage war if commanded so to do by a prince or by the pope.[85] Rufinus (+ before 1192) strongly disagreed. "Some of our predecessors," he wrote, "have tried to distinguish, more drunkenly than soberly, which clerics can take up arms and which cannot." As for himself, Rufinus wanted no part of such dangerous casuistry. No cleric of any kind, in his view, should fight in a war. To this he admitted two possible exceptions: a cleric might, under most extraordinary circumstances, fight to defend himself when required by necessity, which knows no law; and clerics might conceivably fight against pagans on the orders of a superior.[86] Although other decretists—the anonymous authors of the *Summa Parisiensis* and the *Summa 'Elegantius'*, as well as Sicard of Cremona (+1215), for example[87]—agreed in principle with Rufinus, they expressed their views less pungently. Huguccio was inclined to join Rolandus in distinguishing the question, but on different grounds. Clerics, Huguccio thought, could legitimately accompany an army and they could bear weapons, but only defensive weapons: shields, helmets, body armor, and the like. It was wrong for them to employ offensive weapons—lances, swords, bows and arrows—and if they did so they could be punished.[88] One anonymous glossator thought, on the other hand, that bishops not only could, but should, fight in defense of their sees. He went on to add that a bishop who failed to resist the enemies of the Church ought to be punished; apparently he reconsidered and thought this last sentiment too daring; at least, this statement is deleted in the manuscript that reports it.[89]

Following generations of popes, seeing that this aspect of the canon law was unclear, took pains to remedy the defect. A series of conciliar enactments and papal decretals flatly forbade clerics of whatever rank or grade, to engage in warfare directly and personally, even against the Saracens. Clerics could, however, give aid and counsel in just wars and might thus be indirect participants.[90]

The notion of a law of war, of a set of rules that defines the limits within which war can be waged, has in our own times been labeled a myth,[91] and certainly is somewhat paradoxical.[92] In medieval Europe, however, the notion of a functional set of laws of war was taken with extreme seriousness and, within limits, actually did dictate the bounds within which organized fighting usually took place.

Toward the very beginning of his *Decretum,* Gratian defined the law of war in a canon drawn from Isidore of Seville (ca. 560–636). The terms of this definition were broad enough to embrace not only the formalities attending the declaration of war and such matters as military discipline within an army but also, what was more important, the division of the spoils of conquest.[93] In a later canon, drawing this time on Saint Augustine, Gratian outlined the general principles that should govern conduct in war. The basic thrust of this canon was to rule out unnecessary cruelty, conquest for its own sake, and savage treatment of defeated foes.[94]

The canonists who commented on these passages were interested in part in the theoretical problems that they presented for the nature of law: What was the relationship of the law of war to other kinds of law? Their observations on this matter, though interesting in themselves, are not much to the point for our purposes. More relevant is the way in which they drew upon the Roman law to establish a distinction between public enemies (*hostes*) and mere brigands or robbers (*latrunculi vel praedones*).[95] The significance of this distinction lies in its consequences, since goods and persons captured from public enemies became the legitimate property of the conqueror, while those captured by brigands or robbers did not become the property of their captors. Similarly, the soldier fighting in a properly established army had a public function, which also created property claims, and this, too, helped to differentiate him from the ordinary predator.[96]

The importance of all this was stated most clearly by a civilian lawyer, Cino da Pistoia (1270–1336/37). A time of war, Cino declared, is different from a time of peace; it follows that what is lawful in wartime differs from what is lawful in time of peace.[97] The implications of this insight both for the criminal and civil jurisdictions are fundamental.

In a just war, for one thing, killing in battle was no crime; war, in other words, legitimized homicide and no legal action lay against the slayer. This was laid down by Gratian.[98] The implications of the principle were stated succinctly by an anonymous Anglo-

Norman decretist: "Homicide is licit in three ways, namely when
God secretly inspires one person to kill another; or when a judge
having the power of the sword slays someone; or when, on command of a prince, a soldier slays an enemy."[99] Interesting as the
first two conditions are, it is the third one in this series that is
germane here—slaying a public enemy in time of war is licit
homicide. The topic was treated by other legal writers as well, but
the statement of the anonymous glossator represents the general
opinion.[100]

Solutions to questions of liability for damages in wartime were
resolved differently, depending on whether the war was legally just
or not. In a war against the infidel, which Hostiensis labeled a
"Roman" war,[101] enemies who lost property had no claim whatever to restitution, though such a claim might lie in other types of
war.[102] In contrast, the person initiating an unjust war was liable
for all damages arising therefrom, according to Joannes Andreae
(ca. 1270–1348). Joannes further maintained that there was a legal
presumption that every war was unjust. The burden of proving that
a given conflict was just, in other words, lay with the person
advancing that claim.[103] Those who fought in an unreasonable war,
Joannes thought, were not to be distinguished from robbers and
brigands and they bore absolute liability for any damages they
caused.[104]

Innocent IV even earlier had established that participants in an
unjust war had no right to claim against the person declaring the war
for losses suffered as a result of service rendered in the war. Those
who were summoned to fight in a just war had a limited claim; if
they owed military service to the person declaring the war, participants had no claim against him, unless the war was manifestly
evil.[105] This position was adopted by later commentators as
well.[106]

It is the function of human law, according to one of the decretist
writers, to restrain violence.[107] It is well known that the medieval
canon law did, in fact, attempt to fulfill this function, both by
limiting warfare to certain periods of the year and by exempting
certain classes of persons (priests, clerics, monks, lay brothers,

pilgrims, merchants, peasants, and travelers) from attack during time of war.[108] Beginning in the late ninth century, the medieval peace movement sought to use the penal sanctions of the canon law to punish those who violated these norms. By the late twelfth century, these provisions had been incorporated into the general law of the Western Church, particularly as a result of the constitutions adopted by the third Lateran Council in 1179.[109] Other councils sought to impose further limits on violence—by forbidding Christians to procure assassinations, for example.[110] Although these restrictions were in theory supposed to apply to all just wars, the canonists realistically admitted that they failed to work well and that they were not in practice observed.[111]

There was also an attempt to limit war by outlawing weapons that were thought to be too murderous and too effective in their results—the crossbow and the ballista, in particular. In this connection an interesting distinction was drawn between wars against Christians and wars directed against non-Christian enemies. The crossbow and the ballista were outlawed in the former class of wars; in wars against non-Christians, however, the use of these weapons was allowed.[112] The justification for this invidious distinction was not spelled out either in the canon itself or by the commentators on it; perhaps because it was thought to be self-evident. At any rate, these weapons, which contemporary opinion regarded as excessively dangerous and cruel, were in principle restricted to use in the holy war. A few canonists sought to broaden the interpretation of the canon to mean that these weapons might be used in just wars, but not in unjust ones.[113] In practice the effort to restrict crossbows and ballistas to wars against non-Christians had little effect, and these weapons by the beginning of the thirteenth century were coming into common use in European wars.[114]

More effective in practice than attempts to limit the seasons of war, the classes of persons against whom action was directed, or the weaponry used in warfare were the efforts to restrict indiscriminate looting in time of war. Possibly this sort of control was more effective precisely because its implementation depended, in the final analysis, upon the courts, rather than upon soldiers in the field. It made little sense to loot, after all, if subsequently one's possession of the looted goods could successfully be challenged in the courts.

Gratian had thought (relying on Saint Augustine) that soldiers should not loot at all, but should be paid for their service with established stipends,[115] a notion that conformed to the law and practice of ancient Rome.[116] Although the decretists tended to follow him on this point,[117] the question was wholly academic. Medieval soldiers looted and tried to keep what they took, insofar as their leaders did not claim it for themselves. By the thirteenth century canonists had adjusted their treatment of the law to take account of this fact of life. The ordinary gloss to the *Liber Extra* invoked the just war distinction once more in this matter: if the war were unjust, no spoils legitimately could be taken; if the war were just, however, then spoils were legitimate.[118] This rule applied not only to the property of the vanquished but also to the defeated soldiers themselves. They, too, became the property of the conquerors, to be divided among the members of the victorious army and, in the usual course of things, to be held for ransom.[119]

What I have said thus far will hopefully have given you some notion of the place of war in the medieval lawyers' scheme of things. Now we come at last—at long last, you may think—to the holy war.

Before we try to fit the holy war into the larger legal framework, it would be best to define the term, holy war, at least roughly. For our purposes here, I understand holy war to mean a war that is not only just, but justifying; that is, a war that confers positive spiritual merit on those who fight in it. This requires some positive action, in turn, from a religious authority, accepted as having the requisite power to grant official sanction to a holy war, to confer its particular sacred character upon it. Commonly, though not invariably, such a war will be rather closely directed by religious authorities, fought with the purpose of achieving some religious goal. But the outstanding characteristic of the holy war, I repeat, is that it is viewed as securing personal religious merit for those who participate in it.[120] Thus defined, the holy war may be viewed—and I shall shortly show that it was so viewed by medieval lawyers—as a sub-set of the just war. Every holy war, to put it another way, was a just war; but not every just war was a holy war.

Now there was a feeling abroad in Western Europe during the Middle Ages that warriors who died in defense of Christendom or in battles to advance the spread of the Christian faith were *ipso facto* meritorious.[121] It was in fact reasonably common literary form to describe them as martyrs for the Christian faith.[122] The tradition embodied in this thinking was ancient, and it was rooted not only in popular piety but also in ancient legal sources. "Because they died for the *re publica,* they are, indeed, understood to live in perpetual glory," the *Institutes* of Justinian declared, referring to soldiers who died for the Roman *patria.*[123] Tribonian, Justinian's principal legal counsellor, was not fabricating this sentiment *ex nihilo*—it is founded upon statements of the classical Roman lawyers (Papi-nian, Ulpian, and Marcellus, for example),[124] as well as upon common opinions expressed by Roman literary types.[125]

Other scholars have suggested that the emergence of the idea of holy war in Western Europe was favored by the disappearance of the Roman Empire in the West and that medieval wars against the pagans may be seen as a continuation of Roman wars against the barbarians.[126] It has been persuasively argued, too, that during the early Middle Ages there took place a transformation of the classical tradition of glorified death for the secular *patria* into a Christian tradition of sanctified death for the Christian *patria*—heaven; or alternatively for the advancement of the Christian faith here on earth.[127]

Gratian incorporated in the *Decretum* a number of statements from authorities who reflected this view, most especially a letter of Pope Leo IV in which the pontiff stated that those who died for the truth of the faith, the salvation of the *patria,* and the defense of their fellow-Christians merited a heavenly reward.[128] This statement might be construed, though the evidence is rather slim, as a legal foundation for a doctrine of holy war. In any event, it was not until about a century after Gratian's time that a well-developed scheme was framed to fit the holy war into the larger context of legal thought about war in general. For this development, Hostiensis is our most important witness.

Hostiensis divided wars into seven different categories, of which the first is one that he labeled rather curiously "Roman war." This is the war between the faithful and the infidel; it is also our holy war. The other varieties of war in this scheme were, briefly, the judicial war, the presumptuous war, the licit war, the casual war, the voluntary war, and the necessary war.[129] Hostiensis's notion of the "Roman war" was evidently an adaptation of categories used by the medieval Roman lawyers,[130] but used by him to mean the holy war, that is, the Crusade. The holy war, thus, was what other writers called a "hostile war," that is, one in which the enemy were *hostes* in the full legal sense, the result of which was that their persons and property passed fully and rightfully to the ownership of those who defeated them.[131]

There was a further turn to this development, which I mention only in passing, since it has been more fully explored by others.[132] The identification of the holy war with the Crusades seems to have gone one step further in the thirteenth century, so that writers, especially lawyers but also theologians, come to apply to wars declared by secular rulers the full panoply of legal rights earlier assigned to the Crusades. By the end of the thirteenth century some writers attribute to those who fall in battle on behalf of a national interest that eternal glory once reserved for Crusaders and earlier still for the defenders of the ancient Roman empire.[133]

If the principal characteristic of the holy war is the spiritual merit that it is thought to confer upon those who participate in it, then we must take some account of what precisely that spiritual merit consisted. In the medieval Christian tradition the conventional response to a question on this point was: the indulgence. But what is an indulgence?

The answer to that question is unfortunately complex.[134] We have already noted that from as early as the mid-ninth century there are papal letters that link death on the battlefield with salvation of the deceased warrior's soul.[135] The early papal letters on the subject, however, were not indulgences in any recognizable sense of the term. They were rather expressions of pious hope coupled with intercessory prayers for the salvation of the souls of the dead. Shortly after the middle of the eleventh century, Pope Alexander II (1061–73) moved closer to granting an indulgence when he proclaimed a commutation of penance for soldiers fighting in the wars of reconquest in Spain. Participation in war against the Moors was expressly stipulated by the pope as adequate satisfaction for the penance imposed upon these soldiers by their confessors.[136] Now there is a difference between a commutation of penance and an indulgence (at least as the term indulgence is conventionally understood). An indulgence is satisfaction for the temporal punishment required by God in satisfaction for sin. A commutation of penance, on the other hand, is satisfaction for the penance imposed by a confessor for the sins confessed to him. Punishment and penance are not necessarily the same at all; punishment is determined by God and the full extent of it is presumably known only to Him; penance is determined by the confessor and his estimate of the seriousness of a particular sin (and consequently the punishment required for that sin) is not necessarily identical with the judgment made on the matter by God.

When the Council of Clermont in 1095 adopted its provisions for the spiritual reward of the participants in the First Crusade, it specified that this reward should take the form of a commutation of penance.[137] There is some question, however, as to exactly what was meant, or thought to be meant, by that canon. Pope Urban II, who presided at the Council, seems to have felt unsure about the matter. In one of his letters, about a month after the Council, he blandly referred to the Council as having granted Crusaders "remission of all their sins";[138] a few months later, in another letter, Pope Urban was more circumspect and described the spiritual reward granted the Crusaders as a commutation of penance.[139]

Whatever doubts or uncertainties Pope Urban may have had about the Crusade "indulgence," his twelfth-century successors, when bestowing similar spiritual favors, took care to state that they were granting them in the same sense that Pope Urban had.[140] Thirteenth-century popes and councils grew bolder about the mat-

ter and gradually the Crusade indulgence came to have the character of an indulgence proper, that is a remission of the temporal
punishment for sin.[141]

Pope Innocent IV certainly had no doubt that the pope had the
right to grant indulgences to those who went on Crusade,[142] a
power that he thought was linked to the fact that the Saracens
possessed the Holy Land illegally. The holy war and the grant of
indulgence for its participants rested, so far as Innocent IV was
concerned, upon a property claim, fortified by the holiness of the
particular territory involved.[143]

Hostiensis's treatment of the indulgence for the holy war
likewise rested the justification for the Crusade upon the pope's
claims to a peculiar jurisdiction over the Holy Land, in virtue of its
sanctity as the birthplace and home of Christ.[144] The indulgence,
he also argued, was founded upon the papal plenitude of power.
Proclamation of the Crusade and the Crusade indulgence was,
therefore, limited strictly to the pope.[145] Hostiensis also defined
what he meant by an "indulgence"—the first canonist, so far as I
know, to do so—but his definition was lamentably vague and
sweeping: an indulgence, he said, was a remission of all sins, plain,
simple, and without qualifications.[146]

The arguments raised in defense of indulgences for those who
participated in the Crusades, the holy wars par excellence of the
Middle Ages, point in turn to an even more basic question: How is
it that Christians have the right to make war upon the Saracens and,
indeed, on other unbelievers? What is the basis of that right and
whence does its justification spring?

Not everyone, to be sure, agreed that the Crusades were justified. Ralph Niger, for one, writing about 1189 was dubious of the
proposition that Christians had a right to conquer the Holy Land
and maintained that the shedding of human blood was in no way a
fitting atonement for sins.[147] Criticism of the Crusades in the
thirteenth century was even more widespread than in Ralph Niger's
day and created some problems for the papacy in pursuit of its
crusading goals.[148]

Still, such views were distinctly minority opinions and were not at all commonly held, at least not by widely influential writers. From at least the mid-twelfth century, when the question seems first to have been discussed, the general opinion was that the Crusades were undoubtedly holy wars and as such were fully justified.[149] This viewpoint found support among the lawyers. Although the canonists occasionally conceded that in principle Saracens and Jews were their neighbors and that they ought to love their neighbors as themselves, still this tended to be a qualified concession: "In truth, however, we ought to apply all the works of love according to each man's condition," as the ordinary gloss put it.[150]

On one basic matter there was a sharp difference of opinion among the thirteenth-century canonists. This was the question of the legitimacy of the rights of Saracens and other non-Christians to hold lands and to rule them. One view was expressed by Innocent IV, who held that infidels did indeed have a legitimate right to hold possessions and that they were entitled to rule their lands and exercise jurisdiction over them. God, after all, made the sun to shine on the good and the evil alike, said Innocent, and it was not proper for the pope or the Christian faithful to take away the rights and possessions of infidels who possessed these things without sin.[151] This position, Innocent also thought, was perfectly compatible with his views of papal power. The pope, he held, had jurisdiction and power, at least de jure if not de facto, over all men, infidels included. If therefore infidels were guilty of offenses against the natural law, the pope had a right to punish them.[152] Innocent likewise claimed a right to punish Jews who embraced heresies against their own faith.[153]

Although infidels, according to Innocent IV, should not be forced to embrace Christianity, they did have an obligation to allow Christian missionaries to preach the Gospel.[154] Should they fail to do this, or should they fail to obey other legitimate commands of the pope, then the pope had the right to punish them and to declare war against them.[155] Thus Innocent IV assimilated the holy war, that is, a war declared by the pope against disobedient non-Christians, to the category of judicial wars, fought to execute the judgments of a judge against those who disobeyed a lawful command.

A sharply differing view of these questions was expressed by Hostiensis. He held that all jurisdiction and right to rule were taken away from non-Christians by the coming of Christ, who conveyed to His own followers exclusive rights to the exercise of power and jurisdiction on this earth.[156] Infidels were, therefore, subject to the Church; those infidels who accepted the Church's power over them were to be tolerated. Those who demurred, however, and refused to accept the Church's governance forfeited thereby the privilege of toleration.[157] Disobedient infidels were subject to papal punishment, and the pope was entitled to declare war against them, a war that was by definition both just and justifying.[158]

Although Innocent IV and Hostiensis disagreed sharply on the basis for the holy war, they both agreed that the holy war represented a legitimate exercise of papal power and both of them found adequate juristic grounds for it. The grounds of their disagreement had to do with the legitimacy of possession, jurisdiction, and rule by non-Christians. These differences were of great significance for later lawyers, who had to wrestle with the problem of the legitimacy of the governments and property rights of non-Christian Indians in the New World.[159]

We have seen how the canonists legitimized the holy war against Saracens, pagans, and other infidels. The legal commentators similarly taught that under some circumstances holy wars might be proclaimed against Christians whose interpretation of their faith was unorthodox and heretical. There were passages in the *Decretum* of Gratian to support this contention. Causa 23 itself was based on a situation in which heretics were coercing the faithful to embrace erroneous views, and a number of the authorities whom Gratian cited lent support to the view that under such circumstances it was legitimate for the Church to use force to oppose heretics.[160] Some, indeed, held that rebellious churchmen lost the right to use either the material or the spiritual sword, and hence forfeited all ecclesiastical rights and possessions.[161]

Gratian himself sanctioned the use of force against wicked persons and characterized such use as a legitimate employment of authority.[162] Some of his followers went still further. Heretics, according to Rolandus, lost all their rights to property[163] and Huguccio emphasized that princes had an obligation to defend the Church against heretics and schismatics by making war against them.[164]

A concerted holy war by the Church against heretics was first proclaimed by the third Lateran Council in 1179. Significantly, the pope who presided at this council was Alexander III, that same Rolandus who, as a law professor at Bologna, had taught that heretics forfeited their property rights. The decree of the third Lateran Council assimilated those who took up the sword against heretics with Crusaders who fought against the infidel in the Holy Land and granted fighters against heresy the same indulgence and other privileges enjoyed by Crusaders in the Latin East.[165] This proclamation was ineffective, at least in the sense that it produced no immediate practical action. In 1208, however, Pope Innocent III succeeded in translating the conciliar decree into practice when he launched what was to be called the Albigensian Crusade.[166]

The canonists were not bashful about providing juristic justification for this papal action. Joannes Teutonicus in the *glossa ordinaria* to the *Decretum* taught that if there were heretics in a city, the whole city might lawfully be burnt.[167] Doubtless he had in mind the massacre at Béziers (22 July 1209).[168] Raymond of Peñafort (1175–1275) went further still. Not only was it lawful and laudable for princes to undertake holy wars for the repression of heretics, it was a duty required of them and those who failed to take part in such a war sinned by withholding their help.[169] Hostiensis thought it clear that the Crusades could be preached against heretics and Saracens. Although it was not quite so clear that the Church was authorized to proclaim a holy war against rebels and schismatics, Hostiensis finally concluded that it was reasonable and proper thus to extend the holy war concept.[170]

To summarize briefly, the medieval canonists, beginning with Gratian, worked out a structured discussion of war as a Western Christian legal institution. Generally, the canonists sought to limit warfare, to protect property rights, to define the circumstances within which wars could be fought. In the process the canonists combined elements drawn from Christian theology and from the ancient Roman law and welded them together into a doctrine of war. This doctrine, in turn, enabled them to analyze warfare, to establish criteria to classify various kinds of wars. To each variety of war they assigned conditions and limitations, which determined the legal consequences that flowed from that particular kind of conflict. Foremost in the minds of the commentators was the interest of the Christian religion and the interest of the institutional Church. Differing views of what best served these interests are reflected in the clashing views of different canonistic writers.[171]

Within the overall framework of the legal institution of war, the canonists recognized the holy war as a specific variety of just war; one that, like the others, had its own proper legal characteristics and limitations. The holy war was the most favored variety of war known to the canon law, for it allowed the widest latitude of action to its participants, and the fruits of victory in the holy war were more generously allocated to the victors than in any other type of war that the canonists acknowledged.

During the period dealt with here, there was a slow broadening of the circumstances under which a war might be classified as a holy war. Originally the holy war, otherwise known as the Crusade, was authorized only against Muslims and only in the Holy Land. Then it was enlarged to include wars against the Muslims in Spain. Enlarged again, it embraced wars against pagans. Subsequently the holy war was further extended to include wars against Christian heretics, schismatics, and other rebels against ecclesiastical authority.

By the end of the Middle Ages the holy war had become a model for expansionist campaigns by European Christians against non-Europeans and non-Christians in all parts of the world. It was in this way that the holy war institution was employed, for example, by the Spanish conquistadores in Latin America. The Protestant Englishmen and others who played the major role in the expansion of European-based colonies and settlements in North America were not overly concerned with the formal trappings of holy war. Still it is not particularly difficult to see some dim vestiges of holy war ideology and the presuppositions that accompanied it in the westward expansion of the United States.

In the twentieth century people still speak of "Crusades" against one thing or another, but in modern times the term has been stripped of its former juridical content and effect. Some muted overtones of the holy war's older characteristics linger on. They are its legacy to modern thought and modern attitudes toward war.

So long as Europeans derived their cultural identity largely from their self-identification as Christians, the Church was able to exercise considerable control over warfare. This control reached its peak in the holy war. But with the rise of strong monarchies and nation-states, ecclesiastical control waned. Kings and their ministers, however, found it useful to adapt ecclesiastical concepts and the categories of the canon law to serve their own purposes. As cultural identifications have changed, however, the remnants of the older categories of warfare have become increasingly dangerous and misleading. The holy war served particular purposes in a specific social and cultural environment. In modern society its vestiges probably do more harm than good.

1. Thus, for example, Deut. 28:46–53; Lev. 24:26; Judges 2:14, 3:8, 4:1–2, 6:1–2, 10:6–9, 13:1; Isa. 5:24–30; Jer. 5:14–19. Scriptural passages throughout are cited from the Vulgate text, ed. Aloisius Gramatica (Città del Vaticano: Typis Polyglottis Vaticanis, 1959).

2. E.g., 1 Par. 29:11; 1 Mach. 2:19–22; 2 Mach. 10:38.

3. 2 Par. 13:12; Jer. 7:3.

4. 1 Cor. 15:57.

5. 2 Cor. 13:11; Rom. 15:33.

6. Matt. 26:52.

7. Exod. 21:24; Lev. 24:20; Deut. 19:21.

8. Matt. 5:38–48; Rom. 12:19.

9. Rom. 12:17, 21.

10. Carl Erdmann, *Die Entstehung des Kreuzzugsgedankens,* Forschungen zur Kirchen und Geistesgeschichte 6 (1935; rpt. Stuttgart: W. Kohlhammer, 1955), p. 3. Erdmann's book is a basic point of departure for all subsequent studies of holy war in medieval Christian thought prior to the Crusades.

11. Tertullian, *Apologeticum* 37.4–5, ed. and trans. Jean-Pierre Waltzing, 2d ed., Collection Guillaume Budé (Paris: Société d'édition 'Les Belles Lettres', 1961), p. 79. Other evidence is cited by P. L. T. G. Goyau, "L'Eglise catholique et le droit de gens," *Recueil des cours de l'Académie de Droit International* 6 (1925): 129–32, and especially by Adolf von Harnack, *Militia Christi: Die christliche Religion und der Soldatenstand in den ersten drei Jahrhunderten* (Tübingen: J. C. B. Mohr, 1905). See also R. H. Bainton, "The Early Church and War," *Harvard Theological Review* 39 (1946): 189–212, and Remo Cacitti, "Il cristianesimo primitivo di fronte al problema della guerra e del servizio militare," *Vita e pensiero* 54 (1972): 77–90.

12. Augustine, *De civitate Dei* 1.21, ed B. Dombart and A. Kolb, Corpus Christianorum, series Latina 47 (Turnhout: Brépols, 1955), p. 23; Erdmann, *Die Entstehung*, p. 7, maintains that Augustine's *bellum Deo auctore* is synonymous with holy war.

13. *De civitate Dei* 19.7 (ed. Dombart and Kolb, 2:672).

14. *De civitate Dei* 19.12 (ed. Dombart and Kolb, 2:675).

15. Cicero, *De officiis* 1.11.36, ed Hubert Ashton Holden (1899, rpt. Amsterdam: Adolf M. Hakkert, 1966), p. 15; *De re publica* 3.23.35, ed. and trans. Clinton Walker Keys (Cambridge, Mass.: Harvard University Press, 1928; rpt. 1959), p. 212.

16. P. Bierzanek, "Sur les origines de la guerre et de la paix," *Revue historique de droit français et étranger,* 4th ser. 38 (1960): 85; A. Nussbaum, "Just War—A Legal Category," *Michigan Law Review* 42 (1943): 454–55; Cf. Lactantius, *Institutes* 6.9 in his *Opera,* ed. O. F. Fritsche, 2 vols. (Leipzig: B. Tauchnitz, 1842–44), 2:18.

17. Bierzanek, "Sur les origines," pp. 85–86.

18. See the well-documented account of Augustine's writings on these matters by Juan Fernando Ortega, "La paz y la guerra en el pensamiento agustiniano," *Revista española de derecho canónico* 20 (1965): 5–35, and also Frederick H. Russell, "The Medieval Theories of the Just War According to the Romanists and Canonists of the Twelfth and Thirteenth Centuries" (Ph.D. diss., Johns Hopkins, 1969), pp. 47–73. [See now the published version of Russell's dissertation, *The Just War in the Middle Ages,* Cambridge Studies in Medieval Life and Thought, 3d ser. vol. 8 (Cambridge: Cambridge University Press, 1975).]

19. Goyau, "L'Eglise catholique et le droit des gens," p. 136 and passim. On the Christian idea of war generally, see also Robert Regout, *La Doctrine de la guerre juste de Saint Augustin à nos jours d'après les théologiens et les canonistes catholiques* (Paris: A. Pedone, 1935); Kurt Georg Cram, *Iudicium belli: Zum Rechtscharakter des Krieges in deutschen Mittelalter,* Archiv für Kulturgeschichte, Beiheft 5 (Münster: H. Böhlau, 1955); Ernst Nys, *Le Droit de guerre et les précurseurs de Grotius* (Brussels: Muquardt, Merzbach, et Falk, 1882); Alfred Vanderpol, *La Doctrine scolastique du droit de guerre* (Paris: A. Pedone, 1919); G. S. Windass and J. Newman, "The Early Christian Attitude to War," *Irish Theological Quarterly* 29 (1962): 235–47; and especially the works of Erdmann and Harnack previously cited.

20. I cannot agree with the position taken by some writers who hold that the idea of the holy war was universally known and accepted in the medieval period; see, e.g., Michel Villey, *La Croisade: Essai sur la formation d'une théorie juridique,* L'Eglise et l'état au moyen age 6 (Paris: J. Vrin, 1942), pp. 32–33; H. Pissard, *La Guerre sainte en pays chrétien: essai sur l'origine et le developpement des théories canoniques* (Paris: A. Picard, 1912), p. 4.

21. The resemblances are summarized briefly by Albrecht Noth, *Heiliger Krieg und heiliger Kampf in Islam und Christentum: Beiträge zur Vorgeschichte und Geschichte der Kreuzzüge,* Bonner historische Forschungen 28 (Bonn: Ludwig Röhrscheid, 1966), pp. 139–46.

22. Noth's is the most recent attempt, but, at pp. 147–48, he confesses that he cannot prove any direct influence of the *jihād* on the Christian holy war. See also M. Canard, "La Guerre sainte dans le monde islamique et dans le monde chrétien," *Revue Africaine* 79 (1936): 605–23, where the author maintains *inter alia* that the Western Christian holy war idea emerges as a defense mechanism against Islamic pressures. For an account of Muslim holy war ideas, see Emmanuel Sivan, *L'Islam et la croisade: Idéologie et propaganda dans les réactions musulmanes aux croisades* (Paris: A. Maisonneuve, 1968), pp. 9–22. The paper by Adolf Waas, "Der heilige Krieg in Islam und Christentum," *Die Welt als Geschichte* 19 (1959): 211–25, does little to advance the understanding of the question.

23. Erdmann, *Die Entstehung,* pp. 21, 86–106; cf. the studies of Hans-Dietrich Kahl, "*Compellere intrare:* Die Wendenpolitik Brunos von Querfurt im Lichte hochmittelalterlichen Missions-und Volkerrechts," *Zeitschrift für Ostforschung* 4 (1955): 161–93, 260–401, and "Zum Geist der deutschen Slawenmission des Hochmittelalters," *Zeitschrift für Ostforschung* 2 (1953): 1–14. Both of these studies have been reprinted by Helmut Beumann, ed., in *Heidenmission und Kreuzzugsgedanke in der deutschen Ostpolitik des Mittelalters* Wege der Forschung 7 (Darmstadt: Wissenschaftliche Buchgesellschaft, 1963), pp. 156–76, 177–274.

24. F. Prinz, *Klerus und Krieg im früheren Mittelalter: Untersuchungen zur Rolle der Kirche beim Aufbau der Konigsherrschaft,* Monographien zur Geschichte des Mittelalters 2 (Stuttgart: A. Hiersemann, 1971), pp. 195–96. Edgar N. Johnson, *The Secular Activities of the German Episcopate, 919–1024,* University of Nebraska Studies 30/31 (Lincoln: University of Nebraska, 1932), pp. 166–88, 206–18, gives numerous examples of bishops' military involvement; on this, see also Leopold Auer, "Der Kriegsdienst des Klerus unter den sachsischen Kaisern," *Mittelilungen des Instituts für österreichische Geschichtsforschung* 79 (1971): 316–407; 80 (1972): 48–70.

25. Erdmann, *Die Entstehung,* p. 17.

26. Erdmann, ibid., pp. 24–26, was the first to point out and to detail the significance of the liturgical evidence for the development of holy war ideology.

27. Erdmann, ibid., pp. 74–77, discusses these blessings; at pp. 326–35, he gives examples of the prayers and ceremonies employed.

28. Ibid., pp. 30–50, 166.

29. Ibid., p. 171.

30. Pissard, *La Guerre sainte,* p. 10.

31. Erdmann, *Die Entstehung,* p. 161.

32. Ibid., pp. 134–65; more recently, see I. S. Robinson, "Gregory VII and the Soldiers of Christ," *History* 58 (1973): 190–92.

33. Alfons M. Stickler, "Il 'gladius' nel Registro di Gregorio VII," *Studi Gregoriani* 3 (1948): 89–103.

34. Erdmann, *Die Entstehung,* pp. 185–87.

35. *Das Register Gregors VII.* 2.54, ed. Erich Caspar, 2 vols., Monumenta Germaniae Historica: Epistolae selectae in usum scholarum 2 (Berlin: Weidmann, 1920–23), 1:199; cf. Erdmann, *Die Entstehung,* p. 197.

36. Leo IV, *Epistolae* 1, in *Patrologiae cursus completus . . . series Latina,* ed. J.-P. Migne, 221 vols. (Paris: J.-P. Migne, 1844–64; cited hereafter as *PL*), 115:655–57; P. Jaffé, S. Löwenfeld et al. ed., *Regesta pontificum Romanorum,* 2 vols. (Leipzig: Veit, 1885–88; cited hereafter as *JL*), no. 2,642.

37. *PL,* 126:816; *JL,* 3,195.

38. Erdmann, *Die Entstehung* p, 111; J. A. Brundage, *Medieval Canon Law and the Crusader* (Madison: University of Wisconsin Press, 1969), pp. 23–24.

39. *JL*, 4,530 and 4,533. For the literature on these letters, see Brundage, *Medieval Canon Law and the Crusader,* p. 24, n. 90.

40. The letters of Alexander II just cited do refer to expansion in Spain at the expense of the Moors. The situations dealt with by Gregory VII, however, are different in quality, if not entirely different in kind, from the one dealt with by Alexander II.

41. Brundage, *Medieval Canon Law and the Crusader,* pp. 30–32; E. O. Blake, "The Formation of the 'Crusade Idea,'" *Journal of Ecclesiastical History* 21 (1970): 12, 14–15, 18.

42. John Henry Newman, *The Rise and Progress of Universities* 3:77, in his *Works,* new impression, 41 vols. (London: Longmans, Green, 1898–1903), vol. 30.

43. This conjunction was pointed out, perhaps without ironic intent, by Ferminio Poggiaspalla, "La Chiesa e la partecipazione dei chierici alla guerra nella legislazione conciliare fino alla Decretali di Gregorio IX," *Ephemerides iuris canonici* 15 (1959): 148.

44. Stephan Kuttner, "The Father of the Science of Canon Law," *The Jurist* 1 (1941): 2–19; A. Van Hove, "Quae Gratianus contulerit methodo scientiae canonicae," *Apollinaris* 21 (1948): 12–24.

45. Paul Fournier and Gabriel Le Bras, *Histoire des collections canoniques en Occident depuis les fausses décrétales jusqu'au Décret de Gratien,* 2 vols., Société d'histoire du droit, Bibliothèque d'histoire du droit (1931–32; rpt. Aalen: Scientia Verlag, 1972), 2:28–29, 37; Alfons M. Stickler, "Il potere coattivo materiale della Chiesa nella riforma gregoriana, secondo Anselmo da Lucca," *Studi Gregoriani* 2 (1947): 235–85; Robinsin, "Gregory VII and the Soldiers of Christ," pp. 186–88.

46. Ivo, *Decretum* lib. 10 (*PL*, 161:689–746); *Panormia* lib. 8 (*PL*, 161:1303–18). On the dates of his canonistic collections, see Fournier-Le Bras, *Histoire des collections,* 2:55–57, 105–6; on Ivo's career generally, see Rolf Sprandel, *Ivo von Chartres und seine Stellung in der Kirchengeschichte* (Stuttgart: A. Hiersemann, 1962; Pariser historische Studien 1).

47. Stephan Kuttner, *Kanonistische Schuldlehre von Gratian bis auf die Dekretalen Gregors IX.,* Studi e Testi 64 (1935; rpt., Città del Vaticano: Biblotheca Apostolica Vaticana, 1961), p. 255.

48. G. Hubrecht, "La 'Juste guerre' dans le Décret de Gratien," *Studia Gratiana* 3 (1955): 175.

49. Alfons M. Stickler, "De ecclesiae potestate coactive materiali apud magistrum Gratianum," *Salesianum* 4 (1942): 97–119; briefly summarized in his "Magistri Gratiani sententia de potestate ecclesiae in statum," *Apollinaris* 21 (1948): 98–107, and also in "De potestate gladii materialis ecclesiae secundum 'Quaestiones Bambergenses' ineditas," *Salesianum* 6 (1944): 113; Stanley Chodorow, *Christian Political Theory and Church Politics in the Mid-Twelfth Century: The Ecclesiology of Gratian's Decretum,* Publications of the U.C.L.A. Center for Medieval and Renaissance Studies 5 (Berkeley: University of California Press, 1972), p. 86.

50. Chodorow, *Christian Political Theory,* p. 229; Stickler, "De ecclesiae potestate coactiva," p. 9.

51. C. 23 q. 8 d.p.c. 18 and d.p.c. 28. Citations to the *Decretum Gratiani* and the other parts of the *Corpus iuris canonici* are to the standard edition by Emil Friedberg, 2 vols. (1879; rpt., Graz: Akademische Druck- und Verlagsanstalt, 1959). The conventional canonistic citation system is employed throughout; for explanations, see Xavier Ochoa Sanz and Aloisius Diez, *Indices canonum titulorum et capitulum Corporis iuris canonici,* Universa bibliotheca iuris, Subsidia 1 (Roma: Commentarium pro religiosis, 1964), pp. iv-v. See also Chodorow, *Christian Political Theory,* p. 241; Stickler, "De ecclesiae potestate coactiva," pp. 112–13.

52. C. 23 pr.: "Quidam episcopi cum plebe sibi commissa in heresim lapsi sunt; circumadiacentes catholicos minis et cruciatibus ad heresim conpellere ceperunt, quo conperto Apostolicus catholicis episcopis circumadiacentium regionum, qui ab inperatore ciuilem iurisdictionem acceperant, inperauit, ut catholicos ab hereticis defenderent, et quibus modis possent eos ad fidei ueritatem redire conpellerent. Episcopi, hec mandata Apostolica accipientes, conuocatis militibus aperte et per insidias contra hereticos pugnare ceperunt. Tandem nonnullis eorum neci traditis, aliis rebus suis uel ecclesiasticis expoliatis, aliis carcere et ergastulo reclusis, ad unitatem catholicae fidei coacti redierunt."

53. C. 23 q. 1 pr.; q. 3 pr.; q. 4 d.a.c. 16; q. 5 pr. and c. 1–8.

54. C. 23 q. 1 c. 1.

55. C. 23 q. 1 d.p.c. 7.

56. C. 23 q. 1 c. 3, 5.

57. C. 23 q. 5 d.p.c. 7 § 2 and c. 8, 13.

58. C. 23 q. 4 d.p.c. 37 and d.p.c. 54.

59. C. 23 q. 3 c. 6–8, 11.

60. C. 23 q. 3 d.p.c. 10.

61. There is an interesting shift here. At C. 23 q. 2 c. 1, Gratian cites Isidore of Seville's definition of the just war: "Iustum est bellum, quod ex edicto geritur de rebus repetendis, aut propulsandorum hominum causa" (Isidore, *Etymologiae* 18.2). One reading of this definition is that two conditions are necessary to make a war just: public authorization *(quod ex edicto geritur)* and legitimate purpose *(de rebus repetendis, aut propulsandorum hominum causa).* Gratian's interpretation is different. At C. 23 q. 2 d.p.c. 2, he restates the definition in a form which implies that either of these conditions is sufficient: "Cum ergo iustum bellum sit, quod ex edicto geritur, uel quo iniuriae ulciscuntur. . . . "

62. C. 23 q. 2 c. 3.

63. C. 23 q. 3 c. 3–4.

64. C. 23 q. 3 c. 5.

65. C. 23 q. 3 c. 6.

66. C. 23 q. 3 d.p.c. 1.

67. Thus Huguccio did not gloss C. 23 at all (although he dealt with war in some of his other glosses), while Stephen of Tournai's commentary on C. 23 is merely a conflation of statements drawn from Paucapalea and Rolandus: *Die Summa des Stephanus Tornacensis über das Decretum Gratiani,* ed. J. F. von Schulte (1891; rpt., Aalen: Scientia Verlag, 1965), p. 230. Rufinus, although he commented on C. 23, found Gratian's treatment prolix: "Huius causae tractatus est prolixius, sed que dicuntur aperta sunt nec per omnia scientiae decretorum accomoda; et ideo a prudenti lectori satis nobis indulgendum credimus, si moras solitas in presentis cause questionibus non ponamus"; *Summa decretorum* ed. Heinrich Singer (1902; rpt., Aalen: Scientia Verlag, 1963), pp. 403–4.

68. The differences between the ways in which the canonists and the theologians dealt with the subject of war are described by Regout, *La Doctrine de la guerre juste,* pp. 57–58.

69. Many of these legal commentaries, including some of the most important ones, have never appeared in print. The remarks that follow will, for the most part, be confined to the doctrines of writers whose works have been published.

70. C. 23 q. 8 c. 33, and C. 23 q. 4 c. 36.

71. *Die Summa des Paucapalea über das Decretum Gratiani* to C. 23 q. 8 pr., ed. J. F. von Schulte (Giessen: Emil Roth, 1890), p. 103.

72. *Die Summa magistri Rolandi, nachmals Papstes Alexander III.* to C. 23 q. 3, ed. F. Thaner (Innsbruck: Wagner, 1874), p. 89; see also the remarks of Marcel Pacaut,

Alexander III: Étude sur la conception du pouvoir pontifical dans sa pensée et dans son oeuvre, L'Eglise et l'état au moyen age 11 (Paris: J. Vrin, 1956), pp. 324–25.

73. Huguccio, *Summa* to C. 15 q. 6 c. 2 ad v. *materiali [gladio],* quoted in A. M. Stickler, "Der Schwerterbegriff bei Huguccio," *Ephemerides iuris canonici* 3 (1947): 225, n. 2.

74. *Glos. ord.* to C. 23 q. 1 c. 4 ad v. *principes:* "ut infra eadem q. 2 iustum [c. 1]. Nullus ergo bellare potest sine auctoritate principis, ut hic, et C. ut armo. usus. 1.1 libro 11 [*Cod.* 11.47(46).1]; similiter princeps ecclesiasticus potest indicere bellum, ut infra eadem q. 8 igitur [c. 7] et c. omni et c. seq. [c. 9–10]." The *glos. ord.* to C. 15 q. 6 c. 2 ad v. *materiali* also presented an argument that ecclesiastical judges could declare war: "Argum. quod iudex ecclesiasticus bene potest indicere bellum et in bello insequi hostes, ut 23 quest. 8 igitur [c. 7] et c. hortatu [c. 10] et c. ut pridem [c. 17] et 63 dist. Hadrianus [c. 22?]. Item arg. quod iudex ecclesiasticus potest praecipere iudici saeculari ut puniat maleficos, ut 23 quaest. 4 si quos [c. 47] et q. 5 relegentes [c. 45] et q. 8 ut pridem [c. 17]. Argu. contra 23 ult. his a quibus [C. 23 q. 8 c. 30]." The *glossa ordinaria* to the *Corpus iuris canonici* is cited from the edition in 4 vols. (Venice: Apud Iuntas, 1605).

75. Innocent IV, *Apparatus in quinque libros Decretalium* to X 2.13.12 (Frankfurt a/M.: [Sigmund Feyerabend] 1570; rpt., Frankfurt a/M.: Minerva, 1968), fol. 231va: "Vim quomodo hoc licuit, cum essent personae religiosae episcopus et canonici et templarii vix potuit hoc fieri sine poena canonica, ·17 quaestio 4 si quis suadente [c. 29]. Item cum non sit eis licitum mouere bellum, 23 quaest. 3 c. 1 argument. ff. de capti. et postli. hostes [*Dig.* 49.15.24], et si aliis liceret, clericis tamen non liceret, 23 quaestio 8 clerici et c. his a quibus [c. 5, 30] et infra de homicid. suscepimus [X.5.12.10]."

76. Innocent IV, *Apparatus* to X 2.13.12 ad v. *respondemus* (Frankfurt, 1570, fol. 231va): "[O]mnibus esse licitum mouere bellum pro defensione sua, et rerum suarum, nec dicitur proprie bellum, sed defensio, et quando quis est electus incontinenti, id est,antequam ad aliena negotia diuertat, licitum est sibi impugnare, ff. de verbor. obligat. 1. continuus respon. 1 [*Dig.* 45.1.37], ff. de duob. reis, duo § ultim. [*Dig.* 45.2.4], C. unde vi 1. 1 [*Cod.* 8.4.1] ff. de vi et vi ar. 1. 2 cum igitur [*Dig.* 43.1.6.2] et cum hoc a iure sit concessum, nec est authoritas principis necessaria, argum. 28 distinct. de his ad fin. [c. 5], ff. de condi. institu. 1. quae sub conditione § ultim. [*Dig.* 28.7.8.8], nec incidunt in excommunicationem, nisi in personas miserint manus, sed nec tunc, si sine violentia noluerunt exire domum, quod ex loco isto satis euidenter colligitur, et infra de homi. significasti [X 5.12.16] vel nisi modum excesserint, ut hic in fin. Item ubicunque per alium rem suam et ius suum prosequi non potest, licitum est authoritate superioris arma mouere et bellum indicere ad recuperandum sua, et etiam furtiue accipere, 23 quaestio 2 c. 2, C. de iudic. nullius [*Cod.* 3.1.11], tamen si principem super se habet, eius authoritate hoc faciat, et non aliter, 24 quaest. 2 c. 1 et hoc videtur iustum, quia nulli licet iura temperare sine authoritate conditoris iurium."

77. Innocent IV, *Apparatus* to X 5.37.5 (Frankfurt, 1570, fol. 542rb): "Nos credimus, quod licet episcopus ratione iurisdictionis temporalis possit bellum indicere et antequam sit in percussionibus hortari ut utiliter pugnent et bellis interesse et possit semper hortari ad capiendum. Si quis autem, dum esset in percussione, incitauerit ad percutiendum alium, forte irregularis est, idem etiam si forte super bellatores vocem emitteret, dicens audacter pugnate, ar. contra, supra de ho. c. pe. [X 5.12.24] et de cle. percus. c. pe. et ult. [X 5.25.3,4]. Vel dic, quod in defensione possunt gubernare naues et alios ad pugnam defensionis incitare et intantum confligere hostes, quod eos dimittant, ar. de cle. percus. c. pe. et c. fi. [X 5.25.3,4], et nota supra ne cler. sententiam [X 3.50.9], alias autem in iniusto bello hoc non liceret, ut hic."

78. Thus Hostiensis, *Commentaria [= Lectura] in quinque libros Decretalium* to X 1.29.7; 1.34.1; 2.13.12; 5 vols. in 2 (Venice: Apud Iuntas, 1581; rpt., Torino: Bottega d'Erasmo, 1965), vol. 1, fol. 134ra, 176va; vol. 2, fol. 52vb.

79. Hostiensis, *Lectura* to X 5.7.13 (Venice, 1581, vol. 5, fol. 39rb): "[Accinxerint] Ar. quod authoritate ecclesiae bellum fieri potest, ad idem xxiii q. 8 si igitur et ca. hortatu [c. 10], xv q. vi authoritatem [c. 2], lxiii di. Adrianus [c. 2], quod verum est, contra inimicos fidei, vel existunt, quod dic, ut notavi supra eodem."

80. Gulielmus Durantis, *Speculum iuris*, lib. 2, partic. 1 § 5, no. 2 (Frankfurt a/M.: Sumptibus heredum Andrae Wecheli et Johannis Gymnici, 1592), p. 136: "Ipse [*scil.*: ordinarius] enim per se nequit bellum indicere, quia hoc solius principis est, 23 q. 3 cap. 1 et 2. Alii tamen dicunt, et bene, quod ex quo causa spectat ad forum ecclesiasticum, iudex ecclesiasticus, sive sit ordinarius, sive delegatus, sententiam exequetur, et dabit possessionem corporalem, etiam in possessionibus et rebus laicorum ac rg. in prae. § praeterea; alioquin delusoria talis iurisdictio uideretur, ut extra de offi. deleg. ex litteris [X 1.29.29]."

81. Poggiaspalla, "La Chiesa e la partecipazione dei chierici," 141–47, reviews the evidence on this topic.

82. D. 36 c. 3.

83. C. 23 q. 3 c. 2, 10; q. 8 d.p.c. 6, d.p.c. 18; and cf. Chodorow, *Christian Political Theory*, p. 241, as well as Stickler, "De ecclesiae potestate coactiva," pp. 113–14.

84. C. 23 q. 8 c. 26, 27, d.p.c. 27, and d.p.c. 28.

85. Rolandus, *Summa* to C. 23 q. 1 and q. 8 (ed. Thaner, pp. 88, 96–98).

86. Rufinus, *Summa* to C. 23 q. 8 pr; also to C. 23 q. 1 pr. (ed. Singer, pp. 404, 412).

87. *The Summa Parisiensis on the Decretum Gratiani* to c. 23 q. 1 pr., ed. Terence P. McLaughlin (Toronto: Pontifical Institute of Mediaeval Studies, 1952), p. 210; *Summa 'Elegantius in iure diuino' seu Coloniensis* 2.126, ed. Gérard Fransen and Stephan Kuttner, Monumenta iuris canonici, Corpus glossatorum 1 (New York: Fordham University Press, 1969), p. 101; Sicard's opinion is cited by Robert L. Benson, *The Bishop-elect: A Study in Medieval Ecclesiastical Office* (Princeton: Princeton University Press, 1968), p. 321.

88. Huguccio, *Summa* to D. 50 c. 5 ad v. *necesse sit*, in Stickler, "Der Schwerterbegriff bei Huguccio," p. 266, n. 1. A similar view was expressed in the *Glossa Duacensis*; see A. M. Stickler, "Die 'Glossa Duacensis' zum Dekret Gratians," *Speculum iuris et Ecclesiarum: Festschrift für Willibald M. Plöchl* (Wien: Herder, 1967), pp. 391–92; see also Poggiaspalla, "La Chiesa e la partecipazione dei chierici," p. 151.

89. Cambridge, Fitzwilliam Museum, MS. McClean 135, fol. 195va, gloss to C. 23 q. 8 c. 7 ad v. *decernimus:* "Episcopi ergo possunt interesse bellis, nam et Paulus interfuit, ut supra q. 3 Maximianus [C. 23 q. 3 c. 2] et Moyses, ut xxxvi di. c. ult. [c. 3; *MS. del.:*] immo punitur episcopus qui non agreditur hostes ecclesie, ar. extra i de hereticis et brabancionibus [*Comp. I* 5.6.7 = III Conc. Lat. (1179) c. 27]."

90. These enactments are detailed by Rosalio Castillo Lara, *Coacción eclesiastica y sacro romano imperio: estudio juridico-histórico sobre la podestad coactivo materiale suprema de la iglesia en los documentos conciliares y pontificios del periodo de formación del derecho canónico clásico como un presupuesto de las relaciones entre Sacerdotium e Imperium*, Studia et textus historiae iuris canonici 1 (Torino: Libraria del Pontificio Instituto Salesiano, 1956).

91. M. D. R. Foot, "Introduction" to *The Fourth Dimension of Warfare*, ed. Michael Elliott-Bateman (New York: Praeger, 1970), p. ix.

92. Georg Schwarzenberger, "Functions and Foundations of the Laws of War," *Archiv für Rechts- und Sozialphilosophie* 44 (1958): 351.

93. D. 1 c. 10, citing Isidore, *Etymologiae* 5.7.

94. C. 23 q. 1 c. 4, citing St. Augustine, *Contra Faustum* 22.74–75.

95. Thus Stephen of Tournai, *Summa* to D. 1 c. 10 ad v. *in hostes* (ed. Schulte, p. 11); Rufinus, *Summa* to D. 1 c. 10 ad. v. *egressio in hostes* (ed. Singer, p. 11); as well as

Hostiensis, *Summa aurea una cum summariis et adnotationibus Nicolai Superantii* [= Niccolò Soranzo], lib. 1, tit. De treuga et pace [X 1.34], no. 4 (Lyon: Joannes de Lambray, 1537; rpt., Aalen: Scientia Verlag, 1962), fol. 50ra. These canonists incorporate part of *Dig.* 49.15.24. Citations from the Roman law throughout are to the standard edition by Theodore Mommsen et al., 3 vols. (1872; rpt., Berlin: Weidmann, 1963–65). The conventional citation system is explained in Xavier Ochoa Sanz and Aloisius Diez, *Indices titulorum et legum Corporis iuris civilis,* Universa bibliotheca iuris, Subsidia 2 (Roma: Commentarium pro religiosis, 1965), pp. x–xi.

96. *Dig.* 49.16.1; cf. M. H. Keen, *The Laws of War in the Late Middle Ages* (London: Routledge and Kegan Paul, 1965), p. 65.

97. Cino da Pistoia, *In Codicem et aliquot titulos primi Pandectorum tomi, id est, Digesti veteris, doctissima commentaria* to *Cod.* 6.50.1.1 (Frankfurt a/M.: Johannes Feyerabend, 1578; rpt., Torino: Bottega d'Erasmo, 1964), fol. 423ra: "Not. primo quod aliud est ius tempore belli, et aliud tempore pacis. Sic et alius erat modus testandi tempore belli, ut insti. de testa. § 1 [*Inst.* 1.2.10.1]. ADDITIO. Et per hoc colligitur, quod aliud est iustum tempore guerrae et aliud est iustum tempore pacis, quia illud est iustum quod cuilibet in tempore suo expedit, sic et corpori humano aliud expedit tempore infirmitatis et aliud tempore sanitatis, et ita oportet legislatorem legem secundum tempora condere." See also Keen, *Laws of War,* p. 64.

98. C. 23 q. 5 d.p.c. 48.

99. Durham, Cathedral Library, MS. C.III.1, fol. 213ra, gloss to C 23 q. 5 c. 9: "Tribus modis sit licite homicidium, scilicet cum inspiratur aliquis deo occulte ut aliquem interficiat, uel cum iudex habens potestatem gladii aliquem interficit, uel cum precepto principis miles interficit hostem."

100. See the treatment in the *Quaestiones Bambergenses;* Stickler, "De potestate gladii materialis," pp. 121–24; also Hostiensis, *Summa aurea* lib. 5, tit. De homicidio [X 5.12] no. 2 (Lyon, 1537, fol. 241va), and Joannes Andreae, *Novella commentaria in libros Decretalium* to X 5.12.24, no. 2 (Venice: Apud Franciscum Franciscium, 1581; rpt., Torino: Bottega d'Erasmo, 1963), vol. 5, fol. 65ra–rb.

101. Hostiensis, *Summa aurea,* lib. 1, tit. De treuga et pace [X 1.34], no. 4 (Lyon, 1537, fol. 59rb).

102. Hostiensis, *Lectura super sexto Decretalium,* tit. De homicidio voluntario, c. 1 [VI⁰ 5.4.1] (Venice, 1581, fol. 29va): "Ergo in Summa in Romano bello iudiciali licito necessario non tenetur quis ad restitutionem, nec peccat is qui ex tali bello aliquid acquirit, dummodo modum non excedat, nam si potest hominem capere uiuum non licet perimere, ff. ad 1. Aqui., sed. etsi quemcumque [*Dig.* 9.2.5] et secundum hoc intellige supra eodem c. ii et 3. In praesumptuoso vero temerario et voluntario tenetur ad restitutionem et de tali intellige quod loquamur supra de iureiuran., sicut."

103. Joannes Andreae, *Novella* to X 2.24.29, no. 3 (Venice, 1581, fol. 197va): "Potest etiam determinare uerbum 'mouit'; et est sensus, si constiterit, quod mouit bellum, q.d. considerandum, cum quaeritur de restitutione damnorum datorum in bello, inquiri debere quis fuerit bellum mouens, quasi illi sit imputandum totum commissum in illo conflictu, C. de ui pu. uel priua., 1. quoniam multa facinora [Cod. 9.12.5], ff. si qua. pauperi, 1.1 § cum arietes [*Dig.* 9.1.1.11], ff. ad 1. Aquil. si ex plagis § 1 [*Dig.* 9.2.52.1], et sciendum hoc asserenti incumbit probatio, ff. ad 1. Aquil. scientiam § cum stramenta [*Dig.* 9.2.45.3]. Ex his collige, quod bellum mouens tenetur ad restitutionem, quod uerum, quando iniuste mouit, quod prima facie praesumitur; si tamen mouens vult probare, quod iuste mouit, in nullo tenetur; sed facit sua, quae occupauit, ut in glo. 2 de quo remittit Hosti. de homici. pro humani [VI⁰ 5.4.1], et ad id, quod infra dicam et dicit hoc iudicium ratione pacis et pacti spectare ad ecclesiam, de iudi. nouit [X 2.1.13] et de treu. et pace c. 1 et 2 [X 1.34.1–2],

unde etiam dicit lex, quod si praeses ledat subditum suum, recurritur ad episcopum, ut in aut. ut dif. iudi. § si tamen contingit, coll. 9 [*Auth.* 9.10.4 = *Nov.* 86]."

104. Joannes Andreae, *Novella* to X 2.24.9, no. 4 (Venice, 1581, fol. 197ᵛᵃ): "[Bellum] ut dicit Hosti. bellum sine causa rationabili et auctoritate iuris, uel iudicis moueri non debet, licet tota die fiat contrarium, tenentur ergo tales ad restitutionem, quia censentur hic inde praedones et latrunculi, ff. de captiuis et postli. reuer., 1. hostes [*Dig.* 49.15.24], ff. de verbo. signi., 1. hostes [*Dig.* 50.16.118], nisi ubi altera partium dat damnum se defendendo, quod omne ius permittit, ff. de iusti. et iur., ut vim [*Dig.* 1.1.3], dummodo defendens non excedat modum, quod tunc facit quando violentiam infert, qua omissa, salua sibi erat defensio ad arbitrium boni iudicis, de quo remittit ad decre. olim i.de resti. spo. et sen. excom. dilecto [X 2.13.12; VI⁰ 5.11.6]."

105. Innocent IV, *Apparatus* to X 2.24.9 (Frankfurt, 1570, fol. 288ʳ): "Et nota, quod nunquam vocati ad iniustum bellum, habent actionem mandati, vel aliam contra vocantem ad impendia, vel damna contingentia sibi occasione vocationis, vel mandati, quia in re turpi obligatio non contrahitur, insti. mandati. § illud quoque [*Inst.* 1.3.26.7], ff. mand. si remunerandi § rei turpis. et l. si manda. § qui eodem [*Dig.* 17.1.63; 17.1.27.7]. Vocati autem ad iustum bellum, actionem mandati habent contra vocantem, nisi ex debito teneantur, vel nisi causa pietatis, vel humanitatis, vel parentelae faciant, 23 quaestio tertia non in inferenda et in aliis c. eiusdem quaestio [c. 7], 11 quaestio 3 si domino et c. Iulia [c. 23, 94]; et videtur, quod illi qui ex debito faciunt excusantur, nisi bellum esset malum manifeste, 11 quaestio tertia, quid ergo [c. 99], 23 quaestio 1 quid culpatur [c. 4]."

106. Thus Joannes Andreae, *Novella* to X 2.24.29, no. 5 (Venice, 1581, fol. 197ᵛᵃ); Giovanni da Legnano, *Tractatus de bello, de represaliis et de duello,* c. 42, ed. and trans. Thomas E. Holland, Classics of International Law (1917; partial rpt., New York: Oceania Publications, 1964, pp. 259–60.

107. *Summa 'Elegantius'* 1 § 4 (ed. Fransen-Kuttner, p. 2).

108. See Hartmut Hoffmann, *Gottesfriede und Treuga Dei,* Monumenta Germaniae Historica, Schriften 20 (Stuttgart: A. Hiersemann, 1964); for additional bibliography on the peace movement, see Brundage, *Medieval Canon Law and the Crusader,* pp. 12–14.

109. Third Lateran Council c. 21–22 in *Conciliorum oecumenicorum decreta,* 2d ed. by Giuseppe Alberigo et al. (Basel: Herder, 1962; hereafter cited as *COD*), p. 198 [= X 1.34.1–2].

110. First Council of Lyon (1245) c. 18 (*COD,* pp. 266–67) [= VI⁰ 5.4.1].

111. *Glos. ord.* to X 1.34.1 ad v. *frangere:* "Sed quod dicit his hodie non tenet; et episcopi qui non seruant hanc constitutionem, non dicuntur transgressores, quia non fuit moribus utentium approbata huiusmodi treuga, 4 dist. cap. in isti § leges [D. 4 d.p.c. 3]."

112. Second Lateran Council (1139) c. 29 (*COD,* p. 179) = X 5.15.1.

113. Thus Raymond of Peñafort, *Summa de poenitentia et matrimonio cum glossis Ioannis de Friburgo* 2.4.1 (Rome: Sumptibus Ioannis Tallini, 1603; rpt., Farnborough: Gregg Press, 1967), p. 165: "Possunt Christiani exercere hoc officium contra paganos, et nostrae fidei persecutores; contra Christianos autem, et Catholicos nequaquam, extra eodem: 'artem illam mortiferam et odibilem balistariorum et sagittariorum aduersus Christianos et Catholicos exerceri de caetero sub anathemate prohibemus' [X 5.15.1]. Item dicunt quidam, quod in bello iusto possunt exercere hoc officium contra Christianos, quia in tali bello dicit Augustinus, 'cum quis iustum bellum suscepit, utrum aperte pugnet, an ex insidiis nihil ad iustitiam interest' [C. 23 q. 2 c. 2]. Dominus etiam iussit ad Iesum naue, ut constitueret sibi retrorsum insidias, id est, insidiantes bellatores, 23 q. 2 Dominus [c. 2], idem dicit Gregorius 23 q. 8 ut pridem [c. 17]." But cf. Goffredus de Trano, *Summa super titulis Decretalium* to X 5.15.1 (Lyon: Roman Morin, 1519; rpt., Aalen: Scientia Verlag, 1968), fol. 214ᵛᵇ: "Christiani aduersus christianos non possunt hoc officium exercere, ut

infra eodum c. uno. Quid verum est si bellum fuerit iniustum, nam si iustum quolibet genere armoroum est utendum immo ut vincatur dolis est et insidiis insistendum, ut xxiii q. ii dominus [c. 2] et questio viii ut pridem [c. 17], iuxta illud, 'Nihil refert armis contingat palmo dolisue.' Et alibi, 'Dolus virtus quis in honeste requirat [cf. *Aeneid* 2.390: Dolus an virtus quis in hoste requirat?].' Sed contra paganos et persecutores fidei christiane potest hoc officium exerceri." See also the remarks on this topic in the *Summa* of Peter the Chanter, quoted in John W. Baldwin, *Masters, Princes and Merchants: The Social Views of Peter the Chanter and His Circle,* 2 vols. (Princeton: Princeton University Press, 1970), 2:160, n. 128.

114. Paul Fournier, "La Prohibition par le IIe Concile de Latran d'armes jugées trop meurtrières (1139)," *Revue générale du droit international publique* 23 (1916): 471–79.

115. C. 23 q. 1 c. 5.

116. *Dig.* 49.16.9.

117. Thus, Paucapalea, *Summa* to C. 23 q. 1 (ed. Schulte, p. 99); Rufinus, *Summa* to D. 1 c. 10 ad v. *item modus stipendiorum* (ed. Singer, p. 11).

118. *Glos. ord.* to X 2.24.29 ad v. *restituat:* "Quia iniusta erat bellum; sed si iustum fuisset bellum, statim res sic occupatae essent suae, 23 q. 5 dicat [c. 25]." And cf. the *glos. ord.* to C. 23 q. 7 pr. ad v. *nunc autem.*

119. Innocent IV, *Apparatus* to X 2.24.29 (Frankfurt, 1570, fol. 288^v); Joannes Andreae, *Novella* to X 2.13.12 and 2.24.29 (Venice, 1581, vol. 2, fol. 82^{ra-rb}, 198ra). The practical consequences of these considerations are described by Keen, *Laws of War,* pp. 70–71, 82–100. On the application of these doctrines by the Spanish conquistadores in the New World, see Silvio Zavala, *New Viewpoints on the Spanish Colonization of the New World* (Philiadelphia: University of Pennsylvania Press, 1943), p. 50.

120. For other, and somewhat broader, definitions of the holy war, see Erdmann, *Die Entstehung,* p. 1; Villey, *La Croisade,* pp. 21–22; also Russell, *Medieval Theories of the Just War,* pp. 3–4.

121. Though not, apparently, in the Eastern Empire; see Conrad, "La Guerre sainte," pp. 615–22; Sir Steven Runciman, *A History of the Crusades,* 3 vols. (Cambridge: At the University Press, 1951–54), 1:83–84.

122. Examples are numerous; for the period of the First Crusade, see Paul Rousset, *Les Origines et les caractères de la première croisade* (Neuchatel: La Baconnière, 1945), pp. 81–83; for earlier examples, see Erdmann, *Die Entstehung,* pp. 22–24, 111–13, 128–29, and Noth, *Heiliger Krieg und heiliger Kampf,* pp. 96–109.

123. *Inst.* 1.25 pr.

124. *Dig.* 3.2.25; 9.2.7.4; 11.7.35.

125. For a brief sketch of the literary evidence, see Ernst H. Kantorowicz, *"Pro patria mori* in Medieval Political Thought," *American Historical Review* 56 (1951): 472–75.

126. Villey, *La Croisade,* p. 27; Canard, "La Guerre sainte," p. 620.

127. Kantorowicz, *"Pro patria mori,"* pp. 475–77.

128. C. 23 q. 8 c. 9, 46. On the attribution of this latter canon, see Hubrecht, "La 'Guerre juste,'" p. 173, n. 40.

129. Hostiensis, *Summa aurea,* lib. 1, tit. De Treuga et pace [X 1.34] no. 4 (Lyon, 1537, fol. 59rb): "Ut autem in summa predicta recolligamus aliud potest dici bellum romanum puta quod est inter fideles et infideles et hoc iustum: ut nota supra eodem § ver. unum. § Hoc autem voco romanum: quia roma est caput fidei et mater, xxv q. i is ita [d.p.c. 16 § 1], C. de summa tri., 1. fi. [*Cod.* 1.1.8], xxiii q. i. hec est fides et c. quoniam [c. 14,25], infra de here., ad abolendam [X 5.7.9]. § Secundum quod est inter fideles impugnantes

autoritate iudicis: et hoc iudiciale potest dici: et est iustum secundum ea quae notavi supra eodem ver. si fiat, et ver. ergo qui autoritate iudicis. § Tertium quod faciunt fideles iudici contumaces, et potest vocari, presumptuosum, et est iniustum, ut notavi supra eodem ver. ergo qui autoritate. § Quartum quod faciunt fideles autoritate iuris, et hoc potest dici licitum et est iustum. § Quintum quod faciunt fideles contra autoritatem iuris, et hoc potest dici temerarium et est iniustum, ut de his duobus notavi supra eodem ver. idem est. § Sextum quod faciunt fideles propria autoritate alios impugnantes et hoc potest dici voluntarium et est iniustum. § Septimum quod fideles faciunt defendendo se autoritate iuris contra voluntatem impugnatores, et hoc potest dici necessarium et est iustum et de his proximis duobus notavi supra eodem ver. sed si non interueniat, ergo in. § Romano. § Iudiciali. § Licito. § Necessario non tenetur quis ad restitutionem." See also Hostiensis, *Lectura super sexto Decretalium*, tit. De homicidio voluntario, c. 1 [= VI⁰ 5.4.1] (Venice, 1581, fol. 29ʳᵇ⁻ᵛᵃ). Regout, *La Doctrine de la guerre juste*, p. 55, thinks that Hostiensis's doctrine was based on an idealized image of the *imperium romanum;* cf. Russell, *Medieval Theories of the Just War*, p. 259. I am not convinced. Hostiensis was trying to create an analytical scheme for classifying wars. Those public wars in which the enemy were *hostes* in the rigor of the term were dealt with by his Roman law sources. Hence the term "Roman war" had a neat logic of its own within the legal context, without any need to refer to an idealized Roman Empire. When Hostiensis goes further to identify this "Roman war" with war against the infidel, the Rome he is referring to is papal, not imperial, Rome, as even a cursory glance at his legal citations quickly makes plain. Hostiensis's analysis is copied almost verbatim by Giovanni da Legnano, *Tractatus de bello* c. 76 (Holland ed., p. 276).

130. Thus see the *glos. ord.* to *Dig.* 1.1.5 ad v. *ex hoc:* "[B]ella, ergo insurgentium iniquum est, cum iniquum inducat, sed dic quod dicit de bello licito, ut indicto a populo Romano, vel Imperatore, nam hostes sunt quibus populus etc., ut infra, de captivis, 1. hostes [*Dig.* 49.15.24]. Item dicit de bello indicto ad iniuriam propulsandam, quod licet, ut supra eodem, 1. ut vim [*Dig.* 1.1.3], non autem de alio, ne inde iniuriae nascatur occasio, etc., ut C. unde vi, 1. meminerint [*Cod.* 8.4.6]." The *glossa ordinaria* to the Roman law is cited from the *Corpus iuris civilis una cum glossis* 5 vols. (Venice: Apud Iuntas, 1592).

131. Cino da Pistoia, *Commentaria* to *Cod.* 6.50.1, no. 7 (Frankfurt, 1578, fol. 423ʳᵇ).

132. Kantorowicz, *"Pro patria mori,"* pp. 477–92 and *The King's Two Bodies: A Study in Mediaeval Political Theology* (Princeton: Princeton University Press, 1957), pp. 244, 256–57; also Gaines Post, *Studies in Medieval Legal Thought: Public Law and the State, 1100–1322* (Princeton: Princeton University Press, 1964), pp. 438, 452–53.

133. *Glos. ord.* to *Dig.* 3.2.25 ad v. *si quis;* to *Dig.* 9.2.7.4 ad v. *gloriae causa.*

134. I have dealt with this question earlier, in *Medieval Canon Law and the Crusader,* pp. 145–53. My interpretation has not commanded universal agreement; see the reservations expressed by Hans Eberhard Mayer, *The Crusades,* trans. John Gillingham (London: Oxford University Press, 1972), p. 292 n. 13. Mayer's interpretation still does not resolve the problem pointed out in my study, namely, that the texts of the Crusade proclamations and conciliar degrees concerning the Crusade at least up to 1215 describe a commutation of penance and not an indulgence, as that term has been understood since the late thirteenth century. How the earlier "indulgences" were popularly understood and how they were represented by Crusade preachers is, of course, another question entirely.

135. The relevant letters are: Pope Leo IV, December 853, to the Frankish army (*PL*, 115:655–57 = *JL* 2,642 = C. 23 q. 8 c. 9 and C. 23 q. 5 c. 46); John VIII, September 878 (*PL*, 126: 816 = *JL* 3,195).

136. *Epistolae pontificum Romanorum ineditae*, ed. S. Löwenfeld (1885; rpt. Graz: Akademische Druk- und Verlagsanstalt, 1959), no. 82; *JL* 4,540.

137. Council of Clermont, c. 3, in Schafer Williams, "Concilium Claromontanum, 1095:

A New Text," *Studia Gratiana* 13 (1967): 39: "Quicumque pro sola deuotione, non pro honoris uel pecunie adeptione, ad liberandam ecclesiam dei Ierusalem profectus fuerit, iter illud pro omni penitentia reputetur." This version is the oldest text of the Clermont canons and can be dated to ca. 1100. See also Robert Somerville, ed., *The Councils of Urban II*, vol. 1, Decreta Claromontensia, Annuarium historiae conciliorum, Supp. 1 (Amsterdam: Adolf M. Hakkert, 1972), p. 74.

138. Urban II, letter to the Flemings (late December 1095): "Cui calamitati pio contuitu condolentes Gallicanas partes uistauminus eiusque terrae principes et subditos ad liberationem Orientalium ecclesiarum ex magna parte sollicitauimus et huiusmodi procinctum pro remissione omnium peccatorum suorum in Aruernensi concilio celebriter eis iniunximus. . . . " Heinrich Hagenmeyer, ed., *Epistulae et chartaead historiam primi belli sacri spectantes* (Innsbruck: Wagner, 1901), p. 136, no. 2.

139. Urban II, letter to the Bolognese, 19 September 1096: "Sciatis autem eis omnibus, qui illuc non terreni commodi cupiditate sed pro sola animae suae salute et ecclesiae liberatione profecti fuerint, paenitentiam totam peccatorum, de quibus ueram et perfectam confessionem fecerint, per omnipotentis Dei misericordiam et ecclesiae catholicae preces tam nostra quam omnium paene archiepiscoporum et episcoporum qui in Galliis sunt auctoritate dimittimus. . . ." Hagenmeyer, *Epistulae et chartae*, p. 137, no. 3.

140. First Lateran Council (1123) c. 10 (*COD*, pp. 167–68); Erich Caspar, "Die Kreuzzugsbullen Eugens III.," *Neues Archiv* 45 (1924): 303–5.

141. This development begins already with the crusading canon, *Ad liberandam*, of the fourth Lateran Council (1215) c. 71 (*COD*, pp. 246–47), which the first Council of Lyon (1245) c. 5 (*COD*, p. 277) repeats verbatim.

142. His very certainty may, of course, arise from a wish to banish doubts, both his own and those of others, and to stifle criticism of the indulgence. Cf. the remarks of David Daube, "The Self-understood in Legal History," *The Juridical Review*, n.s. 18 (1973): 134.

143. Innocent IV, *Apparatus* to X 3.34.8, no. 1, 7 (Frankfurt, 1570, fol. 429^v–430^v): "Pro defensione: hoc non est dubium, quod licet Papae fidelibus suadere, et indulgentias dare, ut terram sanctam et fideles habitantes in ea defendant, 23 q. 8 omni timore et c. igitur [c. 9, 7]; sed nunquid est licitum inuadere terram, quam infideles possident, vel quae est sua? Et nos ad hoc respondemus, quod in veritate domini est terra, et plenitudo eius orbis terrarum, et universi qui habitant in eo. Ipse enim est creator omnium, idem etiam ipse Deus haec universa subiecit dominio rationalis creaturae, propter quam haec omnia fecerat, ut habemus in 1 c. Genes. et haec a principio seculi fuit communis, quousque usibus priorum parentum introductum est, quod aliqui aliqua, et alii alia sibi appropriant, nec fuit hoc malum, imo bonum, quia naturale est, res communes negligi, et etiam communio discordiam parit, et fuerunt a principio cuiuscunque qui occupauit, quae in nullius bonis erant, nisi Dei. Et ideo licebat cuilibet occupare, quod occupatum non erat, sed ab aliis occupatum, occupare non licebat, quia fiebat contra legem naturae, qua cuilibet indutum est, ut alii non faciat, quid sibi non vult fieri. . . . Quod autem Papa facit indulgentias illis, qui vadunt ad recuperandam terram sanctam, licet eam possideant Sarraceni, et etiam indicere bellum et dare indulgentias illis, qui occupant terram sanctam, quam infideles illicite possident, hoc totum est ex causa, nam iuste motus est Papa, si intendit terram sanctam, quae consecrata est natiuitate, habitatione, et morte Iesu Christi, et in qua non colitur Christus, sed Machometus reuocare, ut incolatur a Christianis." Joannes Andreae, *Novellae* to X 3.34.8, no. 6, 11 (Venice, 1581, vol. 3, fol. 172ra–173ra), follows Innocent IV closely, at times verbatim, in his treatment of these themes. See also the discussion of this facet of Innocent IV's thought by James Muldoon, "*Extra ecclesiam non est imperium:* The Canonists and the Legitimacy of Secular Power," *Studia Gratiana* 9 (1966): 570–80, and by John A. Kemp, "A New Concept of the Christian Commonwealth in Innocent IV," *Proceedings of the Second International Congress of Medieval Canon Law*, ed. Stephan Kuttner and J.

J. Ryan, *Monumenta iuris canonici*, Subsidia 1 (Città del Vaticano: S. Congregatio de Seminariis et Studiorum Universitatibus, 1965), p. 158.

144. Hostiensis, *Lectura* to X 3.34.8, no. 17–18 (Venice, 1581, vol. 3, fol. 128va): "Quod autem papa illis qui vadunt ad defendendum et recuperandam Terram Sanctam dat indulgentias et infidelibus Terram possidentibus bellum indicit, licite facit papa et iustam causam habet, cum illa consecrata sit natiuitate, conuersatione, et morte Iesu Christi, et in qua non colitur Christus, sed Machometus: unde et quamuis infideles ipsam possideant iuste tamen exinde expelluntur, ut incolatur a christianis et ad ipsorum dominium reuocetur. . . ."

145. Hostiensis, *Lectura* to X 5.6.17, no. 20 (Venice, 1581, vol. 5, fol. 34[rb]): "Unde et ex causa plenam indulget veniam peccatorum, prout sequitur, quod nulli alii licitum est, immo limitatur potestas, infra de pen., cum ex eo [X 5.38.14]. Et est ratio, quia ipse Papa vocatus est in plenitudinem potestatis. Ideoque plenam indulgentiam potest facere. Alii vero in partem sollicitudinis, ideoque ad ipsos particularis tantum pertinet et semiplena, ad hoc ii q. vi decreto [c. 11] et supra de usu. pal. ad honorem [X 1.8.4]." See also *Lectura* to X 5.7.13, no. 16 (Venice, 1581, vol. 5, fol. 39[rb]).

146. Hostiensis, *Lectura* to X 5.7.13, no. 17 (Venice, 1581, vol. 5, fol. 39[rb]): "[Indulgentia] quae est remissio omnium peccatorum, ut patet supra de iudaeis, ad liberandam [X 5.6.17] in textu decisionis. . . ."

147. Ralph Niger, *De re militari et triplici via peregrinationis* c. 12, ed. George B. Flahiff, *"Deus non vult*: A Critic of the Third Crusade," *Mediaeval Studies* 9 (1947): 182. Niger was not, however, critical of the just war concept and conceded that under some circumstances a war might be spiritually beneficial.

148. This whole matter has been well treated by Palmer A. Throop, *Criticism of the Crusade: A Study of Public Opinion and Crusade Propaganda* (Amsterdam: N. V. Swets & Zeitlinger, 1940).

149. Jean Leclercq, "Gratien, Pierre de Troyes et la seconde croisade," *Studia Gratiana* 2 (1954): 585–93.

150. *Glos. ord.* to D. 2 de pen. c. 5 ad v. *participes:* "Ergo Iudei et Sarraceni proximi nostri sunt et diligendi a nobis ut nos et verum est: verum tamen omnia opera dilectionis impendere debemus secundum uniuscuiusque conditionem, 86 dis. pasce [c. 21]." See also C. 23 q. 4 d.p.c. 16; C. 23 q. 8 c. 11. The *Glossa Palatina* to C. 24 q. 3 c. 1 presents an intriguing discussion of the question whether it is a greater wrong to kill a pagan or a good Christian: Cambridge, Trinity College, MS. 0.10.2, fol. 32[rb].

151. Innocent IV, *Apparatus* to X 3.34.8, no. 3 (Frankfurt, 1570, fol. 430[r]): "Item per electionem poterunt habere principes, sicut habuerunt Saul, et multos alios, 8 q. 1 licet [c. 15]; sic ergo audacter, et in pluribus aliis c. predicta in quam scilicet dominia, possessiones, et iurisdictiones licite sine peccato possunt esse apud infideles, haec enim non tantum pro fideli, sed pro omni rationabili creatura facta sunt, ut est predictum. Ipse enim solem suum oriri facit super bonos et malos, ipse et volatilia pascit, Matt. c. 5 circa finem et 6; et propter hoc dicimus, non licet Papae vel fidelibus auferre sua, siue dominia, siue iurisdictiones infidelibus, quia sine peccato ea possident, sed bene tamen credimus, quod papa qui est vicarius Iesu Christi, potestatem habet non tantum super Christianos, sed etiam super omnes infideles, cum enim Christus habuerit super omnes potestatem, unde in psal. Deus iudicium regi da [Ps. 71], non videtur diligens paterfamilias nisi vicario suo, quem in terra dimittebat, plenam potestatem super omnes dimisisset."

152. Innocent IV, *Apparatus* to X 3.34.8, no. 4 (Frankfurt, 1570, fol. 430[r]): "Item ipse [Deus] Petro et successoribus eius dedit claues regni coelorum, et ei dixit: 'quodcunque ligaveris' etc. [Matt. 16:19]. Item alibi: 'Pasce oues meas' etc. [John 21:17] supra de elec. significasti [X 1.6.4]. Omnes autem tam fideles quam infideles oues sunt Christi per

creationem, licet non sint et ouili ecclesiae, et sic per praedicta apparet, quod papa super omnes habet iurisdictionem et potestatem de iure, licet non de facto, unde per hanc potestatem, quam habet papa, credo quod si gentilis, qui non habet legem, nisi naturae, si contra legem naturae facit, potest licite puniri per papam, ar. Genes. 19, ubi habes, quod Sodomitae qui contra legem naturae peccabant puniti sunt a Deo, cum autem Dei iudicia sint nobis exemplaria, non video quare papa, qui est vicaruus Christi hoc non possit, et etiam dummodo facultas adsit, et idem dico si colant Idola."

153. Innocent IV, *Apparatus* to X 3.34.8, no. 5 (Frankfurt, 1570, fol. 430^r): "Item Iudaeos potest iudicare papa, si contra legem euangelii faciunt in moralibus, si eorum praelati eos non puniant, et eodem modo, si haereses circa suam legem inueniunt, et hac ratione motus Papa Gregorius et Innocentius mandauerunt comburi libros talium, in quos multae continebantur haereses, et mandauerunt puniri illos, qui praedictas haereses sequerentur, vel docerent."

154. Innocent IV, *Apparatus* to X 3.34.8, no. 8 (Frankfurt, 1570, fol. 430^v): "Item licet non debeant infideles cogi ad fidem, quia omnes libero arbitrio relinquendi sunt, et sola Dei gratia in hac vocatione valeat, 45 dist. de Iudaeis [c. 5]; tamen mandare potest papa infidelibus quod admittant praedicatores Euangelii, in terris suae iurisdictionis, nam cum omnis creatura rationabilis facta sit ad Deum laudandum, senten. 2 di. si queritur [*fortasse:* Petrus Lombardus, *Sententiae* 2.40.2 (*PL*, 192:747–48)]; si ipsi prohibent praedicatores praedicare peccant, et ideo puniendi sunt."

155. Innocent IV, *Apparatus* to X 3.34.8, no. 9 (Frankfurt, 1570, fol. 430^v): "In omnibus autem praedictis casibus et in aliis, ubi licet Papae eis aliquid mandare, si non obediant compellendi sunt brachio seculari, et indicendum est bellum contra eos per Papam, et non per alios, ibi quis de iure suo contendit, nec est contra 2 quaestio 1 multi [c. 18] ubi dicitur, quod non pertinet ad nos iudicare de his qui foris sunt, quia intelligitur quod non debemus eos iudicare excommunicando, vel compellendo ad fidem, ad quam sola Dei gratia vocantur, 45 dist. de Iudaeis [c. 5]."

156. Hostiensis, *Lectura* to X 3.34.8, no. 26 (Venice, 1581, vol. 3, fol. 128vb): "Mihi tamen videtur quod in adventu Christi omnis honor et omnis principatus et omne dominium et iurisdictio de iure et ex causa iusta et per illum qui supremam manum habet, nec arrare potest, omni infideli subtracta fuerit et ad fideles translata; quod hoc iusta causa fuerit probata Eccle. x, Regnum a gente in gentem transfertur propter iniustitias et iniurias et contumelias et diuersos dolos, quod hoc factum sit comprobatur supra de consti., translato [X 1.2.3] et hoc in persona Christi filii Dei vivi, qui non solum sacerdos fuit, sed et Rex: Luce i."

157. Hostiensis, *Lectura* to X 3.34.8, no. 27 (Venice, 1581, vol. 3, fol. 128vb): "[U]nde constanter asserimus quod de iure infideles debent subici fidelibus, non econtra, ut patet in eo quod legi et notavi infra de iudeis, c. i in fi. et c. multorum et c. etsi iudaeos § inhibemus [X 5.6.1, 2, 13]. Concedimus tamen quod infideles, qui dominium ecclesiae recognoscunt, sunt ab ecclesia tolerandi, quia nec ad fidem precise cogendi sunt, ut dictum est supra. Tales etiam possunt habere possessiones et colonos christianos et etiam iurisdictionem ex tolerantia ecclesiae. Etsi de eis contenti non sunt, vel abutuntur, sibi imputent, quia priuelegium meretur amittere etc., super quo vide quod legi et notavi de iudaeis, multorum [X 5.6.13]."

158. Hostiensis, *Summa aurea,* lib. 1, tit. De treuga et pace [X 1.34] (Lyon, 1537, fol. 59ra).

159. See, among others, Kenneth J. Pennington, Jr., "Bartolomé de las Cases and the Tradition of Medieval Law," *Church History* 39 (1970): 1–13; James Muldoon, "A Canonistic Contribution to the Formation of International Law," *The Jurist* 28 (1968): 265–79; D. Carro Venancio, *La teologia y los teólogos-juristas españoles ante la conquista de América,* 2 vols. (Madrid: Centro de Estudios Históricos, 1935).

160. C. 23 q. 3 c. 3; C. 23 q. 4 c. 48.

161. C. 15 q. 6 c. 2.

162. C. 23 q. 5 d.p.c. 48; C. 23 q. 6 pr. and d.p.c. 4.

163. Rolandus, *Summa* to C. 23 q. 7 (ed. Thaner, p. 7); see also the *glos. ord.* to C. 23 q. 7 pr. ad v. *nunc autem.*

164. Stickler, "Der Schwerterbegriff bei Huguccio," p. 217, n. 4.

165. Third Lateran Council c. 27 (*COD*, pp. 200–201); Pissard, *La Guerre sainte*, pp. 27, 31; G. Sicard, "Paix et guerre dans le droit canon du XIIe siècle," *Cahiers de Fanjeaux* 4 (Toulouse, 1969), 89–90, n. 37; Austin P. Evans, "The Albigensian Crusade" in *A History of the Crusades,* ed. Kenneth M. Setton et al., 2d ed. (Madison: University of Wisconsin Press, 1969), 2:282. Similar provisions were made by the fourth Lateran Council (1215) c. 3 (*COD*, pp. 209–11); see also *Comp. V* 1.17.1 (X—).

166. Evans. "The Albigensian Crusade," pp. 284–85.

167. *Glos. ord.* to C. 23 q. 5 c. 32 ad v. *omnes:* "Si argo aliqui heretici sunt in una ciuitate, tota ciuitas potest exuri: et sic ecclesia uel ciuitas punitur pro delicto personarum, ut 25 q. 2 ita nos [c. 25] et C. de sacrosanct. eccl., iubemus nullam (*Cod.* 1.2.10]; Quid iuris sit de hoc, notatur in illo borcardo, an delictum persone etc. Item habes hic, quod heretici occidi potest, ut supra eadem q. 4 quando [c. 19]. Joan."

168. Evans, "Albigensian Crusade," pp. 288–89.

169. Raymond de Peñafort, *Summa* 2.1.10 (Roma, 1603, pp. 157–58): "Idem dico in Episcopo, vel iudice ecclesiastico, qui ob defensionem rerum ecclesiasticarum, vel fidei inuocat, et hortatur contra violentos brachium seculare; et etiam potest eos sequi hortando eos, non ut eos occidant, vel mutilent ipsos violentos, haereticos, vel paganos, sed ut ecclesiasticam fidem et patriam liberent, et defendant, et terram ab infidelibus occupatam redigant ad cultum fidei Christianae: et super hoc facit ecclesia quotidie remissiones magnas: et licet ibi, hinc inde aliqui occidantur, non est hoc praelato, vel ecclesiae imputandum, immo peccaret, nisi se opponeret contra tales: posset enim dici, mercenarius est, qui non est pastor, etc. [John 10:12] et esset merito deponendus, ut supra de haereticis puniuntur, ver. archiepiscopi. Probatur hoc per iura supradicta, et 23 q. 3 Maximianus [c. 2] et q. 8 igitur et scire et omni et hortatu et ut pridem [c. 7–10, 17]. De illis autem, qui mouent arma contra tales propter obedientiam, iustitiam, et zelum fidei, certum est, quod merentur. Immo peccarent alias; et possent cogi principes per censuras ecclesiasticas ad purgandas suas prouincias ab haeretica prauitate, necnon et matrem suam ecclesiam defendendam; cum propter hoc contulerit eis Dominus principatus, et regna, 23 q. 5 principes et Regum et administratores et si audieris et omnium [c. 20, 23, 26, 32, 46] et q. 1 quid culpatur in bello [c. 4]."

170. Hostiensis, *Summa aurea,* lib. 3, tit. De voto et voti redemptione [X 3.34], no. 19 (Lyon, 1537, fol. 178va): "In quo casu et a quo crux debeat predicare. Et quidem contra sarracenos et hereticos predicari potest et debet, infra eodem quod super his [X 3.34.8] et c. se. et c. fi. [X 3.34.9–10] et infra de here. excommunicamus [X 5.7.13]. § Sed nunquid contra schismaticos et inobedientes et rebellen predicari potest? Hoc non est expressum in iure et ideo vidi in alemania aliquos super hoc dubitare, asserentes quod contra christianos non videbatur equum et honestum quod crux assumeretur maxime quia non inuenitur in iure expressum, arg. pro ipsis supra de transla. episcopi vel electi, inter corporalia [X 1.7.2] § sed denique, ii q. v consuluisti [c. 20], supra ne sede, vacan., illa [C. 3.9.2], sed certe non semper debet requiri ius expressum, quia plura sunt negotia quam vocabula, ff. de prescri. ver. 1. iiii [*Dig.* 19.5.4]; ideo iure deficiente est de similibus ad similia procedendum, ff. de legi., non possunt [*Dig.* 1.3.12], supra de rescrip., inter cetera [X 1.3.4] et naturalibus utendem est rationibus, nam et lex ratio commendat, dist. i consuetudo [c. 5], et quod naturalis ratio et c. insti. de iure naturali § quod vero naturalis ratio [*Inst.* 1.1.2.1]. Dicas

ergo quod si crux transmarina que pro acquistione seu recuperatione terre sancte tantum-
modo predicat videtur merito predicanda, multo fortius pro unitate ecclesie conseruanda
predicanda est crux contra schismaticos cismarinam, arg. xxiiii q. i loquitur et c. seq. et c.
schisma [c. 18, 34], xvi q. fi., sicut domini vestimentum [C. 16 q. 7 c. 19]; nec enim filius
dei in mundum venit, nec crucem subiit ut acquireret terram, sed ut captiuos redimeret et
peccatores ad penitentiam reuocaret, nec aridam imo catholicam ecclesiam desponsauit,
cum ergo maius periculum immineat in hac ultima quam in prima, quia pretiosior est anima
quam res, C. de sacrosan. eccl., sancimus [Cod. 1.2.21], id est magis subueniendum est,
xlii di. quiescamus [c. 2]."

   171. Cf. Russell, *Medieval Theories of the Just War,* p. 194.

W. MONTGOMERY WATT

Islamic Conceptions of the Holy War

Before embarking on a discussion of the attitudes toward warfare found in the Islamic religion, it is necessary to say something about conditions in Arabia immediately before the appearance of Islam. [1] The majority of the inhabitants of Arabia were nomads, organized in clans and tribes, and wresting a living from a difficult environment by pasturing camels and other animals. Islam did not originate in the desert, however, but in the small urban community of Mecca, which by the early seventh century was an important commercial center and distinctly prosperous. The people of Mecca were descended from nomads, only a generation or two back, and still retained much of the nomadic outlook and practice. The immediate occasion of the appearance of the new religion was the tension between nomadic attitudes and the demands of a prosperous commerce-based community. It is also to be noted that some nomads had a relationship with Meccan merchants in that the nomads guaranteed the safe-conduct of trade caravans through their territories and in return received payment.

The feature of nomadic life that is of chief concern in the present study is the razzia. This might almost be described as the national sport of the nomadic Arabs. The razzia was a marauding expedition aimed at capturing camels, goats or, less frequently, women from a hostile tribe. Ideally one launched an attack with overwhelming force on a handful of men looking after a herd of camels. Because resistance was futile the herdsmen could flee without disgrace, and the attackers then drove off the camels. Of course the hostile tribe would seize the first opportunity of playing the same trick. In such a razzia loss of life was infrequent; but occasionally, when there was some deep cause of grievance, the tribes became involved in bloodier wars. It was essentially from the light-hearted razzia, however, that the Islamic idea and practice of the jihād or holy war developed.

THE JIHĀD UNDER MUHAMMAD

About the year 610 Muhammad began to receive revelations or messages from God that he was to communicate to his fellow Meccans. Sound scholarship demands that we hold Muhammad to have been sincere in thinking that he could distinguish these revelations from the products of his own mind, though it does not prevent us taking the view that the messages came from his unconscious. By proclaiming these divine messages, and no doubt by also preaching in similar terms, Muhammad gathered round himself in Mecca a band of followers, but at the same time roused opposition. Because of the opposition he made the Hijra, or emigration, to Medina in 622 along with about seventy of his followers. Medina was an oasis in which the inhabitants gained their livelihood mainly from growing date palms and cereals. Because the community there had been split in two by a long-standing feud, most sections of it accepted Muhammad as prophet and became his followers, presumably hoping that he, as an impartial arbiter, would be able to keep peace between the two main factions.[2]

Muhammad and those Muslims who followed him from Mecca to Medina cannot have expected to live indefinitely as guests of their fellow Muslims there. They presumably did not intend to earn a livelihood by agriculture, though some land of poor quality was still available. They may have intended to make use of their trading skills, but such a course, if successful, would almost certainly have brought them into conflict with the Meccans. The remaining possibility was to engage in raids or razzias against Meccan caravans, which were particularly vulnerable when they passed relatively close to Medina on their way to Syria. Whatever ideas Muḥammad may have had when he first went to Medina, after he had been there about six months he seems to have committed his followers to a policy of razzias; and the histories of the Medinan period of Muḥammad's career are essentially a series of accounts of the razzias or, as they are usually called, "expeditions." About ninety expeditions are listed, though a few are not really razzias. The number of participants varied from thirty thousand to five (or even to single individuals).[3]

In the Qur'ān (which is the collection of the revelations received by Muḥammad) the earliest reference to fighting by the believers is said to be: "Permission is given to those who fight because they have been wronged—God is well able to support them—who have been expelled from their homes unjustly, only because they say 'Our Lord is God.'"[4] The Qur'ān is not arranged chronologically, though there are traditional accounts—sometimes contra-dictory—of the occasion on which particular passages were revealed. In the case of the verses quoted, the most likely view is that they were revealed during the first year of Muḥammad's stay at Medina. They apply primarily to the Muslims who had emigrated from Mecca, since it was these who had been "expelled from their homes unjustly" and so "wronged"; and it is known from historical sources that in the first few "expeditions" only Emigrants, that is, Meccan Muslims, took part. It is also to be noted that the reason stated for the permission to fight is that the Muslims had been unjustly treated on account of their belief in God. The fact that in the first few expeditions only Emigrants took part is implied by the distinction in 8.72/3 and 74/5 between "those who believed and emigrated and strove with goods and person in the way of God" and "those who gave shelter and support." The latter are the Muslims of Medina and the former the Emigrants; and, as will presently be seen, the phrase "strove with goods and person in the way of God" implies fighting.[5]

Some other early passages dealing with fighting may now be

mentioned briefly. "When you meet the unbelievers, (let there be) smiting of necks (with the sword); then, when you have made great slaughter among them, bind them fast" (47.4). "O believers, fight those unbelievers who are near you, and let them find a roughness in you" (9.123/4). These passages are addressed to all believers, and thus imply that the Muslims of Medina are participating in the fighting. In January 624 a successful razzia brought up the question of whether Muslims were justified in violating the pagan sanctities of time and place. A verse revealed about this time gives an indication of the temper of the Muslims.

> They ask you (Muḥammad) about the Sacred Month and fighting in it. Say: Fighting in it is evil; but restraining (men) from the way of God, and unbelief, and (from) the Sacred Mosque and expelling its people from it is more evil in God's sight; persecution is more evil than killing; they will not cease fighting you until they bring you back from your religion, if they can; whoever of you is brought back from his religion and dies an unbeliever—the works of such men are vain in this world and the next; and they are the people of the Fire, consigned to it for ever (2.217/4).

These passages suggest a picture of a small community struggling for its very survival against opponents who were using military force to try to get some of the Muslims to apostatize.

Not all the Muslims were enthusiastic about fighting. This was particularly the case in the months after the reverse at Uḥud in March 625. The conflict of opinion among the Muslims at this period is reflected in the passage 4.71/3–78/80 (which is not necessarily one continuous revelation). The objectors apparently did not want to risk losing their lives.

> Have you (Muḥammad) not looked at those to whom it was said, Restrain your hands, perform the prayer, and pay alms; and when fighting was prescribed for them, a group of them feared men with the fear (due to) God or a greater fear; they said, O our Lord, why have you prescribed fighting for us? Would you not give us respite until (our natural) end which is (in any case) near? Say: the enjoyment of this life is slight, and for those who fear (God) the Hereafter is better, and they will be in no way wronged. (4.77/9)

The assurance of heavenly reward, mentioned in the closing section here, is repeated more explicitly. "Let those who exchange this present life for the Hereafter fight in the way of God. Whoever fights in the way of God, be he killed or victorious, to him we shall assuredly give a great reward" (5.74/6). The same assurance is given in several other passages.

The Arabic word commonly used for "holy war" is *jihād*, which properly means "striving" or "expenditure of effort." It occurs only four times in the Qur'ān, though there are over thirty occurrences, in different forms, of the corresponding verb *jāhada*. In 16.110/11 the word "strove" occurs by itself and apparently means "fought": "Then to those who emigrated after being persecuted and who then strove and endured, your Lord after that is forgiving and merciful." On the other hand, it can mean forms of pressure other than fighting, as when God addressing the individual Muslim says: "if (your parents) strive with you to get you to associate with me that of which you have no knowledge, obey them not" (31.15/14). Very often, however, we find the fuller phrase "strive in the way of God" or "strive with goods and person in the way of God," and this seems always to refer to fighting.[6] Occasionally the ordinary word for "fight" also occurs in the phrase "fight in the way of God."[7] In the earliest passages the word "strive" seems to connote "active participation" in contrast to "inactivity," for there is a verse (4.95/7) that expresses the inferiority in God's eyes of those who "sit still" to those who "strive with goods and person in the way of God."

Thus the Islamic conception of the jihād or "holy war" developed gradually out of the circumstances in which the Muslims found themselves in their Arabian environment. Muḥammad's opponents took measures against him and his followers that, in a land where the razzia was normal practice, were bound to lead to razzias or to more serious fighting. On the whole the Muslims were on the defensive. A verse (2.190/86) tells the Muslims to fight those who attack them but not to provoke hostility. If occasionally Muḥammad took the initiative, this would seem to be an instance of attack being the best defense and not the sign of a predilection for fighting, for, once the conflict had reached a certain pitch of intensity, Muḥammad and his followers would have vanished had they not attained military victory.

The original linking of the Islamic religion with fighting was thus the work of Muḥammad's pagan opponents who by their measures against the Muslims put the latter in the position of having to fight for survival. In the course of time, however, a further linking took place, probably due to the fact that the Muslims formed a political community and to the influence of the conception of the razzia. The essential point is that there can be no razzia against allies. From the time he went to Medina Muḥammad's followers constituted in Arab eyes a federation of clans or tribes. To this belonged besides the small groups in Medina, usually called clans, a number of nomadic tribes. As Muḥammad proved himself successful in his struggle against the pagan Meccans, the federation grew stronger and was able to make more effective razzias, though generally less serious and bloody than the fighting against the Meccans. There was, of course, no question of one member of the federation making a razzia against another member, short of some misdemeanor. Thus when some group became tired of being the object of Muslim razzias, it could avoid the unwelcome attentions by joining the federation. To begin with there may have been pagan groups among Muḥammad's allies, but certainly in his later years he insisted that any group that wanted to enter the federation should first become Muslim.

In a certain sense, then, it may be said that Muḥammad gave to the pagans of Arabia a choice of "Islam or the sword." It seems quite clear, however, that the thought in the mind of those who organized and participated in razzias was not the conversion of those attacked but the plunder to be gained from them. It was the almost fortuitous linking of the Islamic religion with the Arab conceptions of the razzia and the federation that led to the expansion of the Islamic community. It was only to pagans, too, that even in this limited sense Muslims gave the choice of "Islam or the sword"; and this seldom seems to have happened outside Arabia. For Jews and Christians in the first place, and then for Zoroastrians, Buddhists, and even Hindus, another status was possible, namely, that of "protected minorities" (*ahl adh-dhimma, dhimmīs*).[8] These were equally members, though secondary members, of the federation and immune from attack. The rationale for this status was that the Qur'ān presented Muḥammad as the last of a long line of prophets, all sent by God with a message that was always in essentials the same. Among these prophets were Moses, who brought to the Jews the book called the Torah, and Jesus who brought to the Christians the book called the Injīl or Evangel. Since Jews and Christians were thus accepted as already believing in God, they were not required to change their beliefs but only to pay a tax or tribute, known as the Jizya, in return for protection.

THE JIHĀD AND LATER ISLAMIC EXPANSION

At the time of Muḥammad's death in the year 632 the territory in which his political authority was recognized probably comprised about half of Arabia. Besides the tribes or sections of tribes included in his federation, some small Jewish and Christian groups were attached to the federation as protected minorities. Exactly a century later in 732 the Muslims were fighting near Tours in the center of France, and they had penetrated just as far eastward. To the Islamic empire, as it may now be called, belonged Spain, North Africa, Egypt, Arabia, Syria, Iraq, Persia, Afghanistan, northwest India, and parts of Central Asia. In 732 it was still essentially a federation of Arab tribes. Non-Arabs who became Muslims were attached as clients to the Arab tribes, but the vast majority of the inhabitants of the empire consisted of protected minorities.[9]

The phenomenal expansion was primarily a political expansion, and was based on the two concepts of razzia and federation together with a third that may be called military aristocracy. As soon as the revolts that broke out in Arabia at Muḥammad's death had been quelled, the Islamic state began to send out military expeditions in the direction of Syria and Iraq. These expeditions were essentially large-scale razzias. For one thing they provided an outlet for the excess energy of former nomads, who could not be allowed to attack other members of the federation. The primary aim of the expeditions, however, was material gain. This might be either in the form of movable plunder (which could be taken away and sold), or in the form of a poll tax and land-rents paid by protected minorities, and collected centrally by the Islamic state. The participants in these expeditions doubtless thought of themselves as "fighting in the way of God" and expected to go straight to Paradise if they died; but the immediate aim of the expeditions seems to have been always material gain or the removal of obstacles to further material gain (as when the resistance of the Tunisian Berbers was overcome). There is no evidence that any expedition was undertaken whose primary aim was to offer pagans the choice of Islam or the sword. The expedition that was defeated at Tours was just such a plundering expedition, and the defeat made it clear to the Muslims that the military cost of plundering in this region was now excessive.

The concept of the military aristocracy was introduced by an arrangement known as the Dīwān of 'Umar (the second caliph, who ruled from 634 to 644). By this arrangement all male Muslims capable of bearing arms, provided they took part in expeditions or performed some other duty for the state, received a stipend from the state, which made it unnecessary for them to do any other work for their living. In other words most of the male population of Arabia was set free for campaigning. Up to the end of his life Muḥammad had insisted that all male Muslims must take part in expeditions when summoned to do so; and early sources show that for a time the jihād was regarded as one of the chief duties of a Muslim. In the course of time, however, things changed. Manpower became more plentiful, and many urban-dwellers were unwilling to risk their lives on distant expeditions. The stipends may also have decreased in purchasing power. Certainly by the first half of the eighth century it had become necessary to recruit men specially for the armies and to offer them material inducements beyond the stipend.

The great expansion of the Islamic state, as already noted, was essentially a political and not a religious expansion. To begin with the only people who became Muslims were pagans like the Berbers who wanted for material reasons to participate in the expeditions. Jews, Christians, and Zoroastrians became protected minorities and retained their religion. Nevertheless, because the member of a protected minority was a kind of second-class citizen, there was some social pressure on him toward conversion to Islam; and Islam, which from the first had been a missionary religion, could hardly refuse converts. On the other hand, nothing was done to encourage converts from the protected minorities; and indeed for a period shortly after 700 conversion was forbidden because it was having an adverse effect on the finances through loss of taxes. Later in the eighth century many Zoroastrians became Muslims. There does not seem to have been any mass conversion of Christians, but rather a steady trickle of converts through the centuries. In other words, though the fighting that led to the expansion of the Islamic state might be called jihād, it was not primarily an operation aimed at conversion.

THE GROWTH OF THE THEORY OF JIHĀD

What has been described so far has been mainly the actual practice of warfare "in the way of God," and this must be clearly distinguished from what the scholars said later as part of their elaboration of the Sharī'a. Since the Sharī'a is often referred to in English as "Islamic law," but differs considerably from law as understood in Europe and America, it is necessary to say something here about the nature of the Sharī'a.[10]

For one thing the Sharī'a is much wider than law as we understand it, and covers every aspect of the daily life of the Muslim. Thus the Sharī'a is concerned with ritual and liturgical matters, and gives precise rules for the performance of the daily prayers and the pilgrimage to Mecca and for the observance of the fast of Ramadan. It also includes matters that we would classify as ethics, etiquette, and even hygiene; an example of the last is the commendation of the use of the medieval equivalent of the toothbrush. More importantly, however, the Sharī'a differs from occidental laws in that it is essentially an ideal law. Much of it is, from its nature, not enforceable by police and lawcourts; but even the rest of it is not actually enforced except in those countries where the ruler or government has decreed that certain courts and judges should administer particular sections of the Sharī'a, such as the rules about marriage and inheritance. The enforceable part of the Sharī'a has never been enforced in its entirety; and nowadays most Muslim countries enforce only small sections of it.

It must not be concluded, however, that the Sharī'a is unimportant because it is thus largely ineffective. On the contrary countless generations of Muslim scholars have devoted their lives to the study and elaboration of the Sharī'a, and it is still highly esteemed by the great majority of Muslims. The reason for this is that it is a divine law, or way of life, prescribed by God for men and revealed to them by Him in its basic principles. During the first century or so after Muḥammad's death the government of the Islamic state followed as best it could along the lines he had laid down; but when new problems arose, as they constantly did because of the great expansion, it tended to decide in accordance with traditional Arab ideas. There therefore arose a body of men anxious to ensure that all the decisions of the state were based on Islamic principles. This meant in the first place such principles as were expressed in the Qur'ān; but it was soon discovered that many aspects of administration were not mentioned there, and the Qur'ānic principles were therefore supplemented by reference to the example of Muḥammad (often spoken of as his Sunna or "standard practice"). The evidence for this is in the collections of "sound" Traditions, that is, of properly accredited stories of what Muḥammad said or did on particular occasions. On the basis of Qur'ānic verses it came to be held that Muḥammad's sayings and doings were divinely inspired just as much as the Qur'ān itself, and were therefore a source for man's knowledge of the Sharī'a.

The Qur'ān and the Sunna, however, are not the whole of the Sharī'a, but only express its essential principles. The Sharī'a is a total ideal for human life, and therefore infinite. Later scholars expended much effort in the detailed elaboration of certain sections of it, such as the rules of inheritance. It was sometimes felt that they did this not to meet any practical need but to show off their intellectual dexterity. Other sections of the Sharī'a were completely neglected. The treatment of the jihād may be said to come midway between these extremes. Here it may be sufficient to look at two stages in the development of the ideal doctrine of the jihād: first, what is found in the Traditions; and second, the views of an eleventh-century writer.

The oldest of the collections of "sound" Traditions regarded as canonical was written down about the middle of the ninth century and includes for each Tradition a list of the scholars who are supposed to have handed it on from the person who actually heard and saw Muḥammad. Whereas Muslim scholars accepted this chain of transmission as literal fact, most occidental scholars consider it to have been in part invented and the saying or act of Muḥammad to have been either invented or greatly modified from an actual happening.[11] For the occidental scholar, however, the Tradition is evidence of a view held in the Islamic community at the period at which the Tradition may be supposed to have come into circulation, though of course this is a matter that is to some extent conjectural. Two Traditions about the jihād may be quoted here. "Abd-Allāh ibn-Mas'ūd said: I asked the Messenger of God, . . . 'Which work is most excellent?' He said, 'Dutifulness to parents.' I said, 'Then which?' He said, 'The Jihād in the way of God.'" And again, "Abū-Hurayra said: The Messenger of God said, 'I am commanded to fight people until they say, "There is no deity but God"; and whoever says, "There is no deity but God," is inviolable to me in goods and person, apart from his due payments.'"[12]

The first of these Traditions is presumably to be dated to a period when at least the more pious Muslims still considered it a duty or a "good work" to take part personally in the expeditions sent out by the Islamic state. This is most likely to have been before the year 700. The second Tradition is perhaps a little later, but the assertion that one of the transmitters was a scholar who lived from 670 to 742 may well be genuine. The wording of this Tradition is to be noted carefully. It does not require the opponents to repeat the whole of the Islamic confession of faith—"there is no deity but God; Muḥammad is the Messenger of God"—but only the first half. That is to say, it does not require Jews, Christians, or Zoroastrians to change their religious allegiance, and the phrase "their due payments" would most naturally be referred to the poll tax paid by such persons. In other words the Tradition justifies and gives a religious interpretation to what had been a prominent feature of the Islamic state in the century after Muḥammad's death—plundering raids and warfare against members of these religions until they accepted the status of protected minorities. Thus, although most of the participants in any expedition probably thought only or mainly of the plunder, it was possible for pious-minded men to regard the expedition as having a religious basis. [13]

With this justification of the wars of expansion may be linked a wider process, namely, the transformation of the image of the Islamic state. In Muḥammad's time and for at least a century afterward the Islamic state could be regarded as a federation of Arab tribes. The original members of the federation (as named in the document known as the Constitution of Medina) were all Muslims, and subsequently those who wanted to join the federation were required to become Muslims; but in itself the form of the body politic was something Arab and not Islamic. Gradually, however, this conception was transformed. It became customary to speak of the world as divided into two "houses" or spheres, namely, the house or sphere of Islam and the house or sphere of war. The first consisted of the territory ruled by Muslims and—ideally at least—administered according to Islamic principles, while the latter consisted of territory not under Muslim rule and not subject to the Sharī'a. Thus the Islamic state was seen as having a universal mission to bring the whole world to confess that "there is no deity but God." It was always added, however, that there was no duty to go to war unless there was a reasonable prospect of victory. Though this new conception of the Islamic state was in part idealized, it nevertheless had an important influence on the course of history.

The theory of jihād as expounded by the eleventh-century writer al-Māwardī (d. 1058) is more elaborate than the conceptions found in Traditions (though the latter contain many details that have not been mentioned here). [14] The religious character of the state is marked by the fact that the first duty of the head of state (usually called *imam* rather than *caliph*) is to maintain religion. Other duties include protecting Islamic territories and defending the frontiers; in this it is implied that the enemies are non-Muslim invaders from the sphere of war. The sixth of the ten basic duties is to fight against those who have been invited to become Muslims and have refused, and to do so until they are converted to Islam or accept the status of protected minorities.

The actual rules for the jihād are found in a chapter dealing with the appointment of a commander or emir for it. Some of the more general points may be mentioned briefly. It is envisaged that there will be both regular soldiers and volunteers. Emphasis is placed on inviting pagans to become Muslims before they are attacked; divergent views among the jurists are recorded, some holding that the commander who attacked without a prior invitation to Islam was liable to a penalty (blood money for those killed). The combatant ought to have the aim of upholding the religion of God "so as to render it victorious over all religion despite the polytheists" (9.33; 48.28; 61.9). In accordance with this aim four possible outcomes of a war are envisaged: the enemy may become Muslims; if the enemy refuse to become Muslims, the men may be killed and the women and children sold into slavery; the Muslims may cease fighting after the enemy has either paid a lump sum or has promised to make an annual payment; the Muslim may, without receiving any payment, make a truce with the enemy for not more than ten years.

Although these are the points of most general interest, there are countless other points of detail. Some are matters of common sense, such as the duty of the commander to choose an advantageous site for his camp and to provide food for his men and distribute it at a suitable time. Others are generalizations from incidents during Muḥammad's battles; thus with regard to the question whether it is permissible to kill the horses of the enemy, one jurist took the negative view because a well-known Muslim had once himself been killed while trying to kill the horse of the enemy commander. On the question of when flight was permissible there was much discussion; because a Qur'ānic verse promised that the Muslims would with God's aid defeat an enemy twice as numerous, some jurists held that the Muslims might flee when the enemy were more than two to one; others, following another verse (8.16), said the Muslims might only flee if they had the intention of renewing the conflict; and so on.

The first thing that strikes the student of Islamic history as he reads this chapter is that most of it is wholly irrelevant to the situation in which al-Māwardī was writing. In the eleventh century the caliph or imam had no political or military power. The Islamic lands were ruled by "warlords" who found it convenient to have a letter from the caliph appointing them governors of certain provinces, but it was they themselves who decided what provinces they ruled by fighting with other warlords. Moreover their wars were not the jihād, nor did they fall into the other categories recognized by al-Māwardī: wars against apostates, against rebels, and against criminals. Why then did intelligent men like al-Māwardī spend so much time in elaborating a practically irrelevant theory? The answer appears to be that they were creating an image of the ideal Islamic state, as a unitary state or empire administered in all respects according to Islamic principles. Although this image had no practical relevance in the circumstances of the time, the fact that it was widely accepted by ordinary Muslims placed certain restraints on the warlords and forced them to pay at least lipservice to Islamic norms.

The influence of the ideal image can also be traced at certain points in later history. It doubtless contributed to the conception of the *ghāzī*, in effect the ideal warrior for the faith, though literally the participant in the razzia. This conception inspired countless men to volunteer for service in Asia Minor on the frontier with the Byzantines from the eleventh to the fourteenth centuries, and thereby seriously weakened the Byzantines. Through the centuries, again, many leaders have declared that the fight against their enemies is a jihād and have thereby roused in their followers a fervor that was both religious and patriotic. Abuses certainly occurred; some African leaders declared a jihād against a tribe they wanted to enslave, claiming that some slight divergence from their own views rendered it infidel; and the Ottoman sultan in 1914 tried by declaring a jihād to rouse the Muslims of British India against their rulers, but failed because these Muslims realized that he himself was in alliance with infidels. Even these abuses, however, show the potency of the image at certain periods.

These reflections, then, lead to the conclusion that, though the Islamic theory of the jihād was of little use to commanders in the field, it was an important part of the self-image of Islam, and as such was not without influence on the currents of history.

Perhaps as a final word some sayings of the mystics or *sūfīs* in a different vein may be quoted. An early ascetic, Sufyān ibn-'Uyayna (d. 814), is reported to have said that the jihād in the way of God consists of ten parts, of which only one is fighting against the enemy while the other nine are fighting against the self. The same thought was expressed in another way by Sahl at-Tustarī (d. 896) when he remarked, "We have returned from the lesser Jihād to the greater Jihād," and then on being questioned added, "The greater Jihād is the struggle against the self." Since jihād properly means "effort," it was claimed that this was the true interpretation of some of the Qur'ānic verses containing the word. [15]

1. A full account of many aspects of pre-Islamic Arab life is found in R. A. Nicholson, *A Literary History of the Arabs,* 2nd ed. (Cambridge: Cambridge University Press, 1930), pp. 30–140. Some old practices still continue in the present century; see Alois Musil, *The Manners and Customs of the Rwala Bedouins,* Oriental Explorations and Studies, no. 6 (New York and Prague, 1928), and H. R. P. Dickson, *The Arab of the Desert: A Glimpse into Badawin Life in Kuwait and Sau'di Arabia* (London: George Allen and Unwin, 1949).

2. For a general account of Muḥammad's career, see W. Montgomery Watt, *Muhammad: Prophet and Statesman* (London: Oxford University Press, 1961; rpt., New York: Galaxy Books, 1974).

3. There is a list of expeditions with the number of participants in W. Montgomery Watt, *Muhammad at Medina* (Oxford: Clarendon Press, 1956), pp. 339–43.

4. 22.39/40–41. Further references to the Qur'ān will be given in the text; where two verse numbers are given, with a slash mark between, the former is the numbering of the Standard Egyptian Edition, now generally adopted, and the latter the older European numbering of Gustav Fluegel, ed., *Corani Textus Arabicus* (Leipzig, 1834). For an English translation see *The Koran Interpreted,* trans. Arthur J. Arberry, 2 vols. (New York: Macmillan, 1955).

5. See W. Montgomery Watt, *Islam and the Integration of Society* (London: Routledge and Kegan Paul, 1961), p. 66.

6. 2.218/215; 4.95/97; 5.35/39, 54/59; 8.72/73; 9.19–20, 24, 41, 44, 81/82, 86/87, 88/89; 49.15; 60.1; 61.11.

7. 2.190/186, 244/245.

8. See Watt, *Muhammad at Medina,* pp. 244–46; *Encyclopedia of Islam,* 2nd ed., s.v. "Dhimma"; W. Montgomery Watt, *The Majesty that was Islam* (New York: Praeger, 1974), pp. 46–49.

9. For the expansion of the Islamic state, see Philip R. Hitti, *History of the Arabs* (London: Macmillan, 1937), pp. 139–68, 209–15; Watt, *The Majesty,* pp. 32–44.

10. For the Sharī'a, see Noel J. Coulson, *A History of Islamic Law* (Edinburgh: University Press, 1964); Joseph Schacht, *An Introduction to Islamic Law* (Oxford: Clarendon Press, 1964); Watt, *The Majesty,* pp. 78–80, 121–30.

11. For the Traditions in the technical sense (Arabic, *hadīth*), see the works mentioned in the previous note and Watt, *The Majesty,* pp. 81–83, 179–80.

12. The first of these is found in the collection of al-Burkhārī, 56.1 and the second in 56.102 and elsewhere. See A. J. Wensinck, *The Muslim Creed* (Cambridge: Cambridge University Press, 1932), pp. 27–29.

13. Worldly motives for jihād are criticized in many of the Traditions in *Mishkat al-Masabih,* English translation James Robson, vol. 2 (Lahore: S. M. Ashraf, 1963), pp. 806–16, especially p. 811.

14. The fundamental work of al-Māwardī, *Al-ahkām as-sultāniyya,* is translated into French as *Les statuts gouvernementaux,* trans. Edward Fagnan (Algiers: A. Jourdan, 1915). Chapter 4 deals with "The Investiture of the Commander of the Holy War" (pp. 71–108). Al-Māwardī's purpose in writing this book is discussed by Hamilton Gibb, *Studies on the Civilization of Islam,* ed. Stanford J. Shaw and William R. Polk (London: Routledge and Kegan Paul, 1962), pp. 151–65. See also Watt, *The Majesty,* p. 217.

15. The first of these sayings is quoted from Margaret Smith, *An Early Mystic of Baghdad* (London: Sheldon Press, 1935), p. 76. The second is from al-Hujwīrī, *Kashf al-Mahjūb,* trans. R. A. Nicholson (London: Luzac, 1936), p. 200.

THOMAS M. GREENE

Renaissance Warfare: A Metaphor in Conflict

The paper that follows needs to be regarded as a kind of epilogue to the proceedings of this conference, since it involves a considerable shift of focus. Its subject is the literary consequences of a cultural collision that occurred in western Europe during the sixteenth century. Thus we must make first of all a leap in time, since most of the men I shall be dealing with were, in terms of the calendar, at least as close to us as they were to Urban II. But we must also shift disciplines, since we shall primarily be concerned with the *imagination* of the sixteenth century, and I shall be zigzagging back and forth across the fuzzy line between literary and intellectual history, a line that is particularly indistinct in Renaissance studies. We must also interpret the phrase "holy war" somewhat freely, since this particular century, for better or worse, was free of Crusades in the medieval sense, although by no means free of religious conflict. In making all these shifts, I can only hope that the altered perspective will shed some measure of light on human responses to conflict that will transcend its era.

The cultural collision that concerns us came about when a civilization ostensibly committed to the values of civic order and Christian love was confronted with the new destructiveness of modern warfare. Trends in social, intellectual, and doctrinal his-

tory encountered trends in military, political, and technological
history, and the strains that resulted were explosive. There can be
no doubt that a new chapter in the history of warfare did in fact
begin roughly at the turn of the century, or more precisely in 1494
when the French king Charles VIII led his troops into Italy to claim
the throne of Naples, proclaiming his intention to use that city as a
stepping stone to the Holy Land. His invasion thus constituted a
kind of holy war *manqué*. The wars that it triggered were new in
several respects. They were no longer fought by purely mercenary
troops led by irresponsible warlords like those which had made
earlier wars in Italy into polite if risky games of military chess. Nor
were they fought, like most earlier wars in northern Europe, between greater or lesser feudal suzerains commanding the personal
loyalties of their vassals and mindful of decaying codes of chivalric
conduct. The new warfare would stem from conflicts between
national states, unified by growing royal power and growing tax
revenue, dependent on the leadership of a sovereign or his ap-
pointed deputy. Modern warfare would also depend increasingly
on gunpowder technology. The devastation of artillery, when skill-
fully used, was demonstrated at the battles of Ravenna and Marig-
nano, and we can measure its growing effectiveness by following a
topos from Ariosto to Milton ascribing its invention to the devil.
Milton in fact took the *topos* away from rhetoric and made it
narrative. But technology finally mattered less than politics; the
emergence of the national state, the consolidation of dynasties, and
the growing art of diplomacy produced wars that were no longer
localized as before but increasingly pan-European. For our purposes the most important effect of these developments was the
terrible increase in destruction and in the suffering of civilian
populations, especially in Italy, which would become the focus of
so much conflict after 1494. And when later in the century war
assumed a religious character, the destruction and cruelty were by
no means mitigated.

The suffering of Italy was ironic because men of the Quattrocento in that country had come to feel a new respect for human

society. The growth of Humanism in Florence had occurred under the leadership of a series of Humanist chancellors, Salutati, Bruni, and Poggio, who incarnated harmoniously a veneration of antiquity together with a proud and loyal devotion to the civic affairs of the city. The old debates over the active and contemplative modes of life paid increasing homage to the ideal of responsible action in the service of a community. Tributes to human excellence and dignity stressed man's role as builder and civilizer, as administrator not only of his own communities but of the entire creation, placed at his disposal by God. Man was believed by many Humanists to demonstrate his fitness for God's trust by cultivating himself and the world about him, and by constructing buildings, cities, laws, governments, and works of art.[1]

Until 1494, the military function of human society was not perceived in Italy as a serious challenge to this optimistic anthropology. In Florence, the Medici staged mock battles, mock sieges, jousts, even imitation Roman triumphs to amuse their subjects, and the very existence of such amusements demonstrates the mildness the face of Mars wore. In fact, literal representations of Mars in the Quattrocento excluded the terrifying and demoniacal aspect he had worn during the Middle Ages and portrayed him rather as a chivalrous and valiant knight, susceptible to the tender charms of Venus.[2] But the French invasions shattered Italian complacency, and as the Italian wars were renewed in decade after decade, adjustments had to be made in Humanist anthropology. *Homo faber* had to be reconciled to *homo homini lupus*. And insofar as Quattrocento Humanist ideals had penetrated northern Europe, this crisis of Italian Humanist faith would become pan-European. It is the fallout from this crisis that I want to survey briefly here. What we discover is a literary search that tries to understand violence by assigning it interpretive images, images designed to explain its relation to human life. Warfare could be perceived more or less lucidly for what it was and still become a metaphor for something beyond itself. The interplay of imagery can be read as a kind of running conflict over the appropriate meaning attributable to violence. *This* conflict by its nature allows of no clear victory.

The earliest literary response I am aware of to the invasion of Charles VIII is the last extant stanza of Boiardo's immense unfinished romance, *Orlando Innamorato.* Boiardo may well have gotten tired of his poem or despaired of putting an end to its labyrinthine plot, but he attributes his decision to break off to heartsickness at his country's helpless posture—"all Italy in flame and fire."[3] There is something fitting in Boiardo's decision, since he and his poem were both in a sense vestiges of an older and somewhat unreal ethos. He was an aristocrat bound by kinship to the ducal house of the d'Este, for whose court he composed the *Innamorato,* and the Ferrarese court itself was notable for its medievalizing cult of chivalric modes. The army that followed Charles to Naples spelled the beginning of the end for that cult and whatever piety was still accorded its archaic gestures. This fact was clearly seized by Ariosto, whose continuation of Boiardo denounces gunpowder precisely because it has rendered impossible the display of valor and individual glory:

> You [gunpowder] have destroyed military glory, and dishonored the profession of arms; valour and martial skill are now discredited, so that often the miscreant will appear a better man than the valiant. Because of you no longer may boldness and courage go into the field to match their strength.[4]

Modern warfare for Ariosto means the end of a heroic myth and an affront to his patrons; it means finally the deepening of his own narrative irony. Yet that irony lifts at least once for a passionate invective against those greedy, wicked, and fierce Harpies who descend on Italy to devour the bread of starving mothers and children.[5] Here the imagery points beyond sentimental nostalgia to the monstrously and hideously inhuman.

Metaphors of inhumanity also focus the jeremiads of the most tireless foe to warfare that the Renaissance produced, Desiderius Erasmus. Erasmus struck out repeatedly against what he saw as a scourge and a scandal to Christian society—in three or four of his *Colloquia,* in the *Praise of Folly,* in the diatribe *Querela Pacis,* and in several of the *Adages,* most notably the "Dulce bellum inexpertis." This last adage, which might be translated "War is sweet if you've never seen it," drew one of the longest commentaries of the *Adages* and was certainly the best known; published in 1515, it was reprinted separately twenty-four times in the sixteenth century and was translated into German and English. It remains one of the most powerful and eloquent polemics against war ever composed. It employs any number of metaphors to carry the polemic: war as a pestilence or a plague, as a product of hell, as a form of insanity, an offense against Nature, as a Christian farce for the amusement of the heathen. But underlying all these is a central metaphor that channels Erasmus's anger and concentrates his argument: war is a debasement of man to the level of bestiality; war turns man into beast. This metaphor is deeply felt, resourcefully developed, and orchestrated by allusions and quotations from a dozen different authors as well as from Scripture. Behind Erasmus's passion one feels the idealizations of Quattrocento Italy and the temperate equilibrium of ancient wisdom, but the supreme appeal is to the charity and forgiveness of Christ Himself. "If Christ is a figment," he asks, "why do we not frankly reject him?"[6] True Christian Humanist as he was, Erasmus drew upon his faith to illuminate a passage in Pliny that distinguishes human anatomy from that of all other creatures. "If one considers," he writes, "the outward appearance of the human body, does it not become clear that nature, or rather God, created this being not for war, but for friendship?"

> For she endowed everyone of the other living creatures with its own weapons. . . . Only man was produced naked, weak, tender, unarmed, with very soft flesh and a smooth skin. . . . The other creatures, almost as soon as they are born, are self-reliant . . . but only man makes his appearance in such a condition that he must depend . . . on the help of others. . . . From this one may conjecture that this animal alone was born for friendship. . . . Nature wished man to owe the gift of life not so much to himself as to loving-kindness, so that he might understand that he was dedicated to goodness and brotherly love. . . . And so even if it were perfectly possible to live a comfortable life without relationships with others, nothing would seem merry without a companion, unless

one were to throw off human nature altogether and sink to the level of a wild beast.[7]

Thus Erasmus argues that war is a bestial violation of that *amicitia* which is so much uniquely human that our very bodies demonstrate its fitness and its necessity. War, he adds, can only be "called *bellum* by antiphrasis, because in war there is nothing either good or beautiful." And then, turning upon his central metaphor, he rejects the etymology that connected *bellum* with *belua,* a beast, because, he now says, armed conflict is worse than bestial.[8]

In denouncing the scandal of universal Christian hypocrisy, Erasmus's outrage is moving and his courage impressive, though it must be pointed out that the basis of his argument stood close to heresy. Here as elsewhere he seems to imply that it remains within man's unaided will to lead a life of charity and purity, and this is a doctrine, of course, that the church has regarded as heretical ever since Saint Augustine denounced its formulation by Pelagius. The Renaissance Humanist believed as a pedagogue in the effectiveness of training; if he was truly a Christian Humanist, he had to accommodate this belief to the doctrines of original depravity and necessary grace. Erasmus might have been less angry had he fully accepted those doctrines. His anger at the brutalization of warfare stemmed from his deep Pelagian hope that men could attain on earth a harmonious Christian community.

Erasmus's distress was shared by a contemporary thinker who ran no risk of the Pelagian heresy and who would publish six years after Erasmus's adage a volume in seven books on *The Art of War.* This was Niccolò Machiavelli. War was a subject that received major treatment in all of Machiavelli's discursive works, including *The Prince,* the *Discourses,* and the *History of Florence,* just as the training of troops and the supervision of military operations preoccupied him as a bureaucrat. He too suffered from what he saw about him, though he suffered not as a Christian but as an Italian at the humiliation and despoilment of his country. Italian armies were the scorn of Europe, he thought, because Italian society itself was self-indulgent, slack, and effeminate. What was needed was a native militia instead of undependable mercenaries, a militia eager to defend the borders of the state against all invaders, and trained in the disciplines of ancient Rome. But also needed was a stern, valiant, clear-sighted leader to restore manhood to a decadent people, thus bringing justice as well as security, for, he wrote, "without a good military organization, there can neither be good laws nor anything else good."[9] All the arts, all the benefits, all the restraints established in a civil society are worthless without a sufficient military force, like a magnificent palace that lacks a roof.[10]

If for Erasmus the opposite of military force is universal friendship, for Machiavelli the opposite is abject ruin, disorder, indolence, and corruption. In the *History of Florence* he seems to see this ruin as one term of an eternal historical shuttle, moving inevitably from valor to peace, from peace to repose, thence to disorder and ruin, which in turn lead back to order, *virtù,* glory, and good fortune.[11] But in the *Art of War,* he leaves room for an individual genius who can arrest historical vicissitude by imposing his own chosen form upon the shapeless matter of a decadent people. In this forming and shaping activity, military discipline becomes merely an extension of civil discipline, and military valor a touchstone of community virtue. Thus the truly strong leader is a kind of artist; in Burckhardt's terms, Machiavelli saw the Italian states as botched works of art that, with severe training, might be redeemed. Thus his spokesman in the *Art of War,* Fabrizio Colonna, dismisses the value of mercenary troops by asking "What good form . . . could I impress upon such matter?" and later, speaking of the need for an Italian prince to make a fresh start, he likens the state to a block of marble:

> Just as no good sculptor can hope to make a beautiful statue out of a block of marble that has been previously . . . spoiled by some bungler, so he will be sure to succeed if he has a fresh block to work upon.[12]

Earlier, Colonna had compared a well-trained army moving to the beat of a drum to a dancer moving in time to music. Thus it is not surprising to find Machiavelli in the closing paragraph of his treatise calling for a resurrection of this supremely important art, a resurrection comparable to the revival of the other arts.

> Let me urge you not to despair of success since this province seems
> destined to revive the arts and sciences which have seemed long since
> dead, as we see it has already raised poetry, painting and sculpture—as
> it were—from the grave.[13]

The military art for Machiavelli becomes the central, crucial art
that, once revived, will restore to an abject Italy the pride of her
Roman forebears. It is the only art necessary to one who commands, permitting the soldier-statesman-artist to become a physician as well, curing the body politic of those ill humors and that
corruption bred from effeminate peace.

> As all religious republics and monarchies must have within themselves
> some goodness, by means of which they obtain their first growth and
> reputation, and as in the process of time this goodness becomes cor-
> rupted, it will of necessity destroy the body unless something inter-
> venes to bring it back to its normal condition. Thus, the doctors of
> medicine say, in speaking of the human body, that "every day some ill
> humors gather which must be cured."[14]

This intervention to prevent civic corruption involved a necessary
and inevitable act of political medicine, calling for the tough and
pitiless prudence of a master healer.

In the literature and thought of the later Renaissance, we can
observe these metaphors of the soldier as artist or physician in
conflict with Ariosto's and Erasmus's metaphors of the soldier as
monster, beast, or devil. To these we can add another, of particular
interest to us here: the soldier as the servant of God, as holy
warrior, and even as sacrificial priest. Needless to say, this conception had roots at least as old as the Carolingian empire, but in a
century when war of conquest came to be or came to masquerade as
war of faith, this age-old metaphor received a new force. This force
may be said to have gathered strength in part from Luther himself,
who discussed at length the moral problems posed by war in several
sermons and tracts. Luther's position on war was too complex and
too qualified to lend itself to a brief summary. But a few points can
be made. In theory he sanctioned only a defensive war waged by a
sovereign against rebels or invaders, and only after the failure of
negotiations in good faith. In *theory,* this position is not unlike

Erasmus's. But in the spirit and tone of their writings, the two men stood opposed. It is clear from Luther's tracts that he felt no deep aversion to the very thought of war as Erasmus did, no loathing of the soldier as soldier. We see this in the way his emphasis falls in the tract "Whether Soldiers can be Saved." Here Luther writes that except for rebellion and aggression, the use of the sword is necessary to maintain peace and protect the innocent.

> Although slaying and robbing do not seem to be a work of love, and therefore a simple man thinks it not a Christian thing to do, yet in truth even this is a work of love. . . . A good physician, when a disease is so bad and so great that he has to cut off a hand, foot, ear, eye, or let it decay, does so, in order to save the body. Looked at from the point of view of the member that he cuts off, he seems a cruel and merciless man; but looked at from the point of view of the body, which he intends to save, it turns out that he is a fine and true man and does a work that is good and Christian, as far as it goes. In the same way, when I think of the office of soldier, how it punishes the wicked, slays the unjust, and creates so much misery, it seems an unchristian work and entirely contrary to Christian love; but if I think of how it protects the good, . . . then it appears how precious and godly this work is.

Thus, Luther goes on, "The hand that wields this sword and slays with it is then no more man's hand, but God's, and it is not man, but God, who hangs, tortures, beheads, slays, and fights. All these are His works and His judgments."[15] In this revealing passage, the medical role of the soldier as surgeon yields to the divine role of the soldier as godly instrument. In a later tract, Luther wrote that the emperor is justified in taking arms against a pope bent on destruction, and he asserts that God will intervene, indeed *has* intervened, to make the right triumph.

> If the pope and his followers were to attack the empire with the sword, as the Turk does, he should receive the same treatment as the Turk; and this is what was done to him by the army of Emperor Charles before Pavia.[16]

Although Luther in other passages counseled Christian meekness and long-suffering before injustice, the conception of the soldier as godly and the sword as potentially divine sufficed to justify wars of religion for many Protestants in the terrible century that followed.[17]

One way to follow the shifts and alterations of attitudes toward war in the sixteenth century is to trace the interplay, the conflicts, the metamorphoses of the metaphors that emerged in its opening decades. As the Humanist ideals of a harmonious civilization grew ever more remote, as violence became almost constant in some regions, and as moral, political, and spiritual issues were fused with the practical issue of survival, the frightful tensions and confusions came inevitably to be reflected in the imaginative representation of warfare. Through all this welter of principles and mythologies, we can make out a few underlying trends. We can note first of all that the Erasmian image of animality became a locus of particular contention and pressure. At the beginning of the century, Leonardo had translated the animalistic metaphor into visual terms by sketching the grimace of a man in combat next to hideous grimaces of warhorses and a lion. "Animals will be seen on earth," he wrote, "who will always fight each other with immense loss."[18] And he leaves no doubt who these animals are. In Thomas More's *Utopia,* the chapter on military affiars opens with the same image:

> War, as an activity fit only for beasts and yet practiced by no kind of beast so constantly as by man, they regard with utter loathing.[19]

The Latin text plays punningly with the resemblance of *bellum* with *belua,* "beast," we have already met. But in the maelstrom of religious controversy later in the century, the image of the beast is accompanied by the counterpoise of a heroic or divine warrior who will destroy it. Thus Ronsard would liken the Huguenot army to a hydra overcome by a Hercules, the future Henri III, who is invited to finish off the monster and to fix its bloody remains over the gate of a holy temple.[20] Equivalent passages can be found in Huguenot authors, for example in Agrippa d'Aubigné's extraordinary epic of the civil wars, *Les Tragiques,* where the Catholic wolves and tigers are to be dealt with in the earthly vengeance and heavenly judgment of Christ which occupy the two concluding books. But mingled with this simplistic opposition, other images appear in d'Aubigné that reflect the suicidal insanity of both parties, and here briefly a kind of Erasmian disgust for all violence gets translated into the poem's lurid rhetoric. Bellona, goddess of war, appears as a monster of self-laceration who tears at her skin with her own nails, and whose hair consists of vipers covering her body with ulcers by their stings.[21]

The struggle of Reformation and Counter Reformation produced of course any number of Saint George figures created deliberately to deal with various dragons, infidels, and heretics. We think immediately of Spenser's Red-Cross Knight, of Camoens' Vasco da Gama, of Tasso's Goffredo. It is interesting to recognize the conflict of a monster with a heavenly champion half-concealed at various levels beneath the surface narrative of Renaissance epic. In the ninth canto of Tasso's *Gerusalemme Liberata,* the monster is reduced to an ornament on the helmet of the pagan leader Solimano, as he leads a night raid on the Christian encampment.

> The sultan's great and horrid helmet shows
> a writhing serpent with his neck upraised:
> his body half in air reveals two wings
> while like an arch his forking tail appears.
> It seems that from three quivering tongues he spits
> a livid foam with a loud hissing sound.
> Now that the fight is thick, with each new stroke
> this serpent, too, pours out new flame and smoke.[22]

This female dragon spitting flame resembles the Fury Allecto who has stirred up the infidels to battle by strewing fire in their hearts, and who will finally be driven off by the angel Michael. Thus the purely human conflict on earth is overlaid by the symbolic conflict of a monster with a heavenly champion. The ultimate version of this archetypal conflict is enacted of course in *Paradise Lost,* where the supreme champion, Christ, overcomes the supreme serpentine Adversary.

Against that current of Apocalyptic imagery, counter-currents of esthetic and medical imagery continued to hold their own. In the *Gargantua* of Rabelais, the hero's army is said to be so well trained that "it seemed more like a concert of musical instruments or a perfect clockwork mechanism than an army or a squadron of

horse."[23] And in Sir John Davies's *Orchestra,* the dance of the
cosmos and the dance of civil government find their counterpart in
the marching and maneuvering of an army:

> For after towns and kingdoms founded were,
> Between great states arose well-ordered war,
> Wherein most perfect measure doth appear;
> Whether their well-set ranks respected are
> In quadrant forms or semicircular,
> Or else the march, when all the troops advance
> And to the drum in gallant order dance.[24]

Beneath the opposition of metaphors and intellectual traditions we
can make out a deeper uncertainty over the organic role of warfare
in a properly constituted society. The Apocalyptic current suggests
that war is either subhuman or superhuman or both at once; here
Erasmus and Luther reach out to each other across the gulf that
divides them. The Machiavellian idea that war is the proper concern of man and is in fact an essential, health-giving function of
society, flourished most vigorously in Elizabethan England, for
reasons that are not far to seek. Tudor England escaped major
armed conflict on its own soil, with the exception of the extreme
north; and thus, despite its expeditions to Ireland and the Low
Countries, Tudor England could contemplate with relative security
the risks of external warfare. But it perceived with correspondingly
greater apprehension the risks of prolonged inaction—what Hamlet calls:

> . . . th' imposthume of much wealth and peace
> That inward breaks, and shows no cause without
> Why the man dies.[25]

It is this relative security that produced Davies's Terpsichorean
army and that produced the ubiquitous medical metaphor that
appealed to the Elizabethan imagination. Typical is the image of
Fulke Greville:

> So doth the War and her impiety
> Purge the imposthum'd humors of a Peace,
> Which oft else makes good government decrease.[26]

Thus Arcite, in *The Two Noble Kinsmen,* addresses Mars as the

> . . . great corrector of enormous times,
> Shaker of o'er-rank states, . . . that heal'st with blood
> The earth when it is sick, and cur'st the world
> O' th' plurisy of people![27]

Spenser's variant of this makes Artegall into a kind of civic gardener cutting back the overgrown "wicked seed of vice"; Artegall and other virtuous heroes "crope the branches of the sient base, / And with strong hand their fruitfull ranckness did deface."[28] War in all these authors preserves the community from that vicious circle of Machiavelli's leading from peace to repose to disorder to ruin. It is absolutely necessary civic therapy.

In several major authors of the sixteenth century, one can follow a conflict of metaphors struggling to dominate within a single canon the author's representation of warfare. This is the case quite clearly of Montaigne who on this subject, as on so many, remained disarmingly ambivalent. On the one hand, Montaigne professed to admire the military life above all others, although he seldom gratified this taste, and he professed to admire most ardently of all great men Alexander, Caesar, and Epaminondas along with Homer and Socrates (Book II, chapter 36). Yet his metaphor for the actions of Caesar and Alexander might give us pause; they were two forest fires or two floods that ravaged the world, he writes, and goes on to quote a Virgilian simile that employs both figures (fire and flood) in a clearly negative context.[29] Elsewhere he considers the argument that an external war drains off a nation's rank humors and preserves it from the mortal fever of internal hostilities. But he doubts that God would favor such cynical and calculating surgery.[30] And in the late essay "On Physiognomy" he represents the savage turbulence of his shattered nation in terms of a disease that has infected the entire body.

> When these epidemics come to last, like ours, the whole body is affected, head and heels alike; no part is free from corruption.

"Monstrous war!" he cries, recalling d'Aubigné:

> It is by nature so malignant and ruinous that it ruins itself together with

all the rest, and tears and dismembers itself with rage. . . . All discipline flies from it. It comes to cure sedition and is full of it. . . . Our
medicine carries infection.[31]

Here the image cuts both ways. The present civil war is monstrous
because the soldier fails to play the physician, which is his proper
and necessary role. Only the present war, then, is evil. Against that
implication still another passage can be cited, from the *Apology for
Raymond Sebond,* where the rejection is absolute, where war is
cited as "testimony of our imbecility and imperfection," and where
an army collectively becomes a single monster whose immensity
deceives the eye in a Swiftian play with perspective.

> This great body . . . which seems to threaten heaven and earth . . . this
> furious monster with so many arms and so many heads is still man,
> feeble, calamitous, and miserable. It is only an anthill stirred and
> wrought up.[32]

The *Essais* clearly provide no single judgment or single metaphor
that circumscribes the subject; what they do provide, what they
always provide, is rather the image of a man trying out judgments
and metaphors, rewriting and recasting them restlessly, trying to
avoid fantasies and conventions, trying to keep in touch with the
actualities, and trying to respond with realism and humanity. The
interplay of imagery corresponds to the incessant movement of that
restive mind.

In the case of Shakespeare, any number of books might be
written, and some have been,[33] on the range and complexity of
soldiering in his imagination. We have only to recall the gallery of
soldiers he created to recognize the manifold faces he attributed to
Mars, including Titus Andronicus, Talbot and Joan la Pucelle,
Prince Hal and Falstaff, Fluellen and Bardolph, Ajax and Hector,
Bertram, Othello, Fortinbras, Edmund and Cordelia, Macbeth,
Coriolanus, Alcibiades, and even Imogen, among many others. If
drama can tell the truth about war, Shakespeare tells as much as can
be told; he renders each figure and each story its own truth and even
all the paradoxes of its truth, its double and triple paradoxes, so that
necessity and folly are somehow conjoined; the farcical and the
noble, heroism and self-deception come together; patriotism fades

into brutality and brutality into prudence. Shakespeare is capable of giving us in a single battle Hotspur crying "An if we live, we live to tread on kings"; and Falstaff, pointing to the corpse of Sir Walter Blunt, "There's honor for you"; and Prince Hal, over Hotspur's body, "Ill weav'd ambition, how much art thou shrunk"; and the guilty king, after the victory, losing control of his ironies, "Thus ever did rebellion find rebuke." But to try to hear all the resonances of Shakespeare's terrible honesty would require a foolish kind of courage, and we can limit ourselves to registering a few of the ways he deals with the imagery we've been tracing.

What strikes one first in surveying these images is the way each usage, emerging from a context of paradoxes, invites ironic scrutiny; the play always supplies us with alternative perspectives to the speaker's, and so supplies us with a basis for skepticism. Shakespeare's pitiless lucidity seldom allows one to accept the metaphor on its own absolute terms. If he echoes the metaphor of soldier as high priest, he assigns it, grotesquely, to Hotspur:

> Let them come.
> They come like sacrifices in their trim,
> And to the fire-ey'd maid of smoky war
> All hot and bleeding will we offer them.
> The mailed Mars shall on his altar sit
> Up to the ears in blood.[34]

Or again, Shakespeare will assign the role of physician to Macbeth, the very breeder of his land's infection. "What rhubarb," asks Macbeth, "senna, or what purgative drug, / Would scour these English hence?"

> If thou couldst, doctor, cast
> The water of my land, find her disease,
> And purge it to a sound and pristine health,
> I would applaud thee. (V, iii, 50–56)

In both of these instances, the whole play is there to underscore the misplacement of the imagery. Othello may be alluding to something like this process of misplacement when he refers to "the big wars that make ambition virtue."[35] But this very remark, coming as it does in his anguished and misguided farewell to his occupation, invites its own ironic consideration.

In those plays of Shakespeare most firmly focused on warfare,
certain images seem to attract to themselves the very crux of the
dramatic contention. In *Troilus and Cressida* one thinks of the
grim climax to Ulysses' speech on degree, where power and will
degenerate into appetite,

> And appetite, an universal wolf,
> So doubly seconded with will and power,
> Must make perforce an universal prey
> And last eat up himself. (I, iii, 121–24)

What Ulysses in fact gives us is an organizing image by which to
understand the rest of the play, and whatever irony intrudes here
lies perhaps in his insufficient awareness that the universal wolf is
already within the door. Priam will refer later to the "hot digestion
of this cormorant war" (II, ii, 6). A similar nexus appears in *Henry
V* where Exeter, the English ambassador, threatens the French king
by urging him "to take mercy / On the poor souls for whom this
hungry war / Opens his vasty jaws" (II, iv, 103–5). This is a form of
mercy to which Henry himself does not yield, and we remember
the play's opening lines ostensibly painting an ideal king who
should

> Assume the port of Mars, and at his heels
> (Leash'd in, like hounds) should famine, sword, and fire
> Crouch for employment. (I, Prologue, 6–8)

Henry V is a play that will always set critics at odds because it is
genuinely ambivalent, because its royal protagonist cannot be
judged adequately from any single moral posture, and because its
imagery localizes the ambivalence of the whole. We might be able
to deal satisfactorily with this elusive play if we could deal satisfactorily with these images of animality and accommodate them to the
king's remark to his footsoldiers on the eve of Agincourt: "War is
his [God's] beadle; war is his vengeance" (IV, i, 175–76). But the
very difficulty of these accommodations is perhaps a key to the
play's knotty strength. And in another context Shakespeare can
employ a military metaphor to resolve a play's intolerable tensions.
This occurs at the conclusion to *Timon of Athens,* where in the last

scene Alcibiades enters as a justicer to scourge what he calls "this coward and lascivious town" of Athens. But then, after listening to the reasonable pleas of the Athenian senators, he chooses to moderate his chastisement and, in the closing lines of the play, employs the medical metaphor we know well to define his middle course. "Bring me into your city," he says

> And I will use the olive, with my sword,
> Make war breed peace, make peace stint war, make each
> Prescribe to other, as each other's leech. (V, iv, 81–84)

In a play about excessive generosity and excessive misanthropy this metaphor of reciprocal healing offers whatever equilibrium the play is able to provide.

The last work I want to discuss in this historical hedgehopping is the long book written by François Rabelais, a book that also reflects the tensions of its age and that exposes them to its own peculiarly perverse and quirky humor. In the first volume of his work, the *Gargantua,* Rabelais pays his respects to the pacifist principles of his acknowledged master Erasmus; and in his second volume he specifically excludes a holy war from those wars of defense which both he and Erasmus acknowledged to be necessary.[36] But mingled with passages deeply impregnated with the values of peace, generosity, and clemency, are other passages that cut athwart those values with characteristic Rabelaisian paradoxicality. Part of the young Gargantua's regimen is training in the use of arms, and Rabelais presents the strenuous training with lance and sword and dagger as great sport. And later when his second hero Frère Jean discovers enemy soldiers pillaging his abbey's vineyard, he uses the staff of his cross to lay about him with relish and sends all the pillagers to paradise, as he says, "as straight as a sickle." The scene of Frère Jean's massacre is written with splendid high spirits, and word-master Rabelais catches in his language the rousing fun of crunching all those bones. Most fighting may be inhuman, but when it is necessary, apparently, it can also be exhilarating.

Only in the *Third Book,* however, do the problem of war and the metaphor of war become absolutely central to Rabelais's story. I venture this remark despite the fact that war is mentioned explicitly only in the great Prologue to that volume and briefly in one or two of the early chapters. In the Prologue Rabelais retells a story he had found in Lucian, a story about the philosopher Diogenes. The story begins with the hasty preparations of the city of Corinth in anticipation of a siege by Philip of Macedon, preparations that Rabelais catalogues in his own exhausting manner until the page comes alive with the teeming and frantic fever of activity. Then enters the Rabelasian hero:

> Now when Diogenes saw them all so warm at work and himself assigned no duties by the magistrates, he watched their behavior for some days in complete silence. Then, as if spurred by the martial spirit, he slung his cloak across his chest, rolled his sleeves up to his elbows . . . and made off out of the town towards Cranium, which is a jutting hill not far from Corinth and a fine look-out place. Thither he rolled his earthen tub, which served him as a shelter against the inclemencies of the weather; and putting out all his strength, in a tremendous outburst of spirits, he twirled it, whirled it, scrambled it, bungled it, frisked it, jumbled it, tumbled it, . . . rolled it from top to bottom of the hill, and precipitated it from the Cranium. Then he rolled it uphill again, as Sisyphus did his stone, so violently that he almost knocked the bottom out of it.
>
> At the sight of this activity one of his friends asked him what moved him thus to torment his body, his spirit, and his tub. To which the philosopher replied that, not being entrusted with any other duties by the State, he was giving his tub a thrashing in order not to seem the one lazy idler among a people so feverishly busy.[37]

Thus ends Rabelais's story. And here, we realize, in this little anecdote he has given us another image for war, an inspired parody of the whole wretched farce, or what he would call on the next page the "tragicomedy" performed on the stage of Europe. All of that meaningless frenzy, all the self-destructive ritual, all the weary Sisyphean futility travestied in the mauling of that poor tub; and the whole rigamarole transmuted into an enduring symbol by the witty malice of a cantankerous barefoot philosopher!

But once this story has been told, there begins a very curious paragraph, which has not in my opinion been adequately weighed. First, Rabelais goes on to refer to the preparations that were being made as he wrote against an invasion of northern France by the Emperor Charles V.

> In the same way . . . I am still not unperturbed at finding myself counted unworthy of employment, whereas throughout this most noble kingdom of France . . . I see everyone today busily and earnestly working, . . . some in repelling the enemy, and some in attacking them: and all this under such excellent direction . . . and with such a clear view to future advantages—for the frontiers of France will soon be magnificently extended, and our people rest in peace and security.[38]

All of this is delicious irony, and when we hear all about that peace and security, knowing what we know of international relations in 1546, we catch the wink of the eye. But then, as he does so often, Rabelais modulates his tone a little, so that we no longer quite know where we are, and he even proceeds to take issue with Erasmus, in the only instance of his career. The passage he takes issue with is one we know:

> I can almost subscribe, therefore, to the opinion of the excellent Heraclitus, to the effect that war is the father of all good things. Indeed, I believe that war is called *bellum* (a fine thing) in Latin, not out of antithesis, as certain botchers of old Latin tags have believed [he means the Erasmus of the *Adages*], because they saw but little beauty in war, but positively and literally, because in war every kind of beauty and virtue shines out, every kind of evil and ugliness is abolished.[39]

Now this paragraph is arresting because it is hard to interpret either as irony or as affirmation. If it is ironic, it seems a little gratuitous; if it is positive, it works against a great deal in this book and in particular against the very first chapter to follow. In fact, we do not yet have the means to interpret this paragraph, because the key will only be given to us by the narrative of the *Third Book* we are about to read.

That narrative is about a man who cannot make up his mind whether or not to marry. On the surface, it has absolutely nothing to do with the morality of warfare. But Rabelais hints indirectly that this question of marriage stands as a kind of comic synecdoche to the much larger question of assuming our full responsibilities as human beings, of participating in that network of mutual bonds and affections which Erasmus saw as the basis of human life. Thus the drama of Rabelais's anxious antihero, Panurge, comes to adumbrate every man's drama because it centers on the problem of courage in a problematic world of contingencies. Panurge's vacillations before the risks of marraige are funny, pathetic, and exasperating at once, but through them we come to see the virtue of courage as the crucial virtue for living in a world of risks, large and small. And finally we understand that only through the risky and the contingent do we attain to the higher courage Rabelais calls "Pantagruelism," which he defines as a gaiety of the spirit contemptuous of accident. When we understand how that inner gaiety stems only from confronting the risky and the painful, then we are ready to understand how war can be said in the Prologue to be the father of all good things. Literal war, shooting war, receives Rabelais's scorn, but he writes his book nonetheless, he tells us, for Pantagruelist soldiers. War is contemptible as the tenor of Diogenes' parody, but as a metaphoric vehicle it comes to adumbrate the whole problematic and purgative struggle to lead a human life. Here for once the Renaissance imagination transcended the terrible immediacy of bloodshed and compelled it to serve the purpose of comic understanding.

---

1. For useful discussions of representative Humanists of the Quattrocento who shared these assumptions, together with generous quotations from their writings, see Charles Trinkaus, *In Our Image and Likeness*, 2 vols. (Chicago: University of Chicago Press, 1970), part 2 (1:173–321) and part 3 (2:461–551).

2. J. R. Hale, "War and Public Opinion in Renaissance Italy," in *Italian Renaissance Studies,* ed. E. F. Jacob (London: Faber and Faber, 1960), pp. 94–122.

3.   Mentre che io canto, o Iddio redentore,
                     Vedo la Italia tutta a fiama e a foco
                     Per questi Galli, che con gran valore
                     Vengon per disertar non so che loco;
                     Però vi lascio in questo vano amore
                     De Fiordespina ardente a poco a poco;
                     Un'altra fiata, se mi fia concesso,
                     Racontarovi il tutto per espresso.

Matteo Maria Boiardo, *Orlando Innamorato*, ed. Aldo Scaglione, 2 vols. (Turin: U.T.E.T., 1963), 2:625.

4. Ludovico Ariosto, *Orlando Furioso,* trans. Guido Waldman (London: Oxford University Press, 1974), p. 109.

> Per te la militar gloria è distrutta,
> Per te il mestier de l'arme è senza onore;
> Per te è il valore e la virtu ridutta,
> Che spesso par del buono il rio migliore:
> Non piú la gagliarda, non piú l'ardire
> Per te può in campo al paragon venire.

(Canto 11, stanza 26)

Orlando Furioso, ed. N. Zingarelli (Milan: Hoepli, 1954), p. 96.

5.
> Oh famelice, inique e fiere Arpie
> Ch'all'accecate Italia e d'error piena,
> Per punir forse antique colpe rie,
> In ogni mensa alto giudicio mena:
> Innocenti fanciulli e madri pie
> Cascan di fame, e veggon ch'una cena
> Di questi mostri rei tutto divora
> Ciò che del viver lor sostegno fora.

(Canto 34, stanza 1)

Ariosto, *Orlando Furioso,* p. 366.

6. Margaret Mann Phillips, ed. and trans., *Erasmus on his Times: A Shortened Version of the "Adages" of Erasmus* (Cambridge: Cambridge University Press, 1967), p. 139.

7. Phillips, *Erasmus,* pp. 108–9. For a fuller discussion of the pacifism of other Humanists, see P. Adams, *The Better Part of Valor* (Seattle: University of Washington Press, 1962).

8. Phillips, *Erasmus,* p. 111.

9. *Discourses on the First Ten Books of Titus Livius,* Book Three, chap. 31, in *The Prince and the Discourses* (New York: Modern Library, 1950), p. 503.
"Il fondamento di tutti gli stati è la buona milizia, e . . . dove non è questa non possono essere né leggi buone né alcuna altra cosa buona." *Opere,* ed. Mario Bonfantini (Milan and Naples: Ricciardi, 1954), p. 391.

10. From the dedicatory letter to the *Art of War.* "I buoni ordini, sanza il militare aiuto, non altrimenti si disordinano che l'abitazioni d'uno superbo e regale palazzo, ancora che ornate di gemme et d'oro, quando sanza essere coperate non avessono cosa che dalla pioggia le difendesse." *Opere,* pp. 495–96.

11. Book Five, chap. 1.

12. Neal Wood, ed., *The Art of War,* rev. trans. Ellis Farneworth (Indianapolis: Bobbs-Merrill, 1965), p. 210.
"Né si troverrà mai alcuno buono scultore che creda fare una bella statua d'un pezzo di marmo male abbozzato, ma sì bene d'uno rozzo." *Opere,* p. 529.

13. *Art of War,* p. 212. "Non voglio vi sbigottiate o diffidiate, perché questa provincia pare nata per resuscitare le cose morte, come si è visto della poesia, della pittura e della scultura." *Opere,* p. 531.

14. *Discourses,* Book Three, chap. 1, pp. 397–98.
"Tutti e principii delle sètte e delle republiche e de' regni conviene che abbiano in sé qualche bontà, mediante la quale ripiglino la prima riputazione ed il primo augumento loro. E perché nel processo del tempo quella bontà si corrompe, se non interviene cosa che la

riduca al segno, ammazza di necessità quel corpo. E questi dottori di medicina dicono, parlando de' corpi degli uomini: 'Quod quotidie aggregatur aliquid, quod quandoque indiget curatione.'" *Opere,* p. 309.

15. Martin Luther, *Works,* 6 vols. (Philadelphia: A. J. Holman, 1915–32), 5:35–36.

"Ob's nun wohl nicht scheint, dass Würgen und Rauben ein Werk der Liebe ist, derhalben ein Einfältiger denkt, es sei nicht ein christlich Werk, zieme auch einem Christen nicht zu thun: so ist's doch in der Wahrheit auch ein Werk der Liebe. . . . Ein guter Arzt, wenn die Seuche so böse und gross ist, dass er muss Hand, Fuss, Ohr oder Augen lassen abhauen oder verderben, auf dass er den Leib errette: so man ansieht das Glied, das er abhauet, scheint es, er sei ein greulicher, unbarmherziger Mensch; so man aber den Leib ansieht, den er will damit erretten, so findet sich's in der Wahrheit, dass er ein trefflicher, treuer Mensch ist und ein gut christlich, so viel es an ihm selber ist, Werk thut. Also auch, wenn ich dem Kriegsamt zusehe, wie es die Bösen straft, die Ungerechten würgt, und solchen Jammer anrichtet, scheint es gar ein unchristlich Werk zu sein und allerdinge wider die christliche Liebe; sehe ich aber an, wie es die Frommen schützt, . . . so findet sich's, wie köstlich und göttlich das Werk ist. . . . Die Hand, die solch Schwert führet und würgt, ist auch alsdann nicht mehr Menschen Hand, sondern Gottes Hand, und nicht der Mensch, sondern Gott hängt, rädert, enthauptet, würgt und krieget; es sind alles seine Werke und seine Gerichte." *Sämmtliche Schriften,* ed., J. G. Walch, 23 vols. (St. Louis: Concordia Publishing House, 1881–1910), 10:492–93.

16. *Works,* 5:117.

"Das meine ich also, wo der Pabst sammt den Seinen auch mit dem Schwert das Kaiserthum angreifen wollte, wie der Türke thut, so soll er so gut sein als der Türke; wie ihm denn neulich vor Pavia auch geschehen ist von Kaiser Carls Heer." *Sämmtliche Schriften,* 2:2148.

17. René Girard's powerful and provocative book, *La Violence et le sacré* (Paris: Grasset, 1972), argues for a necessary and essential relationship between the two impulses denoted by its title. The implications of Girard's thought for a consideration of "holy war" are far-reaching, since for him, religious cult stems directly from fear of social catastrophe and most particularly from fear of violence. "Le sacré, c'est tout ce qui maîtrise l'homme d'autant plus sûrement que l'homme se croit plus capable de le maîtriser. C'est donc, entre autres choses mais secondairement, les tempêtes, les incendies de forêts, les épidémies qui terrassent une population. Mais c'est aussi et surtout, bien que de façon plus cachée, la violence des hommes eux-mêmes, la violence posée comme extérieur à l'homme et confondue, désormais, à toutes les autres forces qui pèsent sur l'homme du dehors. C'est la violence qui constitue le coeur véritable et l'âme secrète du sacré" (p. 52).

18. For the sketch, see A. E. Popham, ed., *The Drawings of Leonardo da Vinci* (New York: Harcourt, Brace and World, 1945), plate 85. The sentence is quoted by André Chastel, *Art et Humanisme à Florence* (Paris: Presses Universitaires de France, 1959), p. 433. "Vedrannosi animali sopra della terra, i quali senpre combatteranno infra loro e con danni grandissimi."

19. *The Yale Edition of the Complete Works of St. Thomas More,* vol. 4, *Utopia,* ed. Edward Surtz, S. J. and J. H. Hexter (New Haven and London: Yale University Press, 1965), p. 199. "Bellum utpote rem plane belvinam, nec ulli tamen beluarum formae in tam assiduo, atque homini est usu, summopere abominantur" (p. 198).

20. Pierre de Ronsard, "L'Hydre desfaict, ou la Louange de Monseigneur le duc d'Anjou" in *Discours des misères de ce temps,* ed. Jean Baillou (Paris: Société les Belles Lettres, 1949), pp. 176–82. See also Ronsard's comparison of Huguenot soldiers to monsters of the apocalypse in his "Continuation du discours des misères de ce temps," line 71 ff., p. 77.

21. "Les Fers," ll. 327-34, in Agrippa d'Aubigné, *Les Tragiques*, ed. A. Garnier and J. Plattard (Paris: Marcel Didier, 1962–), 3:119-20.

22. Torquato Tasso, *Jerusalem Delivered*, trans. Joseph Tusiani (Rutherford, N.J.: Fairleigh Dickinson University Press, 1970), p. 211.

> Porta il Soldan su l'elmo orrido e grande
> serpe che si dilunga e il colla snoda;
> su le zampe s'inalza w l'ali spande
> e piega in arco la forcuta coda;
> par che tre lingue vibri e che fuor mande
> livida spuma, e che 'l suo fishcio s'oda.
> Ed or ch'arde la pugna, anch'ei s'infiamma
> nel moto, e fumo versa insieme e fiamma.
>
> (Canto 9, stanza 25)

Torquato Tasso, *Poesie*, ed. Francesco Flora (Milan: R. Ricciardi, 1952), pp. 227-28. Reprinted by permission.

23. François Rabelais, *The Histories of Gargantua and Pantagruel*, trans. J. M. Cohen (Baltimore: Penguin Books, 1963), p. 141.

"Mieulx ressembloient une harmonie d'orgues et concordance d'horologe q'une armée ou gensdarmerie." Rabelais, *Oeuvres complètes*, ed. Jacques Boulenger (Paris: Bibliothéque de la Pléiade, 1955), p. 137.

24. From *Silver Poets of the Sixteenth Century*, p. 334, edited and with an introduction by Gerald Bullett. An Everyman's Library Edition. Published in the United States by E. P. Dutton & Co., Inc., and reprinted with their permission. All rights reserved.

25. *Hamlet* IV, iv, 27-29. George Lyman Kittredge, ed., *The Complete Works of Shakespeare* (Boston: Ginn and Company, 1936). All quotations from Shakespeare will be taken from this edition.

26. Fulke Greville, Lord Brooke, "A Treatise of Monarchy" in *The Remains*, ed. G. A. Wilkes (London: Oxford University Press, 1965), p. 178. Reprinted by permission of the Oxford University Press, Oxford.

27. V. i, 62-66, *Complete Works of Shakespeare*.

28. Bk. 5, canto 1, stanza 1. J. C. Smith and E. de Selincourt, eds., *The Poetical Works of Edmund Spenser* (London: Oxford University Press, 1942), p. 277.

29. "Ce furent deux feux ou deux torrents à ravager le monde par divers endroits." Montaigne then quotes from the *Aeneid*, Bk. 7, 521 ff. Michel de Montaigne, *Essais*, ed. Maurice Rat, 2 vols. (Paris: Garnier, 1962), 2:166.

30. "Il y en a plusieurs en ce temps qui discourent de pareille façon, souhaitans que cette emotion chaleureuse qui est parmy nous se peut deriver à quelque guerre voisine, de peur que ces humeurs peccantes qui dominent pour cette heure nostre corps, si on ne les escoulle ailleurs, maintiennent nostre fiebvre tousjours en force, et apportent en fin nostre entiere ruine. . . . Mais je ne croy pas que Dieu favorisat une si injuste entreprise, d'offencer et quereler autruy pour notre commodité." *Essais*, 2:87.

31. "Quand elles [ces maladies populaires] viennent à durer, comme la nostre, tout le corps s'en sent, et la teste et les talons; aucune partye n'est exempte de corruption." *Essais*, 2:490.

"Monstrueuse guerre. . . . Elle est de nature si maligne et ruincuse qu'elle se ruine quand et quand le reste, et se deschire et desmembre de rage. . . . Toute discipline la fuyt. Elle vient guarir la sedition et en est pleine. . . . Nostre medecine porte infection." *Essais*, 2:489-90.

32. "Ce grand corps . . . qui semble menasser le ciel et la terre . . . ce furieux monstre à tant de bras et à tant de testes, c'est tousjours l'homme foyble, calamiteux et miserable. Ce n'est qu'une formilliere esmeuë et eschaufée." *Essais*, 1:523–24.

33. I have found of particular use Paul A. Jorgensen, *Shakespeare's Military World* (Berkeley and Los Angeles: University of California Press, 1956). Also helpful is Lily B. Campbell, *Shakespeare's "Histories": Mirrors of Elizabethan Policy* (San Marino, Ca.: The Huntington Library, 1947).

34. *1 Henry IV*, IV, i, 112–17.

35. Othello, III, iii, 349–50.

36. Pantagruel seems to be speaking for his creator when he speaks of religious war in his prayer to God: "In such matters thou wishest for no ally but the Catholic Confession and the Keeping of the Word, and hast forbidden us all arms and defences. For thou art the Almighty, who in thine own affairs, and where thine own cause is called into question, can defend thyself a great deal better than man can conceive." *Gargantua and Pantagruel*, p. 262.

"En tel affaire tu ne veulx coadjuteur, sinon de confession catholicque et service de ta parolle, et nous as défendu toutes armes et défences, car tu es le Tout Puissant qui en ton affaire propre et où ta cause propre est tirée en action, te peulx défendre trop plus qu'on ne sçauroit estimer." *Oeuvres complètes*, pp. 290–91.

37. *Gargantua and Pantagruel*, pp. 282–83. "Diogènes, les voyant en telle ferveur mesnaige remuer et n'estant par les magistratz employé à chose aulcune faire, contempla par quelques jours leur contenence sans mot dire. Puys comme excité d'esprit martial, ceignit son palle en escharpe, recoursa ses manches jusques ès coubtes, . . . feit hors la ville tirant vers le Cranie (qui est une colline et promontoire lèz Corinthe) une belle esplanade, y roulla le tonneau fictil qui pour maison luy estoit contre les injures de ciel, et en grande véhémence d'esprit desployant ses braz le tournoit, viroit, brouilloit, garbouilloit, hersoit, versoit, renversoit, . . . le dévalloit de mont à val, et praecipitoit par le Cranie, puys de val en mont le rapportoit, comme Sisyphus faict sa pierre: tant que peu s'en faillit, qu'il ne le défoncast.

Ce voyant, quelq'un de ses amis luy demanda quelle cause le mouvoit à son corps, son esprit, son tonneau ainsi tormenter. Auquel respondit le philosophe qu'à aultre office n'estant pour la républicque employé, il en ceste façon son tonneau tempestoit pour, entre ce peuple tant fervent et occupé, n'estre veu seul cessateur et ocieux." *Oeuvres complètes*. pp. 322–23.

38. *Gargantua and Pantagruel*, p. 283. "Je pareillement . . . ne suis . . . hors d'esmoy, de moy voyant n'estre faict aulcun pris digne d'oeuvre, et consydérant par tout ce très noble royaulme de France . . . un chacun aujourd'huy soy instantement exercer et travailler . . . part à la fortification de sa patrie . . . , part au repoulsement des ennemis . . . , le tout en police tant belle. . .et à profit tant évident pour l'advenir (car désormais sera France superbement bournée, seront François en repouse asceuréz). . . ." *Oeuvres complètes*, p. 323.

39. *Gargantua and Pantagruel*, p. 283. " . . . Peu de chose me retient que je n'entre en l'opinion du bon Heraclitus affermant guerre estre de tous biens père, et croye que guerre soit en latin dicte belle non par antiphrase, ainsi comme on cuydé certains repetasseurs de vieilles ferrailles latines parce qu'en guerre guères de beaulté ne voyoient, mais absolument et simplement, par raison qu'en guerre apparoisse toute espèce de bien et beau, soit décelée toute espèce de mal et laidure." *Oeuvres complètes*, pp. 323–24.

Panel Discussion

The discussion that follows* was not and is not intended to draw together the papers in this volume as studies in medieval and Renaissance culture. Stanley J. Kahrl's introduction discusses the coherence of the papers as scholarly studies and examines their implications for the study of the Crusades and the holy war tradition in the Renaissance.

In the panel discussion attention shifts from the past as past to the present as both product and analogue of the past. But the present is neither a direct product or a simple analogue of the past, and though, as Mr. Alger points out, there are implications in what is said for teaching and research even outside the earlier periods, this discussion does not come to rest on fully wrought conclusions. The exchange of ideas chronicled here is in the fullest sense a seminar—an effort to plant some seeds and to open a dialogue between the past and present for the sake of the future—Editor.

Professor Stanley J. Kahrl: When we were planning the conference, I did not want to require the medieval scholars or Mr. Greene, the Renaissance scholar, to speak about contemporary events with the same air of authority that we expected them to speak

*Professor Linda Seidel was unable to attend the panel discussion.

about their subject matters. Too often, when talking about "relevance" in teaching, for example, we take a scholar who is a recognized authority in an earlier period and expect him, because he is an authority there, to be an authority on things that we wish to have explained about our contemporary experience. However, there are scholars who take it as the focus of their interest to reflect on the evidence that is accumulating in the immediate past and to read recent documents in the same way that the speakers have looked at documents from the more distant past. So, we asked a representative of the Mershon Center of the Ohio State University, Professor Chad Alger, to join us and to do the direct reflecting on what kinds of connections could be made between the papers that have been presented in the conference and the kinds of warfare that all of us have had as an immediate background to our lives.

Professor Alger, a political scientist by training, will lead off the discussion with prepared thoughts. The other members of the panel will then respond to the connections that he may have seen among their papers and to the remarks that he has made. At the conclusion of that, we will entertain questions.

Professor Chadwick F. Alger: The Mershon Center is a research center where scholars from a number of disciplines come together, hopefully pooling their knowledge so that it can be directly useful to government and nongovernmental policy makers outside the university. Other people in the university are doing the same kind of thing, but at the Mershon Center we see this as our particular mission, and it is quite appropriate for what I'm supposed to do today: conduct an interdisciplinary dialogue with my colleagues on the platform and in the audience and speculate a little bit about what the papers we've heard mean in our present context.

I am quite out of place in the sense that occasionally I look back to the ancient history of World War I. Once in a while I look back on the prehistoric past of the nineteenth century as I work in the area I know the most about, the United Nations system, and try to discern some nineteenth-century roots of the system, and so forth. So, my own work is mainly about what any historian would call "the present" and has largely to do with international organizations.

Rather lately this has stimulated me, on another line of inquiry, to look into the international connections and links of metropolitan communities, beginning with Columbus as a case, in order to unravel and understand a bit better our present international predicament. Part of that predicament is that masses of the public find it difficult to understand how they personally relate to the world as a whole; they find they are unable to evaluate their own participation and involvement and to know how to accept personal responsibility for the international state of affairs. Though you may think that the international relations of people in Columbus, Ohio, is a subject unrelated to the Crusades, near the end of my comments I will forge a link.

Certainly, we don't have to try very hard to find analogies between the events discussed in the papers and the present scene. For example, modern social science tells us of the importance of internal factors as causes of external wars; there is much in the literature about population expansion, about new weapons technology, and about the effect of other internal problems on external wars. Mr. Cowdrey and Professor Watt have shed new light on these that I think is helpful for scholars of more modern wars. Likewise, Professor Brundage has stimulated us to ponder the ways in which more recent lawyers have justified the conduct of holy wars far from home. He makes us feel uncomfortable that we so readily see through the legalisms of the twelfth and thirteenth centuries, and smile as we listen, but have often ourselves been swayed by their twentieth-century counterparts. Professor Greene causes us to think more carefully when we use the word "war" in many contexts such as "War on Poverty" and "War on Hunger" and to examine its subtle effect on how and perhaps why we become engaged in these wars. The visual images provided by Professor Seidel and the words and music provided by Professor Crocker have added depth and vividness to the prose images of the holy wars provided by other speakers.

Now, beyond that, as I try to assess the points raised in a more systematic way, I think that my own reactions will be personal and swayed by the fact that much of what I heard, the interpretations, and so forth, were quite new to me and, I imagine, have a somewhat different impact on me than they might have on others. As I stand back from a multitude of concrete analogies to the present, it seems to me that the holy wars, as analyzed by our speakers, raised three kinds of questions which those of us concerned about the exercise of large-scale violence in our own time might wish to speculate on and about which we might even wish to take some action.

1. What has been the impact of the holy wars in setting cultural and normative patterns that continue to shape thought and action in Western civilization to the present day?
2. What has been their impact on the perspectives and attitudes of organized religion in Western civilization that endures to the present day?
3. What is their relevance as reminders that if we permit certain conditions to develop, *any* society, no matter what its internal values, is capable of holy war?

Now, I would like to briefly talk about those three questions. First, should the holy wars of the eleventh and twelfth centuries be looked upon as a kind of cultural learning or normative development in Western civilization that has been applied and reapplied up to the present day? Professor Brundage suggested this interpretation when he asserted that vestiges of holy war are to be found in Western colonialism in Africa and Asia, in United States expansion westward, with the Spanish *collanges,* and some would wish to add Vietnam. If this is true, those abhorring violence might wish to consider how we might revise patterns of cultural learning. Do wars, holy and otherwise, play too prominent a part in our discernment of who we are as cultures and societies and who we have been? Thus, do they have undue influence on who we wish to become, as cultures and societies, and on the techniques chosen for achieving these objectives? What does this have to do with the selective way in which we teach about the past and particularly the more recent past?

Second, should the holy wars of Christianity be looked upon as a significant turning point for the religious institutions of Western society? Up to that point, there seems to have been a possibility that the Church could become a vital force in the implementation of its doctrines on nonviolence and brotherhood as behavioral norms for Western civilizations, but the Church undermined this potential when it became immersed in large-scale violence itself. This left a heritage of military symbolism that could be exploited by rising interests, and the potential the Church might have had for moral leadership against violence was undermined when the Church itself took up the sword. Thus, and as a twentieth-century historian I simply speculate, it would seem that forever afterward, Western civilization was deprived of what could have been the key institutional base for restraining the use of violence. If this is true, those in the Church concerned about large-scale violence in the present and future might ask how the Church might rid itself of its military symbolism and use symbols more in accord with its nonviolent teachings. They might wish to examine how the Church came to be organized in the image of the nation-state system. They might wish to question the continuing impact of this method of organization on the capacity of Christians to wage holy wars, even against each other.

Third, should the holy wars, both Christian and Islamic, be looked at not purely in terms of the societies in which they occurred but as a kind of phenomenon to which *all* societies and nations are susceptible under certain conditions? From this point of view, we would not look on Western colonialism, in Africa and Asia, as vestiges of earlier holy wars, but as a recurrence of holy war under similar conditions. This perspective would assert that these holy wars would have taken place even if the Crusades had not. Under what conditions does this kind of war then occur? The papers seem to provide four main conditions: (1) the ability to define some out-group in such a way that restraints on violence within your group do not apply to them, and certainly a condition for this is ignorance about out-groups, an ignorance based partly on considerable lack of contact with these out-groups; (2) inability to use certain skills, equipment, and human energy in any other enterprise within the society, and therefore, the need to use it in foreign ventures of this kind; (3) an available external target—such as resources, holy places, markets, infidels—against which in-group feelings can be exercised with available technology; (4) an ideology in which this activity can be clothed so that mass support can be obtained for the activity.

What are the obligations of researchers and teachers to help their own society understand that, no matter what the ideals of the society, they are not immune from holy war? How might this be done? All three of these questions have implications for thought, for research, for teaching, and for action. Each question reflects a number of other questions and further concerns, and before I conclude I would like to come around again to each of these questions and make some comments on them.

First, I will return to the question of the impact of holy war on our cultural and normative heritage. The symposium has convinced me that the historical roots of militarism through symbols, selective history, models of heroes, and so forth has a greater impact than I had realized. In my own teaching, which I indicated focusses on international organizations, particularly the UN system, I have long recognized the problem of obtaining interest in, and disseminating information about, the economic and social activities of the UN system. Whereas there is tremendous interest in the peacekeeping activities of the UN system, the press, the public, and the university courses are much less concerned with the economic and social progress of the UN. Now, I had always believed that this was because American society thinks it has more of a vested interest in peacekeeping than in economic and social activities; because wealthy, healthy, powerful societies have a vested interest in preserving the status quo, and therefore, they want law and order. Those that don't have economic and social justice want it, and they are more interested in these activities. That has been my explanation; now I'm not so sure. I think perhaps there is some deeply engrained cultural interest and fascination in military activities, and this carries through today so that the UN is continually perceived as mainly involved in peacekeeping activities and not very much perceived as an organization engaged in a variety of economic and social good works. So, in the context of my own scholarly activity, I perceive a challenge to my assumptions about why Americans have such a strong interest in peacekeeping.

Turning back to the second point, related to the impact of the Crusades on the Church, I see a new perspective, the widespread military symbolism of the Christian Church, and understand a little better why the Christian Church lacks the capacity to provide strong moral leadership in support of its nonviolent precepts. This reinforces my own belief that international violence is in part a consequence of the fact that nongovernmental institutions, such as churches, so thoughtlessly mirror the nation-state system in their own organizations. This form of organization has a pronounced effect on the perspectives and activities of churches and inhibits their capacity to restrain leaders of violence against other nations. The international ties of churches are not strong enough to overcome the impact of their basic nation-state form of organization, and the international ties do not touch the activities and perceptions of members at the grass roots.

Let me turn now to the third point, that any society, no matter what its internal values, is capable of conducting holy wars, and to the problems and responsibilities this creates for us as scholars. I think that the term *holy war,* not in my personal vocabulary before yesterday, is an exceedingly useful concept for considering the conditions under which *all* nations and societies will violate their own fundamental values in military campaigns against *them* (i.e., those defined as out-groups) and will usually do this in the name of defending these internal values. Although we have superb analyses of holy war, as revealed in this symposium, we have not adequately expressed the notion that all, even *us,* are susceptible to involvement. This is more the fault of those of us who teach about men and events that are closer to the present time and closer geographically to the locale where we are teaching. It is more our responsibility than that of the other scholars who are sitting at the table here. This is partly because scholars, like churches, are organized in the image of the nation-state system. As a result, no national academic community is as able to analyze with insight the holy wars in its own society as it is to analyze the holy wars of *them*.

I would like to give an example that relates to events about two and one-half miles from here. I would imagine that quite a number of the graduates of the public schools in Columbus, and of this university, are aware of the burning of books during the Hitler regime in Germany, and that this has created negative attitudes toward *them* that still endure, while at the same time reinforcing a sense of the superiority of *us*. Although I have been a resident here for less than three years, I would guess you would find only a handful of graduates who know about the burning of books in Columbus during World War I. I would like to read a paragraph from the history of that period that is buried near the end of a somewhat lengthy analysis of Columbus during World War I:

> The study of German in the public schools was first restricted and later banished entirely. Unpatriotic actions and comments by teachers were so persistently reported that the Board of Education in May 1918 adopted a resolution warning all employees that all reports of disloyal acts and utterances would be promptly investigated and that proof would be followed by speedy and positive discipline, regardless of all considerations of service. The banishing of German from schools was made the occasion of the public burning of German textbooks. Wood-piles were made on the street corners on East Broad Street and books brought to them were burned April 19, 1918, while members of the Columbus Reserve Guard stood by to see that there was no interference. The Board of Education was more thrifty than individuals: it sold its German texts at 50 cents a hundred pounds on condition that they be reduced to pulp. The proceeds totaled more than $400.[1]

Likewise, I would imagine that few citizens in Columbus would know of the restraints that were at the same time placed on those who attempted to give a more literal interpretation to Christian scriptures about nonviolence and peace. I read again from the same page: "More than 6,000 copies of Pastor Russell's *The Finished Mystery* and 20,000 copies of the *Kingdom News,* organ of the International Bible Students' Association, were seized here as dangerously pacifist, and distribution was prohibited except to bonafide members. A map maker in state employ, for distributing this sort of literature, was dismissed from his place as a result of his arrest."[2] The point is, that, whereas we teach sometimes quite effectively about *their* holy wars, we are negligent in helping develop better understanding of our own.

In conclusion, I hope the panel will react to the three themes I have selected in order to apply the main currents of their papers to a present context. I hope, too, they will have some thoughts on how the academic community can more adequately make citizens understand the mechanism whereby they become susceptible to holy wars. By academic community I mean not only national communities of scholars but also the more vital international communities of scholars that might provide an essential guarantee against holy wars. Our deliberations on these issues are exceedingly important. If history teaches us anything, it teaches us that holy wars will continue until we develop more adequate knowledge, educational programs, and public policies for preventing them. It would be folly to believe that Vietnam was the last holy war of this society. It would be irresponsible for scholars to entirely shift guilt for past and future holy wars to policymakers and off their own shoulders.

Professor James A. Brundage: Since you are interested in the United Nations, why not point out what may be a blood-chilling thought to you: that while there was no United Nations organization in the medieval period, the closest thing they had to it was the medieval church, the only viable international society the Middle Ages knew, and it was precisely that international society which become involved in the holy war.

Professor W. Montgomery Watt: The holy war seems to be found everywhere, and therefore, as one thinks about the future peace of the world, one shouldn't hope to eliminate the conception of the holy war from man's makeup, but to see rather whether this can be sublimated in some sense.

I have something like twenty Muslim post-graduate students working with me in Edinburgh, and I read the paper to them that I read to you. Now, when I did this, there was a surprising reaction. As you realize, for part of the paper I was trying to defend Islam from the charge of spreading by the sword, but the students took up an entirely different point of view. In a sense, they were all for the holy war, but they were all for it because it is a necessary part of their conception of the Islamic "commonwealth," since there was also a kind of Islamic commonwealth of nations in the medieval period.

Part of our conception of ourselves as members of a community or a society requires both a belief in certain positive values for which we stand and a belief in certain negative values against which we campaign and which we strive to eliminate. Thus, if we are to have a universal society of mankind, I think it has to have both positive values in which it believes firmly and negative values, though we would hope that the negative values are not all projected onto one unfortunate group of people, but are perhaps things we have to struggle against inside ourselves, a point that came out in several of the papers.

Professor Richard L. Crocker: I would like to continue briefly exploring the idea that Professor Watt just mentioned. In studying the text of the trouvére Crusade songs, I became impressed with the nature of the inner experience as one of the great motivating forces, and this idea was buttressed by what Mr. Cowdrey had to say at much greater length and with much more substantial documentation: the inner conviction of the pilgrim as he goes on the holy war seems to be one of the important contributing factors.

But then I look at our experience in the Vietnam War and that kind of inner sense of mission either seemed to be lacking or so extraordinary that when somebody did pop up with a sense of mission, there was usually a news article written about him, some special mention made of this person who really felt he knew what he was doing in Vietnam and had no doubts about his purpose there. Yet it would seem that a comparable mechanism in the absence of a strong internal sense of mission was operating in the minds of many of us. I would translate it by saying we were so concerned with our own problems, whether or not we had a solution and therefore a mission, that we were not able to see clearly the problem of the man standing in Vietnam, the Vietnamese, his view of the world, his needs, his problems, and how they were focussed in this particular situation. If there were some cultural mechanism through which we could gain self-consciousness of our own total absorption in our own needs, perhaps this would be one way out of this situation.

But I think it was remarkable in the Vietnam War that the sense of mission apparent in the First World War, and the Second World War, and perhaps even in the Korean War seemed to me to be absent. Professor Alger, your fourth point was the need for an ideology that justifies the particular holy war in question. My feelings about the Vietnam War was that had there been an ideology at the beginning, it had drastically deteriorated towards the end of the war. Did you feel that was the case?

Alger: I certainly agree with you. My impression is that, as the war began, the leadership believed that anticommunism, which had sustained a tremendous variety of U.S. public policies ever since the McCarthy period, would sustain the war. Midway through the war the degree of anticommunism fell below the level necessary to sustain the war, and in the end large numbers of Americans viewed that war in quite a different sense from the other wars you spoke of.

Professor Thomas M. Greene: I would like to comment primarily on the first point raised by Professor Alger, a question of enduring influential normative patterns set by the holy war. One might argue that, on the basis of twentieth-century history, normative patterns last all too briefly, and are derived simply from the experience of the immediate past. One might say, for example, that all the nations who engaged in World War I, engaged in that war on the basis of the long relative peace that prevailed in Europe after the Napoleonic wars; one might then argue that democracies were so slow in recognizing the dangers of Hitlerism in the thirties because they were still reacting to World War I, and were feeling the revulsion from war that stemmed from World War I. One might also argue that the Korean War was fought on the basis of some kind of false analogy with World War II. And one might then argue that the Vietnam War was based on a false analogy with the Korean War, and so on. We may well be condemned to misunderstand

Vietnam and react badly to some future situation. The indication seems to be that we need a sense of the particularity and uniqueness of each historical situation.

The lessons that we draw from events are always simpler than the events themselves. We can't stand the intolerable complexities of events, and it's important for us, if we are going to remain sane, to draw interpretations from them. We must not, then, become the victims of those inadequate interpretations. For example, I remember that Secretary of Defense Forrestal, who served under President Truman, spoke of the Cold War—America confronting Russia—in terms of the Peloponnesian War in the history of Thucydides. I would see that as a more flexible, less rigid, less determining pattern than the pattern of the Crusade or the pattern of the holy war itself; it leaves more open to the human intelligence in dealing with contemporary events. Perhaps, still more refined patterns might emerge.

I think ultimately, if we are going to be talking about these issues at all, we have to decide whether we are basically Erasmians or Machiavellians; few of us perhaps are Lutherans in this particular sense. If we are going to speak intelligently about what we are told, we have to decide whether we think with Erasmus that war is really something essentially inhuman, something inappropriate for human society, or whether, on the other hand, we have to admit, reluctantly, that indeed, armed conflict is something inevitable, an essential part of human experience. Only if we put ourselves on the line facing that issue, can we go on and talk intelligently about all these subsidiary questions.

Mr. H. E. J. Cowdrey: One of the most impressive things about all that has been said in this conference is that from very different standpoints, we all seem to be basically of one mind about this whole problem of holy war. This, in a sense, underlines the one point I would like to make, and that is the tremendous responsibility the scholarly community has to the world at large in respect to holy war and all the problems it raises in society. I speak with terrible shame as not just a committed Christian but an ordained minister of a Christian church, that the churches must be admitted to show up so badly in this respect. You Americans have been talking about your trauma in Vietnam; our trauma is in our own United Kingdom, in Northern Ireland. In many ways the situation there is more depressing than Vietnam and probably more intractible. It doesn't augur well for the capacity of the Christian churches, at least at the moment, to ward off holy war ideas and ghetto mentalities, when internal pressures and tensions in a society generate the kind of ideas that are current on both sides in Christian Ulster.

On the other hand, I am very much heartened as a scholar. No book, I think, has been of greater importance on this whole subject of the holy war than one written in 1935—and that date is very significant—by a German scholar, Carl Erdmann, and called *The Origins of the Crusading Idea.* This is one of the finest and most influential works of modern Crusading scholarship, as I think almost any medieval scholar would allow; and it was written as a deep protest against Nazism by a scholar who remained in Nazi Germany. In his own way, though an indirect one, in the end he died for his convictions. See the obituary by F. Baethgen, in Erdmann's posthumous *Forschungen zur politischen Ideenwelt des Frühmiltelalters.* A long-term result of such witness has been to enable us to have the kind of discussion we are having today and to achieve from our very different standpoints so large a note of agreement, at least about the basic approach to this problem. I suppose it is the great vocation of the scholar not just to retire into medieval studies or even into modern studies and escape from the modern world, but always to try to see his study as a means to self-understanding and to try to communicate that to the world at large. Perhaps, in particular, Erdmann did this, with his tremendous influence not only in German scholarly circles but, since the war especially, beyond them as well.

Kahrl: The defining of out-groups is certainly one of the most crucial aspects in developing a sense of the mission of a holy war, and, in focussing on the responsibilities of the academic community, Professor Alger has raised questions that all of us can reflect on at leisure later. Mr. Cowdrey, you have certainly provided a case of the type that we ought to consider. Halberstam's book *The Best and the Brightest* makes it clear that the people in American academic and public life suffered in the early fifties for the same kind of witness, if you would like to use that word, against the policies of that day, notably McCarthyism. And though they suffered rather horribly, some of them at the cost of their careers, the majority of the academic community stood by and did very little to support them.

But I suppose the real issue is that nobody speaking at this conference seems to be in favor of holy wars, and yet many of the texts that we deal with are very much in favor of holy wars. Perhaps, with the exception of Machiavelli, this is not true of the ones Mr. Greene cited; but I think of the *Chanson de Roland* and there is no question that is a propaganda text for the kind of attitude which we all now deplore. I think it is worth teaching those things because they are not texts which are isolated in time but texts which have connections with the present of the type we have been exploring today.

Question: The Crusade as a holy war continued until the pontificate of Gregory X, and probably really ended with Acre's fall in 1291. Thereafter, numerous propagandists called for a renewed Crusade, yet none ever occurred. In the indifference expressed after 1291, is there any comparison to the reaction that is taking place today, i.e., an indifference toward the events in Southeast Asia or the indifference of many in the United States to the future of the countries that at one time we felt we had to support as a crucial part of our national interest?

Brundage: That's a very difficult question. Of course, after 1291 you do have crusading armies raised. They didn't get very far, but they were raised; and they tended more and more to take the characteristics of plundering expeditions rather than anything else.

There is one other reflection along that line I might mention. One of the reasons why I think you have so little reaction after 1291 to these repeated appeals for Crusades, is that the impetus, for monarchs in particular, to pursue Crusades is largely dormant, since the "perfection" of a system of taxation to support Crusades was a constant enticement for monarchs to declare their intention of going on a Crusade, to levy a crusading tax, which was enormously profitable, and then to postpone going on a Crusade, hopefully, *ad infinitum*. This left them with a bag full of money, which they could then deploy for other, and sometimes deplorable, purposes. It enabled them to buy internecine wars, although, of course, one of the reasons for starting the Crusades in the first place had been to deflect internal conflicts. There is a possibility the thing had come full circle.

I wouldn't like to suggest that this is an analogy that will be repeated. It is what you see in the fourteenth and fifteenth centuries very largely. You do have crusading armies raised until the time of Pius II, who raised one, and then he died at Ancona just as he was about to set off, but that is the last I know of.

Kahrl: Mr. Crocker raised the whole issue when he suggested, on the basis of his evidence, that the middle classes and the bourgeois elements of northern France, at least, seemed to have a considerable indifference to the idea of the Crusades. Would you feel there is any historical justification to this suggestion?

Brundage: The cities that get involved are primarily maritime cities, as in Italy: the Genoese get involved, the Pisans get involved, the Venetians get involved. But inland cities, having less direct economic interests in the Levant, tend to be relatively uninvolved except where the Crusade takes the form of an eschatalogical religious movement, as it does, for example, in the popular Crusade of Peter the Hermit. Other than that, cities seem to take a relatively small part in it. One exception would certainly be Milan, in the Crusade of 1101. That's the only major exception I can think of.

Cowdrey: The second part of the question—about the withdrawal of responsibility after a trauma like the failure of a Crusade—suggests a danger in modern society, certainly in the Common Market countries of Europe, but also in the United States. I sense that we are getting very preoccupied with our own problems, economic problems particularly, and one danger is that both in Europe and America, we shall find good ideological reasons, of one kind or another, for no longer trying to help underdeveloped countries—for example, for genetic reasons, or cultural reasons, or what have you. I see a very big danger in both American and European societies, that we shall find excuses of that kind for turning in on ourselves and trying to solve our own problems in isolation. This could set off a chain reaction resulting in a kind of backlash from the underdeveloped world, which could prove extremely dangerous to civilization. A lesson we could well learn in the long term from over-reaction against the holy war, is the danger of reacting against international involvement and turning right back into one's own society, to the neglect of the world at large.

Question: In Mr. Cowdrey's lecture he referred to a hierarchy of reasons for war in medieval Europe—rights, interests, and ideas. When he inaugurated the growth of ideological warfare in the time of Gregory VII and Urban II, he left somewhat ambiguous the problem of which came first. Did ideological warfare rise after the fact of wars for interest or was ideological warfare a new species of *raison d'être* for warfare?

Cowdrey: In the quotation from Stubbs's *Constitutional History of England,* Stubbs was saying that the sequence of rights, interests, ideas is largely postmedieval rather than medieval. Warfare for rights really occurred in the late Middle Ages when the kings took over, so to speak, with the secular wars, after the crusading epoch. Henry V of England was his great example of warfare for rights. Warfare for interests is more a seventeenth- and eighteenth-century phenomenon, and insofar as modern history is concerned, warfare for ideas crops up again subsequent to the French Revolution.

Crusading, however, back in the eleventh century, had been a warfare for ideas, and we can see modern warfare for ideas as being, in some sense, a resurgence of the older crusading kind of warfare. As regards the relationship between ideas and what one might call interests in the First Crusade itself, we've got a sort of chicken and egg situation here, partly, I think, because the medieval people were less demanding than we tend to be in expecting people to have some sort of consistency in their motives. The text about the

Lisbon Crusade of 1147, the *De expugnatione Lyxhonensi,*
shows very clearly how Crusaders could go off at one and the same
time trying to glorify God and win the remission of sin and spiritual
benefits by their crusading activities, and also in search of booty.
These two things seemed quite compatible in their minds. I don't
think they were aware of a contradiction, as we probably would be,
in this kind of thing. On the First Crusade, too, not long after the
Crusaders set out from Constantinople toward Antioch, they had to
do battle against the Turks, and they won. There was a war cry,
"Stand fast all together; trusting in Christ and in the victory of the
Holy Cross. Today, please God, you will all gain much booty"
(*Gesta Francorum,* ed. Hill, pp. 19–20). I'm not, therefore, sure
that one can really talk about priorities, but in the West, anyway,
warfare for ideas took a big leap forward in the late eleventh
century. That certainly is true.

> *Question:* Now that Professor Watt has given us a more sympathetic
> view of the supposedly fanatic Muslims, I wonder what the Muslims'
> reaction was to these strangely motivated invading Crusaders?

Watt: The point to be stressed is that the Crusades occupy a
large part in European history and have had, as we have seen from
this conference, a continuing influence on the thinking of Europeans and Westerners. This is a much greater part than the one they
play in Islamic history, where, I think, the Crusades are best
described as a kind of frontier incident. They were relatively
unimportant. At this period you are dealing with Islamic territories
that stretch into Central Asia (Bukhārā and Samarqand) and include North India, a large part of Central Persia, Iraq, and eastern
Syria, which were at that time under the Seljuqs, whose capital was
somewhere in the center of Persia. Things happening in a few
square miles on the Mediterranean coast were of no interest at all.

I spent quite a lot of time studying a man called al-Ghāzalī, who
was in Jerusalem a year or two before it fell to the Crusaders, and
nowhere in his writings or any of the accounts of his life is there the
least reference whatsoever to the Crusades. If you take the general
histories of Islam, some of the chief events of the Crusades do get a

paragraph or two here and there, but it was a thing of no importance.

At that period this part of the world—Syria, Palestine—was not securely controlled by the Seljuq sultan who ruled Persia and Iraq. The local princes, who were princes in a very small way, were relatively independent, and the Crusaders just looked like another of these little princelings you see squabbling with one another. This is all it was in the eyes of the Muslims. To be fair, perhaps I ought to say that there were certain Muslims who were more closely affected by it, and we do find poems about the Crusades and they are mentioned in local histories.

By and large, however, the Crusades were quite insignificant in the histories of Islam, and, therefore, it is wrong to speak about the Crusades as damaging relations between Christians and Muslims. Muslims had been dealing with Eastern Christians from the very beginning of the Islamic state, and to deal with Christians and to have intellectual defenses against the Christian ideas was nothing new. For the Europeans, on the other hand, it was necessary, along with the Crusades, to set up their intellectual defenses against Islam. It was in the twelfth, thirteenth, and fourteenth centuries that Europeans set up their intellectual defenses against Islam in the form that I call the distorted image of Islam, which is something that still affects us. As I like to put it, we in the West are still influenced by the aftermath of medieval war propaganda.

Kahrl: One of the points Mr. Crocker made in his talk was that the attitudes expressed in the songs were those of people who knew nothing about Islam. Is there any evidence that increased tolerance for the Muslims developed in the Western communities that were in contact with them as opposed to the communities that remained at home?

Brundage: There's a certain amount of evidence that this happened, for example, in the Latin settlements in the East. The people who settled in the East became to some degree acclimatized. For example, the memoirs of Usāma ibn al-Munqidh, the twelfth-century Syrian writer, clearly indicate he was aware that the newly arrived Franks from the West were more barbarous and less polite than the ones who had been settled there for a while. And this is also perceived more in a negative sense, by Crusaders who arrive fresh on the scene and are rather startled, shocked, and indignant at the way Latin populations of the Kingdom of Jerusalem had gone native. They didn't like this a bit, and they find the notion of a Latin ruler wearing Arabic dress, eating Arabic style foods, and even having a harem totally abhorrent. Probably you would find the same sort of thing on the Spanish frontiers; Burns's studies of the crusading Kingdom of Valencia, for example, I think would bear out this thought.

Kahrl: I asked that question because it relates to an issue Mr. Alger raised: the more one can get to know about the people who have been defined as aliens, the less easy one finds it to treat them as aliens, the less available they become as a target for hostility and intolerance. From what little I know of the activities of the Crusaders, once they had settled down in the area, their fervor seemed to be considerably less than the Franks who followed them out.

Crocker: Mr. Kahrl, I have a question on the mechanism of the identification of the out-group. I was meditating on this point which Professor Alger raised, and it seems to me there is a slight complexity in the mechanism involved. On the one hand, the out-group needs to be singled out, identified, given attributes that would make them worthy targets of aggression, and, on the other hand, this is made possible by, as he pointed out, ignorance and lack of contact on the part of the people partaking in the holy war. It occurs to me that these two aspects possibly weren't carried out by the same people. Some of the people are ignorant, and somebody else is articulating the out-group against which their aggression can be directed. Since this point was brought up in at least one of the lectures, and I wasn't aware that there was so much information on it, I would like to ask to what degree were the out-group and the aims of the Crusades articulated, defined, even proposed by highly placed authorities, not welling up from below but set forth by the pope. And then, if we could ask Professor Alger, as a scholar looking at a recent event, to comment upon to what degree he thinks the articulation came from above?

Cowdrey: If I may just say a word with the First Crusade mainly in mind. With all the reservations I made in my paper about our poor documentation of what those who preached the Crusades actually said, one's impression is they said very little about the Muslims or about the character of their religion, simply because they knew next to nothing about Muslims. One authority on this subject, Sir Richard Southern, in *Western Views of Islam in the Middle Ages,* says he has found only one mention of the name Muhammad in a Western source outside Spain and Southern Italy before the twelfth century. They were as ignorant as that about the Muslim religion; they knew just nothing about even the prophet himself. Urban seems to have talked about the Holy Sepulchre, the familiar place of pilgrimage that people had been visiting frequently, particularly in the eleventh century, since the Christianization of Hungary made it possible to take an overland route to the Holy Land. Urban also spoke of the subjection of Eastern churches to the Muslim yoke, without, of course, defining very clearly what the Muslim yoke involved. It was these two decidedly Christian things—the Holy Places and certain churches that were subject to an alien yoke—rather than anything intrinsic in Islam itself that people were talking about, insofar as people talked about the Muslims at all. The only connection, I think, in which this came up, was some of the "propaganda" literature at the time of the First Crusade, which turned on the destruction of the Church of the Holy Sepulchre in 1009 by the Fatimid Caliph Hākim. But this was fabricated and secondary, and I doubt whether it had a very wide influence.

It is also noteworthy both in the First Crusade and in the Second Crusade that much of the case against the Muslims, insofar as it was intellectually formulated, didn't concern their religion so much as the fact that both at Antioch in the First Crusade and at Lisbon in the Second Crusade Muslims were unjustly detaining land that had once been Christian. These Crusades were seen as attempts to win back justly for Christian domination land that rightly belonged to Christians anyway. I don't think there was any authentic awareness whatsoever of Islam in the early stages of the crusading movement.

Kahrl: That comment of yours reminds me of nothing so much as the attacks that were made on various presidents during the last twenty years for "losing China" or "losing Vietnam"and Johnson's own feeling that he was not going to go down in history as the man who "lost Vietnam," somehow or other thinking it was something he had to lose in the first place.

Alger: I would like to respond to Professor Crocker's excellent question. We certainly have learned that the relationship between contact and degree of conflict is complicated. Too many of us carry around in our heads the notion that if there would only be more contact, somehow conflict would vanish, but we all know that there can be no conflict without contact. A potential enemy has to be seen, and you have to have ways to get at him before you can have any conflict at all. On the other hand, it does seem that the situations and roles through which cross-cultural contact takes place are rather important. For instance, it is quite possible for an American tourist to circle the globe in his Western bubble—inside a Hertz car drinking Coca-Cola and staying in intercontinental hotels—and there is really no intercultural contact except with citizens from the other countries in lowly service positions. So that's the image you get. We have the same kind of phenomena in cross-cultural relations in our own society, where stereotypes generate because of the roles that people are assuming when they engage in this kind of contact. I'm not sure exactly how that relates to the Crusades. I think it relates very importantly to the kinds of things that American servicemen said: what I, in my war, said about Japanese and what other people in this room said about their wars in Korea and Vietnam. "Gooks," "Japs," these kinds of things are a result of contact, but contact of a very special kind.

The question also causes us to take note of the ways in which different people in a society play different kinds of roles. In this regard, the rights, interests, and ideas trichotomy is a very useful mode of analysis. In large-scale modern war, the leadership may well initiate a military action on the basis of rights or interests for the total society. But it is easiest for the leadership to obtain popular support by proclaiming a war of ideas, some kind of an ideological war. This brings me back to Professor Greene's comment. I disagree with his tendency to say that most of these wars are unique. I agree with him that the Pearl Harbor analogy applied in Korea, and the Korean and Pearl Harbor analogies in Vietnam were quite misleading. But there were aspects of all these wars that can be placed in the holy war context. Particularly for most of the populations that supported the last two wars, for as long as they supported them, it was a war of ideas. For more people than not, it was a matter of simple anticommunism, whereas for some of the more sophisticated leadership, those wars had more limited objectives and were also waged out of some analogy to some other situations.

> *Question:* I am concerned that we have isolated the phenomenon of holy war from a whole spectrum of different types of cultural imperialism, if you want to call it that. If we look at the Islamic case, the greatest degree of conversion actually occurred through relatively peaceful means; I can't comment on a Christian experience in this respect. Are the causes of what we are calling holy wars and the conflicts they involve really so different from the causes of our human conflict in general? Is our question not whether we can keep people from having positive values that they want to impress on other people, but whether we can keep the exercise of this kind of cultural contact on a nonviolent plane?

Kahrl: There is a distinction, which I found illuminating, between the just war, the definitions of which apparently go back to Augustine, and the holy war. When the Japanese attacked Pearl Harbor, they seemed to have fulfilled completely the conditions for the just war defined by Augustine, as Mr. Brundage gave it in his paper, and, therefore, that conflict had a sense of moral rightness that Roosevelt would never have been able to achieve though persuading the country that the war in Europe, for example, involved our interests. Mr. Cowdrey, at the end of his talk, asked us to reconsider "just war" as at least something that one might substitute for ideological war. I do think that the distinction that Mr. Brundage and Mr. Cowdrey are making is a real one, and one that lies at the root of positive response to one kind of conflict, that is, World War II, and negative response to a more recent one.

Brundage: I think we ought to be very clear that in talking about the Crusade, the holy war, as an ideological war we do not mean that it is a war in order to convert. There is very little effort on the part of the Crusaders to convert the indigenous Muslim population to Christianity; there is some, but it is very minor. Conversion is not the main thing they're after. What they want to do is repossess this territory and to get it for themselves. They want to plant Christian communities there, and they want to plant them, as it turns out, almost entirely in the cities. There is no effort to penetrate the countryside, simply to exploit it.

Question: Do the leaders of any country ever really wage war for ideas? They may preach ideas to the people, but don't they really go to war for their political interests?

Cowdrey: Obviously, these things are usually very mixed in people's minds. I saw the Second World War coming on when I was a boy, and as I look back on it, it seemed clear even then that the Germans found themselves in a position where they could not solve their own domestic problems. It was those domestic problems that generated Nazism, and ideas really were fundamental there—ideas that had terrible consequences, particularly for the Jews. One had to face oneself the question of joining up to fight in the Second World War. The critical thing, I think, was that a whole people was being slaughtered by the Nazis. This seemed to me, in Europe, an absolutely classic case of the just war: doing what was necessary to restrain this act of terrible crime against a whole people, quite apart, of course, from the Nazi occupation of so much of Europe. But certainly it was not in Britain's interest to fight the Second World War. It finished us as a great power; we knew it was going to, and it has. I think, perhaps, that's the difference in the way we saw going into the Second World War and the way the Americans saw going into it; we knew it was finishing us as a great power, i.e., as a power with the economic and political capacity to act on its own.

Greene: I would like to comment briefly on that question by citing the situation in Europe in the fifteenth and sixteenth centuries involving the Turkish menace, which was very real into the sixteenth century, and which might have constituted an ideal cause for a holy war, which never really occurred.

It was not for the lack of the Holy See attempting to organize a Crusade; a whole series of popes tried very hard to do that. One of the most interesting popes of the fifteenth century, Pius II, called an international council to discuss this, and almost nobody turned up as representatives of the armed heads of Europe. There was clearly nothing in it for anybody. There was not much booty to be gained by repelling the Turks, and there was clearly the risk of much bloodshed. Thus, the Turks were able to maintain very strong military pressure annually throughout the fifteenth and sixteenth centuries in Eastern Europe. Nobody was interested in fighting them except those who were immediately under the menace, and those were the only people who did fight them. On the contrary, the Very Christian King of France, François Premier, proved his right to that title by allying himself with the Turks against their common enemy, the emperor.

Watt: There's a lot of truth in the assertion that people are moved to war by material motives; at the beginning, Islamic holy war was a razzia to get booty. But it should be noticed that insofar as people mention ideas as part of their reason for going to war, even if there are also material factors, these ideas can dictate their actions at a later period. The razzia contributed to the growth of the Islamic empire because the people realized that if they joined the empire, they ceased to be the object of the razzia. Similarly, you could say in the First World War, European powers talked a great deal about national self-determination because it was going to help them to split up the Austrian Empire, and so forth. Once they had talked about that, however, this came back like a boomerang on their own heads in the events after the First World War. So, I think that if you say you are going to war for certain ideas, you reinforce these ideas, and they then determine certain of your later decisions.

Question: One of the things Western cultures and Western European cultures particularly have been significant for is the scientific and academic study of the out-groups. This began probably around the sixteenth century, and has continued through to today; we have Africanists, Orientalists, and Arabists in a way that few other cultures have ever had. This study seems to me to have been employed, almost from the beginning, for two reasons. One of these was curiosity about the out-group for the sake of understanding, for the sake of pure knowledge. But another one, and a very significant one, is the idea of intelligence about the enemy, finding out about him. Certainly the whole support that the United States government has given to the study of other cultures has been largely under the label of national defense. We find, therefore, in the Arab world, for instance, a good deal of reaction against Western Orientalism as just a brand of intellectual imperialism. I don't think this is necessarily a very well advised reaction on their part, but nonetheless the reaction exists.

Now—and I am addressing Alger's point about the responsibility of the academic community—our academic structures, our faculties in most Western universities, reflect the need for further knowledge of the out-groups. We know something; we have a fair amount of background from Arabists and Islamists, but we know very little about the Far East. A comment was made a couple of years ago that ten years of involvement in Vietnam had generated not more than half a dozen experts in the field of Vietnamese studies. This, I think, is a very sad thing, and I would really appreciate the members of the panel addressing the problem with the academic and disciplinary structures for the study of the out-groups, the objects of most Crusades. How do you feel this study should be approached by Western universities? Do you think it will lead only to propagandistic or military usage, or do you see this as leading to some sort of understanding? How do you see it as advancing our knowledge of the out-group in such a way as to obviate, eventually, the necessity of the Holy War mentality?

Alger: The way we have gone about studying the out-group has had tremendous impact on how we see out-groups, and I don't think we completely understand the consequences of this as yet. When one society looks at another, it often goes there looking for contrasts, images of itself, and how this foreign society differs from itself. As a result, it often finds things that, while they're true, may be rather irrelevant. Take, for example, political scientists like myself. The first thing we're inclined to study will be parliamentary elections, and you just can't learn very much about certain societies by studying parliamentary elections. Vietnam is a good example of how we reached all kinds of wrong conclusions by looking at the wrong things. Now, that's one thing.

Another thing is that many societies that are studied by the stronger and more powerful cultures have the advantage of an external image of themselves. Some of these smaller, weaker societies, therefore, see the world as a whole much better than we do because they have the benefit of these studies. Looking mainly in the political areas, I don't think since Brice and de Tocqueville we have had very widely distributed images of ourselves done by people abroad. One of the problems, then, is that the resources for foreign study are unevenly distributed, and this has very important consequences.

The third item is that the best way to learn about other cultures—and I think scholars are beginning to learn this—is jointly, in a reciprocal, symmetrical relationship between those that are interested outside the culture and those that are being studied inside. This is more and more the case, and the more this happens and the more that ethnocentric college administrations realize that work abroad has to be done cooperatively if we are going to get real insight, the more likely we will be able to see others as they are and the more they will have a capacity to see us as we are. This will, in general, require more flexible organization than funding and research by national governments permits—perhaps by state governments and universities—and more flexible staffing of research institutes and more movement of scholars across national boundaries.

If we were discussing universities in the Middle Ages, I have the impression that we would have noticed more of an international community of scholars in those periods than there is now. Certainly your question focusses on an important point, the unwitting, unconscious, unthinking ways in which scholarly communities have allowed their forms of organization and financing to affect how they see the world.

---

1. Osman Hooper, *The History of the City of Columbus, Ohio* (Memorial Publishing Co., 1920), p. 83.

2. Ibid.

NOTES ON THE CONTRIBUTORS

Chadwick F. Alger, professor, Department of Political Science, and faculty, Mershon Center, Ohio State University.

James A. Brundage, professor and chairman, Department of History, University of Wisconsin at Milwaukee.

H. E. J. Cowdrey, fellow and tutor in modern history, St. Edmund Hall, University of Oxford.

Richard L. Crocker, professor, Department of Music, University of California at Berkeley.

Thomas M. Greene, professor and chairman, Department of Comparative Literature, Yale University.

Stanley J. Kahrl, professor, Department of English, and director, Center for Medieval and Renaissance Studies, Ohio State University.

Linda V. Seidel, lecturer in fine arts and Allston Burr Senior Tutor at North House, Harvard University.

W. Montgomery Watt, professor, Department of Arabic and Islamic Studies, University of Edinburgh.

214